To: Jennifer Jarreau.

With appreciation

For your friendship

Hope you enjoy!

My very best regards

3/23/98

FRANKLY, FITZ!

FRANKLY, FITZ!

Former Lieutenant Governor
James E. Fitzmorris, Jr.
and
Kenneth D. Myers

Foreword by Lindy Boggs

PELICAN PUBLISHING COMPANY
Gretna 1992

Library of Congress Cataloging-in-Publication Data

Fitzmorris, James E. (James Edward), 1921-
Frankly, Fitz! / by James E. Fitzmorris, Jr., and Kenneth D. Myers : foreword by Lindy Boggs.
p. c.m.
ISBN 0-88289-915-5
1. Fitzmorris, James E. (James Edward), 1921- . 2. Lieutenant governors—Louisiana—Biography. 3. Louisiana—Politics and government—1951- I. Myers, Kenneth D. II. Title.
F376.3.F58A3 1992
976.3'063'092-dc20
[B]

92-14678
CIP

Manufactured in the United States of America

Published by Pelican Publishing Company, Inc.
1101 Monroe Street, Gretna, Louisiana 70053

For my wife, Gloria, who sacrificed so much in sharing my life; for our precious daughter, Lisa, who made our life complete; and for my wonderful mother and father, "Romolia and Jim," who made it all possible.

Contents

Foreword

For nearly a collective half-century, my husband, Hale Boggs, and I were privileged to represent Louisiana's Second Congressional District in the United States House of Representatives.

During these years of service, we came home to New Orleans as often as possible to meet with the people and the leaders of our district. One of the most anticipated events on these trips home was a visit with our friend, Jimmy Fitzmorris.

Because he was vigorously involved at every level of the community—politics, business, religious activities, or one of the scores of community projects on which he was tirelessly working—each conversation with Jimmy Fitzmorris was equivalent to gaining a social, economic, religious, and political synopsis of the events and challenges of our area since we had last been home.

Often, Jimmy, one of the wittiest men and best storytellers in public life, had a humorous anecdote about one of our colorful political figures. Sometimes, as one of the most active laymen in town, he gave us the latest news from the religious community. On many visits, Jimmy, who practiced the art of politics daily and joyfully, recounted stories of the current political intrigue or his latest proposals as a member of the city council during the administration of my beloved cousin, Mayor deLesseps "Chep" Morrison. On each visit, Jimmy passed along some request from an ordinary citizen for help in Washington, for he has been and remains one of the most compassionate men in public life.

I am pleased that he has taken the interest to assemble this autobiography of the turbulent times of which he was a part and the colorful characters he knew. It would have been a shame to lose this valuable and vanishing history for the members of our generation and those to follow.

I remember, fondly and vividly, the young Jimmy Fitzmorris, tall, handsome, eager, in his first race for the city council. Jimmy entered politics sharing Hale's and my belief that politics is an honorable profession, and he has worked with diligence and dedication during his long career to make it so. Throughout his years of involvement he has been encouraged and accompanied by his loyal, highly intelligent, and lively wife, Gloria, and cheered from the moment she could speak by his lovely daughter, Lisa.

For over thirty years, his campaigns for the city council, for mayor, for lieutenant governor, and governor had one constant, recurring theme: positive leadership. I have always respected Jimmy for exhibiting the personal qualities of leadership: compassion, singular integrity, vision, and courage, not to mention his unshakable optimism, born of deep religious faith and his wonderful Irish wit. Over his lifetime, Jimmy has come to represent the high standard against which others' public careers will be judged.

As a member of Congress and as a concerned citizen of our community, I have had the opportunity of working with Jimmy Fitzmorris for many years on numerous occasions. He enjoys my respect and affection, and I am pleased and honored to be a part of this unique account of one of the most distinguished careers in Louisiana public life.

LINDY BOGGS
Member of Congress, Retired

Preface

Every political figure who has ever held statewide office has heard it a hundred times at meetings from one end of the state to the other: "You ought to write a book." Next to "You've got my vote," it is the sweetest refrain this side of heaven.

Yet, so many of the political autobiographies I've read seem hollow, sometimes bitter, and for years I resisted the urging of my friends and associates to add to that number. I determined, in my own mind, that I would only tell my story when I was sufficiently removed from the political turmoil and spotlight that I was certain I could avoid being mean-spirited or self-serving.

The story that follows is more than just a recounting of the political triumphs and tragedies of Jimmy Fitzmorris. In a larger sense, it is the story of the colorful, changing face of life in Louisiana since I was a child in the 1920s.

Frankly, Fitz! attempts to be an honest portrait of what was good and bad about the way we were, the genuinely monumental ways in which the landscape of our lives has changed during the last half-century, and some thoughts about the social and political challenges which will face a new generation of Louisiana leaders.

Finally, this is a celebration and a tribute: a celebration of the rich tapestry of public figures I have known during those years, from Huey P. Long through this morning's newsmakers, and a tribute to the thousands of friends I've made in all walks of life and every part of Louisiana, whose friendship and support sustained me throughout my political career. Some of these stories are very private and personal and have never been told before. Others are recollections and memories from a misty time in siana history that is long past, interesting stories worth telling, which only a small, surviving handful of public figures can still recall.

This is a candid story told without rancor or regret, but with fondness, humor, and honor as, poised on the threshold of a new century, we look back on a unique period of epic changes.

JAMES E. FITZMORRIS, JR.
New Orleans, Louisiana

ACKNOWLEDGMENTS

The authors are grateful to the following publishers, individuals, and companies for permission to reprint excerpts from selected materials as noted below:

Martin Baxbaum, from *Inspirational Thoughts: Quotes to Light Up Your Life*, edited by Mac Anderson. Copyright 1985. Reprinted by permission of Greater Quotations.

Endorsement of James E. Fitzmorris, Jr., for mayor of New Orleans, from the New Orleans *Times-Picayune*, 1965. Endorsement of Moon Landrieu for mayor of New Orleans, from the *States-Item*, 1969. Iris Kelso's column "Votes for the Birds," following the primary election for governor, from the *Times-Picayune*, 1979.

From WWL Television broadcast editorials by Phil Johnson on the occasion of the dedication of the Chep Morrison Memorial in May 1964 and following the first primary for governor in 1979.

From "Personal Sonnets–To My Mother" in *Collected Poems*, by George Barker, edited by Robert Fraser. Copyright 1987. Reprinted by permission of Faber and Faber, Ltd.

From *Selected Poems*, by Stephen Spender. Copyright 1934 and renewed 1962 by Stephen Spender. Reprinted by permission of Random House, Inc.

Introduction

The Plains Indians preserved their heritage through the elders, who told stories of the tribal history around the campfire at night. The young braves were encouraged to demonstrate that they could adapt these historic lessons to contemporary times by creating their own stories, combining the old myths and legends with current challenges. The tragedy of the Indians was that most of their stories were only passed along verbally, little was written. Over time, many of the old dialects have died out, and much of the Indian lore and history has been lost forever.

Jimmy Fitzmorris is one of Louisiana's most accomplished storytellers. Many of his stories are of a Louisiana political and social structure that is now almost forgotten and provide useful insights into current challenges. He felt it important to put this unique history into writing, to preserve it for the enjoyment and benefit of future generations.

This book grew out of an interview I conducted with him in 1989 on the subject of "life after politics." Begun as a collection of personal anecdotes, the subject soon became broader and deeper as we attempted to put Louisiana's colorful political past into perspective.

We were uniquely fortunate that the Fitzmorris files represent one of the most comprehensive collections of political and social history available anywhere in the state. We began with thirty-eight oversized, thick scrapbooks with press clippings dating back to the 1920s, compiled by countless volunteers through the years. Each of the thousands of clippings was read and studied as part of the political chronology. They became the basis for five hundred hours of interviews with Fitzmorris, sandwiched into his hectic schedule over a period of two years. For the section on campaign reform, I listened to seventy-six hours of tape-recorded hearings of the joint legislative committee created following the disputed 1979 gubernatorial election. By the time we were ready to begin writing the book, the stack of notes and interviews stood over a yard high in my office.

The result is a unique, personal political history that only Jimmy Fitzmorris could have recounted, for his career spanned several generations and new technologies. He began his political involvement in the Huey P. Long era, when campaigns were largely conducted through "handbills," before Long first experimented with that new device, radio, as a means of communication. In Fitzmorris's own campaigns he eventually spent millions on television commercials, a campaign tool which was almost unknown at the beginning of his career but which is taken for granted today.

Writing this book eventually became the equivalent, in time and effort, of earning a master's degree in political science. I benefitted greatly from the encouragement of his wife, Gloria, and from the unique, personal insights of his daughter, Lisa. The anecdotes and experiences of Fitzmorris's political family—a whole generation of protégés drawn to him by his example of how public life is capable of honor—were especially useful in compiling this book. The secret weapons of this assignment were Carol Daigle and Joe Willis, Fitzmorris's longtime associates, whose remarkable memories for names, dates, and events were invaluable and whose friendship and encouragement sustained me.

I must acknowledge the vital assistance of others: This book would never have been published without the patience and tenacity of my agent, Henry Berry, and the dedicated efforts of Julie Vicknair, who took the ramshackle manuscript and molded it into proper format.

Hundreds of reporters have written thousands of words over the last forty years, attempting to analyze Jimmy Fitzmorris's complex personality and philosophy. Actually the key to understanding him is basic and straightforward, as he explained it, almost casually, during one interview: "I believed I had a calling for public service." He answered that calling, almost in the sense of a religious vocation, with all the dedication, sacrifice, and self-denial it required. His patience in helping me to understand, examine, and explain the complex, controversial political events of parts of eight decades was crucial to this book. Ultimately, the real Jimmy Fitzmorris shines through this story of one of the most decent men in Louisiana public life.

KENNETH D. MYERS
New Orleans, Louisiana

FRANKLY, FITZ!

Chapter 1

Reaching for the Brass Ring
The 1979 Campaign for Governor

The clock on the wall of the International Suite at New Orleans' Fairmont Hotel showed just after 7:00 P.M. when our small, tired band of friends and family arrived. It was Saturday, October 27, 1979; we had been on the road virtually without stopping for well over a year, traveling to every nook and cranny of Louisiana seeking the governorship.

We had worked harder than we ever imagined we could, raised and spent more money than we ever dreamed possible. We had done literally everything we knew to do in running a gubernatorial campaign and now, in a matter of hours, it would all be over. The result of my lifetime in public service, the verdict of the people of Louisiana, was about to be revealed to me and to the entire state. By morning either I would be the most likely man to lead Louisiana into the next decade as I headed for the runoff election or I would be just months away from becoming a private citizen after a long political career. It was not by accident that I had chosen Suite 1276 of the Fairmont Hotel. This was called the "International Suite" but, in reality, it served as the Presidential Suite for the Hotel. Presidents as far back as Harry S Truman had utilized this suite and now, a quarter-century later, it remained virtually unchanged from his visit. Since handsomely redecorated, in 1979 the International Suite was more distinguished by size than decor. Double doors with ornate knockers opened onto a parquet foyer and private bath. The foyer led into a main room the size of a small ballroom, replete with grand piano. A telephone, mounted on a china lion, stood at one end of the room near a completely furnished bar.

A nearby anteroom held a large refrigerator and sinks and offered a private doorway leading discreetly onto the corridor outside. At the other end of the suite was a large, private, master bedroom which boasted rather dowdy, brown-plaid carpeting and brown-flowered drapes. There was a spacious, private bath, but no way outside without exiting through the main room. Once secluded in the master bedroom, I would be a virtual prisoner until election night was over. I paid little attention to my surroundings. I was concerned with what was happening outside that room, around Louisiana, where my future was being decided. The only furnishing important to me was a large console television receiver in the middle of the room. That set was to be my link to Louisiana for the following, most important hours of my life. I was neither the first nor the last Louisiana official to headquarter, for at least part of the campaign, in the Fairmont. During the Huey and Earl K. Long years the hotel had been called The Roosevelt, indeed many Louisianians still refer to it that way, and the Longs had made it their command center. It had been a mostly lucky location for them. I hoped it would be for me as well. The notion of a candidate taking a hotel room from which to view the election returns is a fairly new development in Louisiana.

Of course, I could have watched from home and probably been more comfortable, but there were scores of people in and out throughout the night and almost four thousand people in a nearby downstairs ballroom waiting to celebrate a primary victory, so it was important that I be close at hand. I stayed almost entirely by myself in the master suite throughout the night. My brother, Norris, was with me occasionally as were my wife, Gloria, and daughter, Lisa, but they also tended to our guests in the outer room. I still have almost no recollection of the persons outside my private inner sanctum that night. As is the way with political events of this kind, we kept the location of our top campaign team that evening a closely guarded secret. As always, it soon became the worst-kept secret in Louisiana and well-wishers poured into the suite. Mostly, I avoided them. I wanted to concentrate on the returns; there would be plenty of time for self-congratulatory posing later. I remembered Pres. John F. Kennedy's supposed comment upon hearing his 1960 campaign team described as "coruscatingly brilliant." "Those guys should never forget," JFK reportedly said, "that fifty thousand votes the other way and we'd all be coruscatingly stupid." This night the jury was still out on

Waiting for the returns, election night, 1979. Behind me is Lt. Kenny Delcambre, Louisiana State Police.

whether our campaign would be remembered as brilliant or stupid, and I wanted to be left alone to watch.

I was largely satisfied with the campaign we had run, but I had been at this business, in victory and defeat, all my adult life and I could sense a cliffhanger when I saw one. My pollster, Ed Renwick, saw the same likelihood. He called interim results to Carol Daigle, my longtime assistant, in the Bayou Room of the hotel. He was working that night as commentator for WWL Television in New Orleans, where he continues to be a respected analyst. It was his station I watched. We knew the votes would be badly split because there were strong candidates representing every geographical area of the state. The Acadian parishes of southwest Louisiana were being hotly contested by both Sen. Sonny Mouton and Sec. of State Paul Hardy. North Louisiana had a keen interest in House Speaker E. L. "Bubba" Henry's chances, and Public Service commissioner Louis Lambert came from the Mississippi River parishes. In the New Orleans area I faced competition from each of them for the large metropolitan area vote. Lambert, with strong labor and black support, was making a real run at my natural base. Henry had been endorsed by both the Alliance for Good Government, a progressive civic group, and by the *Times-Picayune*, the major local newspaper. The loss of the *Times-Picayune* endorsement was a particularly bitter blow. In my career I had won endorsements and lost them.

I had won and lost elections with or without key endorsements. But I must admit that I had counted on the *Times-Picayune*'s blessing in the most important race of my life. I was clearly the leading local candidate. I genuinely believed that I understood the needs of the metropolitan New Orleans community better than any other candidate. I had worked so long and so hard for the people in the area that I honestly believed I had earned and deserved the endorsement. To see it given to another candidate, primarily because he was a fresh and interesting new face in statewide politics, seemed like a bitter and personal repudiation of a lifetime of service. It was even more painful because the newspaper's choice, Bubba Henry, had no real chance to win, so getting the endorsement was of little practical use to him. I did, however, have a real chance to win, and losing the endorsement was a very serious blow to me. I had an even greater problem at home, in the person of Republican congressman David C. Treen. He had been my friend for many years and was to remain so. I cannot imagine any possible outcome to the election which could have changed our friendship. We shared a similar basic philosophy and a reputation for businesslike, honest administration in addition to our respect and friendship.

I recognized from the outset that he would be my most serious challenger. This was the first time in modern history that a Republican had any realistic possibility of winning the governorship of Louisiana, and the GOP, hungry for a chance for one of its own to sleep in the governor's mansion, remained loyal and unshakable in its support of Treen. Since many of Treen's Republican backers would otherwise have voted for me, his strength harmed me the most. It was against that backdrop that I prepared to watch the votes trickle in. Renwick had predicted that I would win by a very close margin, and that was good enough for me. That narrow window of opportunity meant that we could leave nothing to chance election night, however, so we put our own group in motion in the key precincts, which Renwick had previously identified. In each of those precincts a Fitzmorris loyalist awaited the results in the clerk of court's office. As soon as that precinct reported, our supporter called Carol's command post from which she relayed the data to Renwick at the television studio and to my suite upstairs. By this means, our returns from the most important precincts in the state ran well ahead of the wire services and other more traditional reporting systems.

Even that system was not foolproof. Many of the clerks of court were longtime friends and supporters of mine and they let our volunteers call in the results directly from their offices. In three crucial precincts, however, the results simply were not reported until the next day. All night long the lead shifted, again and again, as I sat literally hypnotized in front of the television set. Occasionally I would stand and stretch, sometimes looking out into the city night, watching the traffic at the corner of Elks Place and Canal Street in the heart of downtown New Orleans which was visible from my window. I loved this city, genuinely and passionately. Twice I had tried to win the right to lead it as mayor, and twice I had been narrowly denied. I did not reflect on those races this night, however, for I was too concerned with the handful of votes in precincts far away that held the key to my future. The endurance required in gathering these returns, especially from the rural precincts, cannot be overemphasized. In many of Louisiana's rural precincts it may be thirty miles or more from the precinct polling location to the clerk of court's office.

With such a long ballot as the 1979 election it took literally hours for all the votes to be counted and then delivered to the clerk's office. So we were forced to wait, along with the assorted political analysts and the other candidates, until well after midnight before the consensus emerged that Jimmy Fitzmorris would face David Treen in the runoff election. Renwick called me just before his final television appearance of the night in which he projected our victory by one-half of one percent. Only then did we dare go downstairs to greet our four thousand supporters, claim victory, and anticipate the frenetic pace of the campaign ahead. I thought that we might face a deserted hall downstairs because of the lateness of the hour. Instead, the sprawling Imperial Ballroom was a sea of faces. It seemed as though every inch of standing space was taken up by cheering, celebrating Fitzmorris friends and supporters. We had carefully planned who would appear on the rostrum with me for the victory speech. Those plans went immediately awry as scores of people, some of whom I barely knew, clamored onto the stage to share this moment. I had planned to single out and thank various key friends and supporters around the ballroom. The blaze of television lights and cameras made it absolutely impossible even to begin to see specific faces on the other side.

I barely remember, through the blare and the blur a few old friends like Sen. Mike O'Keefe, then the senate president, Clerk of Court Ed Lombard, a veteran of thousands of miles of travel around Louisiana in my behalf, my dear friend Fr. Harry Tompson, then president of Jesuit High School, and New Orleans councilman Mike Early, a former member of my staff. A speech claiming victory is supposed to put the past campaign in perspective and to set the stage for the next. It is, at best, an opportunity for the candidate to shine rhetorically, to utter some key phrase central to the conduct of the next campaign as Sen. John F. Kennedy unveiled the "New Frontier" in his acceptance speech before the 1960 Democratic National Convention in Los Angeles. In some deep recess of my mind that is the kind of speech I had hoped to make at the Imperial Ballroom that night. I wish I could tell you that brilliant speech came to pass, that future students of campaign rhetoric would study the brilliant, lyrical, sparkling language of Jimmy Fitzmorris. Alas, it was not so. For one thing, the ballroom was crowded far beyond capacity and few could hear above the roar of the general celebration. For another, the candidate was emotionally drained and physically exhausted.

I summoned the strength to thank my family and my friends, to exhort this audience to the even more daunting challenge that lay ahead and then, with the cheers of four thousand friends, who had waited through the night to share my joy, ringing in my ears, I was literally carried through the crowd by my state troopers, Billy Booth and Eric Durel, and former trooper Jim Borgstede to the elevator for the brief ride back to my suite. From there, as the New Orleans dawn was about to break, I went home to Emerald Street and to bed. A press conference, scheduled for my home, was only hours away and the runoff campaign was about to begin in earnest.

Announcing for Governor

I announced my candidacy for governor on March 12, 1979. My intention to seek the highest elected post in Louisiana had been known to friends and associates for many months. In fact, on October 13, 1976, I had gathered a large crowd of supporters in the Fairmont Hotel in New Orleans to put to rest speculation that I might run that year for mayor of New Orleans. Incumbent mayor Maurice "Moon" Landrieu's second term was ending, and a large number of community leaders had urged me to run, particularly those who were opposed to the candidacy of the late state senator Nat Kiefer.

While I was flattered, I was then midway into my second term as lieutenant governor, and my ambitions were statewide in nature, so I regretfully declined. That election was won by the late Ernest N. "Dutch" Morial who was a longtime friend and whose support for me in the subsequent race for governor was of inestimable value. So it was that I found myself, on a beautiful, clear Monday morning, announcing my candidacy for governor at a breakfast press conference at the Chateau Capital Riverdome, the historic political gathering place in Baton Rouge which has since closed. A large, enthusiastic crowd was on hand, generated by my Baton Rouge campaign coordinators Billy McGee, the late Stanley Gross, retired colonel Steve Bailey, and Rolfe McCollister, Sr. From Baton Rouge we flew directly to an announcement gathering

Mayor Ernest N. "Dutch" Morial was an invaluable ally in the 1979 governor's campaign and a great friend.

at New Orleans' Lakefront Airport. With me were Gloria, Lisa, press aide Kirk Melancon, my assistant Pat Gallwey, and state trooper Billy Booth. I've staged and attended more political gatherings than I want to remember over the past thirty-five years, but few could rival the air of excitement and optimism of that morning at the airport. There were banners, hats, signs, campaign buttons, and people everywhere. We formed an enthusiastic procession from the plane to the Walnut Room, led by the Olympia Brass Band.

I was especially touched that the band from my cherished alma mater, Jesuit High School, was on hand to play as well. Many of Lisa's classmates from Mount Carmel Academy were there too, cheering us on. Young people played a very important role throughout my campaign. I believe that ours was one of the first to invite representatives of high school newspapers to attend the announcements. They were encouraged to ask questions important to their specific readers, to really participate—not just stand on the sidelines and observe. We crowded into the Walnut Room for my brother Norris's introduction followed by my formal announcement. Some of the best television footage in our campaign commercials came from that golden morning, and I will never forget it. It is a cornerstone of our democracy that any person meeting the statutory qualifications may offer himself for governor or any other office, but I have always believed that when a man asks the voters to entrust him with the highest office in the state, he owes them some explanation of his vision and his purpose. I tried to spell out the dreams I had for Louisiana during my speech. I said, "I will make continued economic development the number one priority of my administration."

I tried to share with the audience the dream for Louisiana that was in my heart, for I believed genuinely and deeply that jobs were at the absolute center of the peril or the prosperity of this state. More jobs meant increased stability and a higher living standard, more tax dollars for education, roads, and public transportation. More jobs would mean less crime, less welfare, and a rebirth and renewal for the whole state. In that way I tried to define myself and my mission. I answered a whole spectrum of questions from the media about my campaign theme, my priorities and intentions if elected, and my background. One question, in particular, came back to me later that day. One of the prominent news stories of the time had to do with the activities of South Korean lobbyist Tongsun Park, perhaps best known for his relationship with Edwin Edwards when he was a congressman and with Congressman Otto Passman. In fact, Park was in Louisiana that day in connection with a trial involving Passman. Asked about my knowledge of Park, I said, accurately, "I have never met Tongsun Park." From the airport we flew directly to Shreveport where we repeated the whole announcement for the area press. Our supporters George Crane, Rome and Cora Blair, Sam Little, and Carolyn Mosley had assembled an enthusiastic crowd.

We then went on to Monroe, where Leo McStravick, Evelyn Blackmon, Fred Huenefeld, and Dick Harper had done a similar bang-up job of assembling supporters. As we were visiting with supporters in the hotel, my campaign assistant, Joe Willis, said, "Governor, Tongsun Park is coming up behind you." And so he was. The controversial man I just said I had never met introduced himself. We chatted briefly and I introduced him to friends and press representatives around the room including Iris Kelso, reporter for WDSU Television in New Orleans, now with the *Times-Picayune*, who accompanied us on that trip. The next morning we flew on to Alexandria, repeated the announcement and met with the late Jack Mulé, Charlie Cantrell, Joe Fuller, and a large group of backers. Then it was on to Lake Charles. Much of the advance work setting up the announcement celebration there had been done by my dear friend, Ed Prendergast, at that time the owner of KOAK Radio in Lake Charles and one of the pioneers in Louisiana public television, aided by Buddy Carter, franchisee for Popeye's Chicken, son of the late Zack Carter, president of Avondale, a longtime friend and supporter in New Orleans.

With the help of Louis Mann, the late Lewis Cook, Bob Oden, and Chuck Zatarain, we restaged the whole show yet again in Jacob's Four Corners Restaurant, one of Lafayette's finest and a favorite local gathering spot for business and political leaders, before finally returning to New Orleans. You might well ask the purpose of re-enacting the announcement for governor in these far-flung locales, especially since, in this age of mass communication, the original announcement could simply have been picked up by the wire services and reported on the evening news without the extra expense and effort. There were several reasons for making individual announcements on location: First, it was a way to provide access to the local media who probably would not have traveled all the way to New Orleans to cover the major announcement session. This kind of access is particularly important to the many weekly newspapers scattered throughout Louisiana, most of which do not have access to the wire service reports. There were some seventy-five weekly papers published in Louisiana during that campaign and, in many cases, they were the primary source of printed information for the people in those communities.

This local press conference format gave those papers a chance to ask about issues important to their own communities, local projects, and concerns. Second, it was a way to get off to a solid and enthusiastic start with our campaign supporters in each area. They were in for a year of hard, often thankless work, and this cavalcade allowed them to share in the action and excitement from the very beginning. Third, it was a way to reach individual, local contributors who were essential to the success of our campaign. Finally, it made sense for a candidate from the New Orleans area. No candidate from New Orleans had been elected governor. My friend and mentor, New Orleans mayor deLesseps "Chep" Morrison, had been rebuffed in three attempts, largely because people from other regions of the state didn't feel that they knew him or because they considered him a "city slicker," more interested in helping New Orleans than the remainder of Louisiana. That was an issue that I, as a New Orleans resident, needed to address from the outset. In order to win, I had to be seen as a candidate *from*, not just *for*, New Orleans. I had been able to convey that feeling in my previous elections as lieutenant governor, and I wanted to continue it in this race.

On the Job Training

In fact, I had used my second term as lieutenant governor as a kind of tutorial for the governorship. I knew that Gov. Edwin Edwards would not be able to succeed himself for another consecutive term and I had determined that, if I were physically capable and the Lord were willing, I would offer myself for this job.

Consequently, I used the four years of my second term to learn everything I could about the management of Louisiana state government. I studied the budget process. I watched how the Edwards administration dealt with the issues facing the state and tried to formulate approaches I might wish to take to the same problems. I tried to meet as many people as possible in all parts of the state, to identify talented, capable individuals—men and women from all backgrounds—who I thought would be able to serve effectively in a Fitzmorris administration. I studied the workings of every state agency and how state government might work more effectively in partnership with business, labor, and local government.

I worked sincerely and diligently at this task, and I still believe that I was the best versed, most thoroughly prepared non-incumbent candidate for governor in this century.

We have seen firsthand the difficulties a governor experiences when he is elected without any real understanding of the inner workings of our complex state government. It is rather similar to attempting to learn to fly a jet airplane when one is already in the air. I believed that I had already mastered the controls in the cockpit, and I was personally acquainted with the key personnel in the aircraft and on the ground. In short, I was ready to take firm control of state government in a decisive, knowledgeable manner from the moment I took the oath of office.

Pondering the Polls

Every modern campaign for major political office, and many minor races as well, begins with public opinion surveys, polls. Edwin Edwards made very effective use of polls in breaking out of a crowded primary field in his first race for governor, but I think political polling in Louisiana really came into its own in our race in 1979. There are several basic kinds of polls. Some are taken on behalf of organizations that have an interest in contributing to or working for a candidate. Others are taken by news organizations and published during the course of a campaign. The most complex polls are taken by candidates' own organizations.

Some campaigns, including ours, conduct "tracking polls," frequent surveys during the campaign designed to show changes in candidates' support or interest in various issues. Polls are very costly—the candidates for governor in 1979 spent some $690,000 conducting them—and sometimes they are contradictory and confusing. It is not uncommon for a candidate's poll to show one probable result at the same time a newspaper or television poll is released showing exactly the opposite. Why the difference? The time period in which a poll is conducted is very important. It must be understood that a poll is merely a snapshot in time, a vignette of how people feel at the specific moment they answer the pollster's questions, and those feelings can change daily during the course of the campaign. I also find that many news polls suffer from a lack of effective screening of the respondents; that is, some news polls contain a large number of responses from people who did not vote in the past election and probably will not vote in this one either. I did not conduct extensive polling early in the campaign, primarily because of the cost and because so many factors change so dramatically by the time the campaign actually gets underway.

For example, one of the early polls showed that then Jefferson Parish assessor Lawrence Chehardy was a leading candidate for governor. Actually, he did not even run and has since retired as a state appeals court judge. Most early polls by others, however, were very encouraging to me. A June 3, 1979, poll by the Baton Rouge newspaper, *Gris-Gris*, showed that 29 percent of state legislators thought the eventual contest would be David Treen versus some other candidate. The survey showed that 20 percent thought it would be Treen versus me, 10 percent thought the race would match Treen and Paul Hardy, 7 percent predicted Treen versus Lambert, 6 percent guessed Treen versus Henry, 5 percent envisioned Treen versus Mouton, and 17 percent thought it was too early to tell. I was particularly interested in the fact that, of the 111 legislators who thought Treen would be one of the final two candidates, only twenty-two thought he would win. A candidate must have great confidence in the professionalism of his pollster. I was fortunate to have the services of Dr. Edward F. Renwick, a respected university professor, television analyst, and the chairman of Loyola University's Institute of Politics.

Much of the actual compilation of the telephone polls for Dr. Renwick and the election day "get-out-the-vote" phoning was done by Multi-Quest, a Metairie firm operated by John Grimm. A visit to Multi-Quest's crowded headquarters was a real experience. Reams of paperwork, questionnaires, and responses were stacked around the room and, at the center of it, sat Grimm, an intense man in his mid-thirties, who survived the brutal hours major political polling requires by consuming copious quantities of popcorn from huge containers set strategically around the office. Later in the campaign we used additional tracking polls conducted by Thomas Kielhorn.

Our first poll, in July 1978, showed that the registered voters who responded were almost evenly divided between those thinking Louisiana was going in the right direction and those who believed we were headed in the wrong direction. I mention this only to show that just taking a poll does not necessarily provide all the easy answers to winning an election. Ultimately the candidate has to make his own personal choices about how to proceed and how to utilize the information provided by the poll.

Our poll showed that I was more recognizable to the voters than any public figure except Edwin Edwards. It also revealed that some 40 percent believed I was doing either an excellent or good job in office. My highest marks were for doing a good job and being a good and honest man. No one responding thought that I was too old, that I had been around too long, or that I was dishonest. These results compared with Lambert, who scored an excellent or good rating of 17 percent, and Treen, who scored 35 percent. Half the respondents thought the next governor should be an experienced public official, but only one in five thought it was necessary that person be a Democrat. It also showed that I was the early choice of 24 percent of those polled, followed by Treen and the late representative Gillis Long, then thought to be a probable candidate. Lambert scored 5 percent. This poll simply confirmed my belief that Treen had strong, probably intractable support and would likely be our toughest competitor.

Our next poll, in April 1979, showed significant changes. Now, 48 percent reported that they saw Lambert on television either daily or once or twice a week. Edwards still led in name recognition with 63 percent, which was only natural for an incumbent. Treen had risen to 50 percent, and I now stood at 28 percent.

That meant that my television recognition had fallen from 31 percent to 28 percent in that period while Lambert's had gone from 12 to 48 and Treen from 19 to 50. Similarly, a third of those polled said they now knew a lot about Lambert compared to 41 percent for me and 52 percent for Treen. In this poll, my approval rating, excellent or good, now stood at 55 percent. Lambert had 37 percent, and Treen, 53 percent. We also explored voters' perceptions of the personal traits of the candidates. The terms most often applied to me were "hard working," "intelligent," "decent," and "a strong leader." The terms least often applied to me were "not smart," "wishy-washy," "lacking in imagination," and "weak." Treen scored a little ahead of me in the areas of hard work, intelligence, and leadership. If the choice were between Treen and Lambert, Treen won by 15 points. The poll also indicated that 64 percent said that an endorsement by Edwin Edwards would make no difference in their choice, while 14 percent said they would be more likely to vote for his pick, and 10 percent said Edwards' endorsement would make it less likely they would vote for that candidate. Crime and education were the most important issues with lack of jobs a strong third.

The Kielhorn polls of September 15 and October 15 were designed to show changes in voter support. They showed that Treen had slipped 2 percent, I had gained 4 percent, and Lambert 1 percent. They also showed that one in five voters was still undecided, which some might have considered a disquieting note considering the millions of dollars the candidates had by then poured into television commercials! It also showed that, matched against any of the other candidates, I would win: 46-42 over Treen, 54-30 over Lambert. It showed Treen defeating Lambert 50-34 when matched one-on-one.

The Kielhorn poll also showed that one-third of the voters had changed their position in the thirty-day period, but mostly from undecided to making a choice, a natural progression in such a campaign. Treen, Lambert, and I all held about 70 percent of our original strength. Lambert, who was running a series of negative commercials at that time, did not manage to switch any votes from Treen to himself in this poll, although it appeared the spots did result in some previous Treen voters switching to me or Hardy. It showed that I picked up 40 percent of those voters who made up their minds in that period.

Most of everybody's money, by that point in the campaign, was going into television commercials, which would wind up costing almost $10 million, not counting the expense of professional services. Thus, I was particularly interested in the ratings for best and worst television commercials. Paul Hardy's commercials were rated best by 27 percent of the respondents. Indeed, most of those who said they had switched to Hardy reported doing so because of his television commercials. Treen's were thought best by 20 percent, mine by 18 percent, and Lambert's by 18 percent. I was more intrigued by those who rated the *worst* television commercials. Mouton's commercials were disliked by 17 percent and Lambert's by 12. Treen's commercials, by comparison, were thought to be worst by only 4 percent and mine by 3 percent. I think, at the very least, when a candidate is spending almost a quarter-million dollars a week on television spots, as I was at this point, he should avoid having his commercials make people mad at him. Television advertising is incredibly expensive, and the polls' rating of its effectiveness can be very discouraging. For example, Lambert was running a costly spot showing why Dave Treen should not be elected governor.

This poll showed that 34 percent of the respondents had never even seen the spot, and that 41 percent of those who saw it thought it was too negative. It also showed that more than a third of those who saw the ad had no idea who sponsored it. The poll also revealed that only 19 percent knew Edwards had made a television spot endorsing me, 64 percent had no idea he had taken a position in the election, and 52 percent said it would make no difference in their selection anyway. Clearly, despite a television commercial cost which came to look like the national debt, television campaigning is still more art than science!

Identifying the Issues

One of the major uses for a poll is in the identification of issues for the campaign. It is important to get a pulse of the people to find out what they are thinking. That is more important than what the candidate thinks the issues should be. After eight years as chairman of the Louisiana Board of Commerce and Industry, I believed strongly that economic development and employment would be my major and most logical issue. We used the term "jobs" over and over in the campaign, and it is interesting to note that other candidates have followed suit.

Education surfaced as the other major issue, a recurring concern for the people of Louisiana. The other issues that quickly came to the fore were the right-to-work question, the environment, and the death penalty. Equal rights actually got to be a major issue in the governor's campaign, despite the fact that it was really a national issue. One of the saddest days in my campaign was when an influential group of Catholic women, with whom I had worked for many years, walked into my office and said, "You've been our friend for many years and you've done everything we asked, but you are for the Equal Rights Amendment; we're against it, and so we have to be against you." The heart of that issue, of course, was legalized abortion which, more than ten years later, became such a raging legislative controversy that Louisiana gained national notoriety.

As a Roman Catholic, I am morally opposed to abortion, but I was for ratification of the Equal Rights Amendment. I have been in business and government enough years to know that women still are not always treated fairly or paid equitably, and I support them in their effort for equality, even though that position cost me dearly in many areas of the state.

We tried to run a positive campaign, partly because I think the voters deserve a positive discussion of the issues and partly because that is just my personal nature. There was, however, a lot of fear and hysteria sown in that campaign. Louis Lambert actually filmed one major television commercial in the middle of Three Mile Island. To this day, not one person has died as a result of the incident at Three Mile Island, but it became an issue in the campaign anyway.

Some issues are really political gimmicks. Tolls on the Mississippi River Bridge is an excellent example of a political gimmick. We saw that when the one-dollar toll was put back on the bridge, in order to pay for construction of a second span, the world as we knew it did not end. That bridge lost the election for Chep Morrison because his opponent, John McKeithen, had made up a huge sign saying, "If you vote for me, I'll take the tolls off the bridge." Chep should never have allowed himself to be drawn into that issue because it cost him the election.

In my own race for governor, many of my friends from across the Mississippi River, which divides New Orleans from the West Bank, urged me to come out against tolls on the bridge. I said that we needed tolls to pay for new bridge construction; that position cost me votes.

All issues work that way. Every issue has its price. When a candidate takes a position on one specific issue, he does so knowing that it will cost him some votes from people who would have backed him except for his stand on that one single issue. The only alternative is to run a campaign that is pleasant but completely devoid of issues, just based on platitudes and personality. I've never run that kind of campaign in my entire career—that just isn't Jimmy Fitzmorris. When I began developing issues for the campaign, I believed that people expect a governor to be able to deal with a whole range of issues. Bubba Henry was a fine Speaker of the

House and a close personal friend of mine, but he chose to concentrate almost exclusively on education. It became virtually his sole issue and, I believe, contributed to his limited appeal and, consequently, to his low showing in the election returns. I tried to make my campaign issues reach out to a much broader audience, but always understanding the inherent risks in running an issue-oriented campaign.

The hard fact is that people rarely judge the overall position of a candidate. Rather, they make their decision based on how the candidate squares with their personal position on one or two specific issues. It is the kind of occurrence that can cost an office-seeker lifelong friends. Once that happens it is difficult to move that person back to the center again. It's difficult to say, "OK, we disagree on one or two issues, but what about the other six?" If a candidate has taken a position which may be unpopular in a particular area, the local news media highlights that controversy to the exclusion of all other issues. I understand that principle, and I don't necessarily disagree with the way the media operates, but in politics you soon learn that you do not necessarily make news by being positive.

Meet the Candidates

The 1979 campaign for governor saw a crowded field of six major candidates. Each of my opponents was well known and highly regarded by me. With the exception of David Treen, each had served in the legislative branch during the time I presided over the state senate. In my view, any could have done a respectable job as governor.

Unlike some elections in which a candidate emerges whose only apparent qualities are ambition and personal wealth, each of the six candidates in 1979 had governmental experience. David C. Treen had been my personal friend for many years. His honesty and integrity were never called into question during the election nor during his term as governor. One-on-one, Treen is one of the most charming, entertaining men I've known in public life. I have often thought that his public career might have been considerably easier if more people had been able to see that side of him. His basic shyness made the roughhouse style of campaigning we use in Louisiana difficult, almost painful, for him—and, frankly, he wasn't very good at it. I remember once, after the first primary, when he attended a crowded affair in the St. Bernard auditorium. I was supporting Dave and went with him to this gathering. We arrived together but I left his side as we entered the auditorium, making my own way through the crowd, shaking hands and greeting everyone I saw. It took the better part of an hour to spend a personal moment with everyone I met and I finally made my way back to the door, exhausted but exhilarated by the experience—for I genuinely loved the process of meeting people.

There stood Dave Treen. He had never made it past the door and had spoken to a bare handful of his closest friends. His administration was marked by the same sense of precision and guardedness. When presented with a difficult decision, it was Treen's nature to study every conceivable aspect and angle, weighing every pro and con before reaching a decision. In the fast-moving pace of state government, that inability to study the issue rapidly and reach a quick decision worked against him. In terms of his public image, it was devastating. Edwin Edwards, who often treated Treen unfairly and teased him mercilessly, was very close to being right when he jibed that Treen was so cautious it took him an hour and a half to watch "Sixty Minutes."

I had known for months that Treen would be the probable Republican choice for governor under Louisiana's unique "open primary" law, and his candidacy spelled trouble for me. Treen represented the suburban Metairie area in Congress. He had also been the Republican nominee for governor eight years earlier and had built up a considerable recognition and following among Republicans and Independents around the state. He and I shared the same geographic base, the same business-oriented reputation, many of the same friends and, frequently, the same contributors. Virtually every vote Treen received was a vote that would have otherwise been mine.

Louisiana's open primary law bears mention. When Edwin Edwards was first elected governor, he had just survived a grueling and expensive primary battle. Then, personally and financially exhausted, he had to face Treen—who had virtually skated through his party's primary, having been able to hoard his financial resources for the runoff. Edwards decided that he would never again face such a financial "double whammy," so he convinced the legislature to change state law so that all candidates ran together in the primary and the top two—assuming that no one had a majority vote that day—faced each other in the runoff. The theory was that, since Democrats comprised such an overwhelming majority in voter registration, the result would be two good Democrats in the runoff.

It never quite worked out that way. The GOP moved quickly to endorse an "official" candidate in the open primary, leaving the assorted Democrats to fight it out. The fact that only one serious Republican was in the race against a host of Democrats usually meant that he was assured a place in the runoff. Add to that situation the huge increase in Republican registration, and you can easily see how potent this "single shot" Republican entry came to be.

For example, when Treen first ran against Edwards, there were only 12,000 registered Republicans in the entire state. By 1990 that number had risen to almost 364,000. Any candidate who can virtually count on a base of 364,000 votes, plus what additional votes he might siphon off from registered Democrats and Independents, is nearly a cinch for the runoff in a crowded election. At the same time the Republican registration was ballooning, the statewide Democratic organization was falling apart. That disintegration began with the election of Edwin Edwards, who preferred to build a personal machine rather than rely on the traditional Democratic parish network. It accelerated after the first primary in 1979 when the four defeated Democratic challengers endorsed the Republican candidate in the runoff at the risk of censure by the state party organization. It continued thereafter with the defection of major Democratic officeholders to the Republican ranks. That situation, and the national Democratic party's history of nominating presidential candidates who were unpopular in Louisiana, meant that the Louisiana Democratic party, despite overwhelming registration advantage, struggled to survive. All those factors combined to help Treen in 1979 as he faced five strong Democratic challengers which included:

Louis Lambert: I first knew Louis as a state senator when I was lieutenant governor and presiding officer of the state senate. He had gone on to become a member of the Louisiana Public Service Commission, a body that had previously served as a springboard for the gubernatorial ambitions of Huey Long and John McKeithen. He was a striking figure and a persuasive and articulate speaker, especially strong with labor and minority forces in the state. I had not thought that he would be a particularly strong candidate in the early part of 1979 because most observers still believed that the late Rep. Gillis Long would also run. Representative Long, a charismatic liberal, had one of the great last names in Louisiana politics and had long nurtured an ambition to be governor. He also came from the same general area as Lambert. When he opted out of the race for reasons of health, Lambert's chances were heightened.

Paul Hardy: Hardy was a skilled speaker and friend from his days in the state senate as well. He had gone from the senate to election as Louisiana's secretary of state, succeeding the late Wade 0. Martin, Jr., who served longer than any individual in modern times. I had strongly urged Hardy not to seek the governorship that year because, with Sen. Sonny Mouton also in the race, it was evident to me that their home-base support would be so split that neither could win. I also pointed out that no secretary of state in recent times had been able to mount a winning race for governor. I thought that since he was a very young man, Hardy had plenty of time to continue building statewide recognition and support. Hardy later went on to serve in the Treen administration and switched parties to become lieutenant governor by beating the incumbent, Bobby Freeman, but lost his re-election bid in 1991. Hardy's strongest suit was his television commercials, often filmed both in Cajun French and in English.

Edgar "Sonny" Mouton: State senator Sonny Mouton was probably the most skilled operator on the floor of the senate of my lifetime. I have often said that if I had a bill I really wanted passed or defeated, I would turn first to Senator Mouton.

Short, wiry and intense, Mouton was widely respected and admired in the senate. In 1960 people used to say that if the president of the United States were chosen by the U.S. Senate, Lyndon B. Johnson would be the landslide winner. Mouton had much the same kind of support in the Louisiana senate. Unfortunately, he had relatively little statewide exposure, and gaining the necessary exposure in a crowded field is a painfully expensive process—doubly so when there is another strong contender from your home area (Hardy). I urged Senator Mouton to run for lieutenant governor and would have been pleased and proud to have put together a Fitzmorris-Mouton ticket in 1979 if he had agreed. I believe we would have been successful.

E. L. "Bubba" Henry: Henry had been one of the "young Turks" who seized control of the Louisiana house of representatives and became its speaker. In that role, he presided over the house at the same time I presided over the senate. Together, we had fashioned a whole series of reforms to bring some order and decorum to the previously chaotic legislative process. In doing so, Henry had won a loyal statewide following. Tall, lanky, and thoughtful, Bubba Henry brought a quiet, earnest, homespun sense of order and purpose to his political life and to this campaign. All candidates admired and respected him.

He also earned the support of the New Orleans *Times-Picayune*, the powerful daily newspaper, and of the Alliance for Good Government, perhaps the most effective and respected of the city's various reform organizations. Both those elements detracted from support I had otherwise hoped and expected would be mine. He came from Jonesboro, also home of a highly regarded former governor, my old friend Jimmie Davis, and had considerable regional support from those who thought that part of the state deserved to elect a governor once again. Throughout the long campaign, we met again and again in public debates and forums. I enjoyed these public appearances and found them generally useful. In a public debate you often get to speak to and meet voters who are truly uncommitted or who are only nominally supporting some other candidate. Thus, there is always the potential to gain a new voter, worker, or contributor at such a forum. In that sense, at least, those multi-candidate forums are more useful than a meeting comprised of only your own, already-committed, campaign supporters. Debates are not, however, very useful forums for the dissemination of new or novel campaign positions.

The fact is, after the first time all candidates meet together in one of these sessions, everyone pretty well knows what each candidate will say. After that, very little new information comes out during the remainder of the campaign. From the first meeting onward, it is mostly a question of each candidate's refining and polishing his already-stated position and seeking to reiterate his own positions in a way that will catch the attention of the voters and the media.

The highest point of the debates, from my perspective anyway, was that we each admired and respected the other candidates. I cannot recall a single word in anger or any attempt to belittle one another throughout the campaign. In fact, these appearances got to be so routine that we all got together at one point and concocted a "group answer" to one of the questions that invariably surfaced at every such forum. Someone always asked, "If you are elected, who will be your commissioner of administration?" This question was generated by the perception, probably correct, that the commissioner is the second most powerful man in state government. Certainly that was true with respect to the relationship between Edwin Edwards and his commissioner, Charles Roemer, father of a subsequent governor.

On this particular night, each of us approached the podium in response to that question and replied that we intended to name Bubba Henry to that post, to which Henry coyly replied that he would accept. This response was only partly in jest for Henry was clearly qualified by training and temperament for the job and, in fact, he performed exactly that role in the Treen administration—with great distinction.

The lowest point of the debates had to do with the inability to ration time accurately and to judge which appearances would be worth the time and travel. I remember specifically one day when all the candidates spoke in Shreveport in the morning. Then I flew to Metairie, at the other end of the state, after a full day, for a forum at the Donelon Office Building. Only Treen and I made the trip, although I believe everyone had promised to show. The candidates and our aides easily outnumbered the handful who bothered to turn out, a really disappointing end to a hard and wasted day "on the road." Perhaps the other candidates had a better "sixth sense" about the relative importance of this gathering, but I doubt it. How can a candidate force a group to guarantee him that a specific number will be on hand for a forum?

In the end, every candidate becomes famous among his staff for asking the rhetorical question, "Why are we here and who set this schedule?"

Paying the Piper

Our time on the road was about evenly divided between appearances, jointly and alone, and the dreadful, daily task of raising campaign funds. In my lifetime I have raised millions of dollars, mostly for charitable organizations. I have no trouble at all raising money for others, but it became increasingly distasteful and painful to maintain the daily drudge of raising the $4 million I needed to run my campaign. I had originally said that I thought I could run for governor with somewhere between $2.5 and $3 million. I turned out to be almost a million dollars too conservative in terms of what I finally spent. Much of campaign costs must be raised by the candidate himself. We all have fund-raising volunteers, and thank God for them, but when it comes down to the bottom line, most contributors want the individual candidate to know, personally, that they have made a donation to his effort. You would be amazed at the number of people—including very small contributors—who said, "You tell Jimmy Fitzmorris that if he wants a contribution, he should come by and see me himself."

I understand that attitude, but such people fail to realize the tremendous amount of territory each candidate must cover and the heavy demands on his personal time. It was always interesting to me that the major contributors to my various campaigns almost never asked for a favor. By the same token, many persons who made very small contributions thought nothing of asking extraordinary, and sometimes highly inappropriate, favors. I sometimes said, "I'm sorry, but what you are asking me to do could send both of us to prison," but the response invariably was, "But I'm just asking you to do this one thing." The fact is, the average person looks just at his particular problem, and the successful candidate has to be able to find a way either to satisfy him or to explain why he can't. That requires a certain temperament. A candidate cannot allow such experiences to eat away at him or make him cynical or bitter. Many people just believe that they elect their officials who are public servants in every sense of the word. The truth is, after raising the first million dollars or so, the rest comes very hard indeed. When raising $4 million, ten- and twenty-dollar checks just don't go very far at all.

It is terribly discouraging to say to previous contributors, "I know you already gave, but now I need you again, this time, more than ever." That was particularly hard for me because I always put myself in the other fellow's shoes. He wants to help. He may have already given five hundred or a thousand dollars. That may be all he can afford to give. Yet, I am between a rock and a hard place. I desperately need additional money, and the available sources are growing more limited each day. It is always possible to raise some money from people who expect to own your soul. But if you want to raise money the proper way, it is a daily grind.

Early in the campaign we established a monthly fund-raising goal and quickly learned that didn't work. For one thing, despite our best intentions and efforts, everything cost more than we thought it would or should. Second, many people who offer to help raise money soon find that it is more time-consuming and difficult than they had anticipated and they fade from the scene, which means that the candidate must pick up the load himself. Whenever I was going out of town, I would call our people in each community I planned to visit and ask them to set up a breakfast, a lunch, and a dinner—and sometimes two or three of each on one day—so I could meet some potential contributors and ask for money.

The fact is, any person who now thinks about seeking public office must first ask himself whether he can raise the necessary money. That question is now more important than background, qualifications, issues, and all the rest. And that money has to come from a wide variety of sources.

I remember one elderly lady in Shreveport. In her seventies, she lived in a nursing home. Out of her little allowance she sent us a handwritten check for ten dollars every month. I went to see her after the election; she has since passed away. I also remember Heather Ann Iseley, the pretty, eight-year-old daughter of a Slidell minister. She came with her father to meet me at a rally there and later wrote me a touching letter, wishing me luck and enclosing her week's allowance, one dollar, for our campaign. As a parent I've learned two basic lessons about children: Children are great judges of character; they recognize and respect an adult who treats them with respect. Second, children are basically sincere; they know more about what's going on in their communities than we sometimes give them credit for. Her mother told me that Heather remembered me in her prayers, and I remembered her in mine. Heather must be nearly of voting age herself now. I hope she still has that same confidence, enthusiasm, and interest in the political process.

I began the system of contributions on the installment plan, an idea which was way ahead of its time but which is becoming popular all around the nation now. The idea is that a person can give two hundred dollars a year for six years, for example, to a senatorial candidate. It has come to a situation where a candidate's strongest supporters must be asked to contribute every month because campaign costs are so high hardly anyone can raise what he needs in one or two checks.

In Louisiana, I think the availability of money has gotten so limited that few campaigns will be able to spend what we did. The

1979 race was in the twilight of the golden "oil years" in the state, and many of those who were active contributors in those days did not survive the oil crunch. The high cost of campaigning has a lot to do with why we elect almost 98 percent of all incumbents—the money just isn't available for a challenger.

Incumbents now depend almost entirely on political action committees for their funding, and I think those days are numbered as well. PACs, as they are known, are becoming so distasteful that I believe one day they will be outlawed. When that happens, we will have to face an entirely new set of realities about fund-raising.

What will we do? For one thing I suspect that we will have to establish very strict spending limits. We have already adopted some meaningful reforms about how we report political contributions, but much more effort is needed. In Louisiana, for example, it should be possible for us to have strict spending limits and then to turn to the public television stations to provide free public forums at which all candidates would have an equal opportunity to explain their views. The same could be done for spot announcements, perhaps even by members of the Louisiana Broadcasters Association. We also need a way to limit "soft money," contributions spent by private organizations or the parties themselves, which are not subject to the spending limits or the reporting rules, if that can ever be done without violating the rights of those organizations to speak out on the issues. Of course, getting such reforms enacted is hard because the present system works to the advantage of incumbents, and it is difficult to convince them to change the system. In the meantime, candidates will have to do what I did. I developed a system of filing cards containing the names of people I had been involved with over the past thirty years in public life.

That list represented a lot of history, personal contact, and lifelong friendship. We had no single contributors of the quarter-million-dollar variety, but a great many substantial contributors below that level. I doubt that 1 percent of my money came from outside Louisiana. I have always thought that the candidate who raises most of his money away from home is less effective than the candidate who gets his money from the home folks, the people who know him best. That is obviously not true in national or congressional elections where the PACs raise the lion's share, but it is certainly so in local and statewide races. I always tried never to neglect those who had more enthusiasm than cash to contribute because both are important. I had some wonderful and dedicated folks who had no wealth but were working for us every day, talking to their family, neighbors, and friends. When running a campaign, the important thing is not how many people promise to vote for you, but how many actually do. The secret is not how many people you can get to sign a petition or how many organizations endorse you. The petitions are only as good as the votes that go into the machine.

I was fortunate in that my campaign finance effort was run by some of Louisiana's most successful business executives: Robert H. Boh, president of Boh Brothers Construction; Joseph C. Canizaro, president of Joseph C. Canizaro Interests, who almost personally changed the New Orleans skyline; and James R. "Jim Bob" Moffett, chairman and chief executive officer of Freeport-McMoran. "Jim Bob," through the "Citizens for Fitzmorris Committee," deserves some special place in my heart. He was very helpful during the campaign but afterward, when we were defeated, discouraged, and nearly bankrupt, he almost singlehandedly raised enough money to wipe out the lion's share of our debt and never asked for a thing. My longtime friend Louis J. Roussel, oil producer and self-made millionaire, is a Horatio Alger story all his own. Roussel could make miracles happen. He gave us space for our headquarters in his American Bank Building for twenty years. George A. Fischer, secretary of the Department of Transportation under Gov. Edwin Edwards, and banker Robert E. Thompson worked with major contributors. Fischer, now a successful lobbyist, put together the "Fitzmorris Testimonial Committee." Floyd Guillot, CPA, retired vice president of Industrial Finance and Thrift, served as campaign treasurer.

Still, better than half of each candidate's day is spent raising hard cash. By the time my campaign and subsequent court challenge were completed, I had spent $3,660,211.85 and had a debt of $853,704.68. Two years later I had whittled that debt down to $221,750, which I discharged through forgiveness of some of the campaign notes and loans and through the sale of fifteen thousand cookbooks as well as World's Fair posters and commemorative plates, and through special events like a Sun King preview party at The Cabildo. The other candidates faced similar staggering deficits. Some candidates are literally destroyed by campaign debts, their marriages ruined, their businesses and careers toppled.

My 1979 gubernatorial campaign treasurer Floyd Guillot, close friend Jim Mehle, and me during the campaign.

In retrospect, I cannot say that political life is worth the awesome personal toll. There were two entities which funded much of my campaign: The first was the Citizens for Fitzmorris, formed by Jim Bob Moffett to raise money from oil-related interests. Moffett was a miracle-worker and when he got serious about raising money he didn't fool around. His Petroleum Club party, for example, cost $10,000 per ticket and that one event netted us $225,000, to which he added his own significant personal contribution. If you think it is difficult to raise money when people believe you have a chance to win, you have no idea how much more difficult it is to raise when you have lost. I simply do not know whether I could have avoided personal, financial ruin without Jim Bob Moffett.

Our other big financial venture was the Fitzmorris Testimonial Committee, formed by George Fischer and Bob Thompson. Contributions to that group were about half by testimonial events and half through notes. The group eventually raised $1,680,392.71.

All in all, we had over six thousand contributors ranging from the lady in Shreveport who gave ten dollars a month to some who gave $100,000 or more. The average was about $1,500. Individual contributions were interesting and challenging to raise because of the many different people one met in such widespread areas of the state and such vastly different occupations. I was astounded, even after a lifetime in politics, at the mechanics of holding a big event such as the $10,000 per ticket dinner. I had never even heard of a $10,000 per ticket dinner, let alone attended one, and I was dubious anyone would come. After all, what do you serve somebody for $10,000? On my way into the dinner I ran into reporter Iris Kelso who asked what we were serving. I told her I had no idea and was afraid to ask. When I walked in the room it was packed—and everyone there had paid for his ticket; there were no "complimentary tickets" to this event.

I was much too excited to eat anything, but the evening was wonderful. That grand gathering of successful friends and well-wishers, who cared enough to share their good fortune with the genuine need of my campaign, went a long way to boosting my confidence. It was a tremendous event in my life.

Most of the campaign contributions went to media and related personnel expenses. The same was true of the other candidates. We spent more money, per voter, than candidates in elections in any state but Alaska—which is misleading since it has so few voters. At the campaign's peak, in the final weeks, I was averaging $165,950 each week in radio and television commercials. I also had French and Spanish radio and newspaper advertising throughout the state. The other candidates spent in a similar pattern and wound up with similar debt, I'm sure. All together, we spent more than $20 million seeking the governorship. Spending per voter ranged from my cost, nearly $2 each, to Bubba Henry's, some 75 cents. Dave Treen spent $2,572,607 in the primary, $1.33 for every registered voter, and followed that up with another $3,277,420 in the runoff election against Louis Lambert. Almost $10 million of our combined expenditures went for the production and placement of media advertising. Professional assistance for advertising is amazingly expensive.

My principal media consulting firm charged $100,000 with the understanding that it might eventually earn more than that in media commissions. High as that might seem, it was nowhere near the record. The Mouton campaign paid David Garth, a nationally known media consultant, $693,000 just in fees and costs of production costs before Mouton's spots ever got on the air. Hardy paid $91,000 just for research and production costs for spots on hazardous waste. The candidates' additional costs for other consultants, attorneys, accountants, researchers, strategists, and the like totaled $2.5 million. One Lambert "voter identification" consultant charged $421,540, and Mouton paid a songwriter $1,500 to come up with a jingle. Our campaign had its own theme song, "The Ballad of Jimmy Fitz," written and performed by "Doc Randolph," who is, in real life, Randolph M. Howes, a distinguished New Orleans plastic surgeon—in addition to being an energetic, talented performer and composer. We first unveiled this song to a festive reunion of some six hundred assorted Fitzmorris relatives.

The spoken and written words are the currency of a campaign, and some of the biggest battles of our race, in spirited discussions with our agency, Cantelli, Killeen and Schaumburg, centered around the proper use and meaning of one or two words in a particular commercial.

We finally came down to two series of television commercials, produced by Tom Buckholtz, aided by Joe Catalanotto and Tom Varisco, one using the theme "Accomplishment you can see," talking about my record, and the second, "Things are getting better and I'm just getting started," giving my position on jobs, crime, the environment, and other issues. I ended by telling viewers, "I'm ready if you are," because I wanted to involve everyone who watched my commercials in my campaign. Media consultants are an emotionally charged and temperamental bunch, never lacking in self-confidence about their own importance. Handling their work requires striking a constant balance between the precision of a Philadelphia lawyer and the showmanship of a P. T. Barnum. It is no easy task. In the final analysis, the candidate himself must decide how he will be portrayed and just how far he is willing to go to attract attention. If you think there is sometimes a barn-burning jealousy between unpaid volunteers who frequently donate eighteen-plus hours per day to your cause and media consultants who, at hundreds of dollars an hour, breeze through headquarters dispensing their wisdom as pearls cast before swine, you are absolutely right. Yet their services are absolutely essential, and I tried to employ the wisdom of Solomon to keep us all yoked together sufficiently to see us through the campaign.

The insane spiral of campaign spending continued into the next gubernatorial campaign where only two candidates—David Treen, then the incumbent, and Edwin Edwards, trying for a comeback—mowed through $18 million, just slightly less than we six candidates spent the previous time. Edwards, in fact, set a national record for spending more money than any winning candidate in America, eclipsing a Rockefeller record (Jay, not Nelson).

Organizing from the Inside Out

It is difficult, even for some otherwise astute business executives, to grasp the tremendous expense and effort involved in organizing a major statewide political campaign. Let me try to explain it in business terms: Suppose I have a product to sell, a product that must be sold in every single parish, city, and town, farm and village throughout the state. Suppose that in order for this marketing campaign to be successful I must contact almost every consumer in the state. Imagine that I must create the marketing organization for this product from scratch, overnight. Then assume that I have only six months in which to make this product accepted in every home in Louisiana, that in six months I must raise more than four million dollars in capital to operate this business.

Understand that I cannot borrow much of this sum since I have no collateral or security. Consequently, I must raise the four million dollars I need from voluntary contributions, ten and twenty dollars at a time, doing so at the same time I am spending those very contributions to market my product. Imagine that I must hire, train, and manage my entire statewide sales force overnight, in order to get this product rapidly into the marketplace, and raise the money to pay its salary at the same time. Finally, assume that even if I manage to accomplish all that, mine is not the only product of its kind. At the same time there are five other major competing products, each claiming to be the best, vying for the attention of the households, competing to raise the same capital and to hire the same sales force. Remember, if I make the sale at the end of the six months (and all sales will take place on the same day), I will have only a month to make the same sale a second time, except that the competition will be reduced to only one other product. On the day of that second sale, my product will either be guaranteed four years "shelf life" or will be off the market, possibly forever. Those, my friend, are the challenges you face when you set out to organize a statewide political campaign. In my case, the product was Jimmy Fitzmorris.

Thus I began the process of creating a statewide political organization. Some personnel I was able to draw from past campaign volunteers and new supporters. Other aides were longtime staff. We also tried to attract the highest caliber professionals we could find because much of the work was sufficiently specialized and complex as to require trained professional assistance. Our campaign was divided into geographic districts and specific functions, all of which required the presence of volunteers who were willing to virtually abandon their families, careers, and private lives for the duration of the campaign. As much for my personal pleasure in reliving the pleasure of their company as to pay them a long overdue tribute for their very substantial personal and financial sacrifice during the long months of this campaign, I have included an appendix recounting some of the hundreds of key volunteers and staff from around Louisiana. As I reflect upon my many willing accomplices through the years, I am reminded of the lines Sen. George McGovern quoted from the poet William Butler Yeats that early morning as he accepted the Democratic party's nomination for president of the United States. "Think where a man's glory most begins and ends. And say my glory was I had such friends."

Other than media, one of the other major costs of campaigning concerns the campaign organization. We set up a whole series of headquarters locations in the eighteen months leading up to the election. In the American Bank Building, Joe Willis and Frances Shay were responsible for receiving, acknowledging, depositing, and accounting for all statewide campaign contributions as well as handling special events and the work of the finance committee. Our computer center was in the Stewart Enterprises Building, donated by Frank B. Stewart, Jr., chairman and chief executive officer of Stewart Enterprises and a key fund-raiser as well. There, Elaine Hartley, Mary Lynn "Cissy" McShane, and Joanne Scheuermann handled our direct mail campaign, statewide meeting notices, and the like.

Through the "Fitzgram," our campaign newsletter, we tried to keep all our statewide volunteers active, informed, enthused, and involved.

As the election drew nearer, entrepreneurs David Burrus and Darryl Berger, then of Berger and Burrus Investments, donated space in Delta Towers in downtown New Orleans. There Jennie LeBlanc coordinated an extensive telephone "boiler room" operation.

It was also the center of activities for Mary Pumilia and Nancy Albert's women's committees and for the Heritage Groups, which were headed by Ricardo Pardo. At 4041 Tulane, in space donated by Russell L. Cuoco, we spilled over onto two floors. Downstairs, Nick and Rita Lapara coordinated area volunteers, busily addressing, stuffing, and mailing campaign material and distributing bumper stickers, signs, and other campaign materials. Upstairs, retired brigadier general Karl N. Smith supervised key statewide operations. We opened a statewide headquarters at 818 Gravier Street where many of our key staff personnel were positioned. George Fischer and Bob Thompson conducted their fund-raising and organizing activities from there. Jim Harris, Kirk Melancon, and Greg Buisson were in charge of media and public relations. Jim Harris, former press secretary to Governor Edwards, is now a successful Baton Rouge lobbyist. Kirk Melancon, a former aide to U.S. senator J. Bennett Johnston, is now public information officer for Jefferson Parish. Greg Buisson, who interviewed me for a school newspaper while still in his teens, later joined my lieutenant governor's staff. He is now public affairs director of WVUE Television in New Orleans. Gay Smith handled most of our campaign scheduling and transportation from that location.

My niece, Beth Ann Simno, and Stephanie Walker Schaff comprised the secretarial staff. Ron Luman and Jesse LeBlanc distributed supplies from this location as well. We kept in particularly close touch with our Jefferson Parish headquarters, which Glenn Gennaro, B. J. (Mrs. Anthony) Corcoran, Lillian Stanton, and Rosemary Duvall had well in hand, and with our Baton Rouge office, where the late Stanley Gross and retired colonel Stephen J. Bailey, Sr., and their wives represented our interests in the capital city. In the late months of the campaign we added headquarters in Alexandria, Bogalusa, Donaldsonville, Hammond, Houma, Lacombe, Lafayette, Lake Charles, Monroe, West Monroe, Opelousas, Ponchatoula, Shreveport, and Slidell. We had at least one office in every major city and town in the state. Oftentimes, the local leadership wanted an office and raised their own money to operate it. Sometimes they found free rent or chipped in to pay the utilities, but we always tried to have at least one paid (though very nominally paid, to be sure,) staffer in each office.

I always wanted someone responsible for making certain that each office was open, because nothing is worse than having a campaign headquarters that is closed. It would be better to have no office at all than to have one that is inoperative. Managing the activities of these locations, as well as the "advance" planning for local events, required skilled field coordinators like Bill Allerton, Ernest Colbert, Jr., Robert H. Tucker, Jr., and Charles C. "Chuck" Zatarain III. These invaluable friends were my eyes, ears, and voice throughout the state. Bill Allerton, a Fitzmorris worker since his youth, has gone on to operate his own highly successful political consulting firm in Metairie. Ernest Colbert, a former official of the Carpenters' Union, is now president of his own consulting firm. Robert Tucker, former aide to Mayor Moon Landrieu, has become an internationally recognized business consultant. Chuck Zatarain is a successful New Orleans attorney. New Orleans lawyer Charles E. Cabibi, Sr., was legal counsel for the campaign. While all this campaign activity was taking place, I was still serving every day as lieutenant governor.

Some of the unclassified employees of the lieutenant governor's office performed campaign duties on their own time: Pat Gallwey

Campaign staffers in the 1979 election Bob Tucker, Ernie Colbert, and Sonny Lacroix—all loyal, dedicated workers.

worked closely with the advance teams, training volunteers and special events coordinators and aiding the finance committee. Carol Daigle, my executive assistant since city hall days, resigned from the state payroll early in 1979 to devote her full-time attention to scheduling the candidate, staffing the various headquarters, designing the campaign contribution and financial reporting system, and organizing the finance committees. She was the only person besides me and treasurer Floyd Guillot who was authorized to sign campaign account checks. The work of lieutenant governor, of course, did not stop simply because I was a candidate for governor. I served as acting governor while Governor Edwards was out of state, and my duties took me from Washington, D.C., to San Francisco, Los Angeles, and Pittsburgh. Carol and Gay coordinated the schedule, perhaps the most exhaustive and unheralded task in politics.

The single most valuable commodity in a campaign is the time of the candidate. Each candidate for public office surrenders all of his personal and family time and privacy and, yet, that is not nearly enough. No matter how crowded my schedule, I tried never to be away from my wife and daughter more than two nights in a row. In the hectic final days of the campaign I came literally to hunger for just a few moments to myself, to read, to think, or just to rest! Hundreds of competing requests for everything from a formal speech to a few minutes' private conversation poured into headquarters daily from every part of the state. Just being able to keep track of the scheduling was one of the major reasons I moved my statewide headquarters from Baton Rouge to New Orleans, my personal base of operations, in fond hopes of keeping my hectic schedule at least somewhat organized. It is sometimes possible to dispatch family or close friends to meetings the candidate cannot make. Gloria, while not terribly comfortable doing intense, issue-oriented presentations before antagonistic audiences, is better than anyone when it comes to speaking to women's groups and the like. Lisa, the great joy of my life, turned out to be a firecracker speaker and organizer with young people's organizations.

On occasion, my brother Norris, and nephew George Simno III, were able and accomplished "pinch hitters." Generally, however, people want to see and touch the candidate, himself. I found it was more acceptable simply to explain that my schedule that day, all the way across the state, made it impossible for me to be with some subsequent group that night. Most were very understanding.

Angling for Endorsements

Anytime you hear a candidate say, "I was not counting on the endorsement of that particular group, and not receiving its endorsement is of no particular importance to our campaign," you can bet that's an endorsement he sought and failed to win. Endorsements are like ball games. You win some, you lose some, but you suit up for every game! I believe that most effective endorsements are like word-of-mouth advertising—incomparable and priceless. I might not be personally well known in a little town, but if leading local citizens, people who are known and trusted in the community, say that Jimmy Fitzmorris is the man for the job, that's at least twice as effective as my buying newspaper space or television time to say the same thing about myself.

My campaign benefitted greatly from the endorsements of community leaders and elected officials. In New Orleans, for example, I had the endorsement and active support of the late mayor Dutch Morial and former mayors Vic Schiro and Moon Landrieu. They were joined by almost a hundred other mayors of cities and towns throughout the state. The ringing endorsement of black ministers all around the state was also very encouraging and helpful. Key white ministers in New Orleans took an active role in contacting their counterparts across the state in my behalf, including nationally respected religious leaders like Dr. J. D. Grey and Dr. Bill Hinson. Their letters praising me opened doors throughout Louisiana. It was highly unusual for key white Baptists to become actively involved in any Louisiana gubernatorial campaign, and I was well known as a Roman Catholic. Our shared vision for the future was more important than our religious differences, and I valued their fellowship and friendship.

Endorsements by local assessors, sheriffs, and legislators— particularly those from the Black Caucus—the New Orleans Regular Democratic Organization, and the late former secretary of state Wade O. Martin, Jr., were wonderfully encouraging. So were the endorsements of college fraternities. We made a particular effort to involve young people in every phase of the campaign. In fact, the average age of my staff was about twenty-five. We paid particular attention to Louisiana's college campuses where Greg Buisson,

Erik Skrmetta, Michele Daigle, Ora Cosse, and Denise Redmann Krouse played a vital role. The process of gaining an endorsement from most groups begins with completion of an exhaustive questionnaire by the candidate, stating his position on issues of interest to that group. Generally, only unions and politically active organizations make such endorsements. Rarely does an individual business or commercial group decide to take the risk of making a public endorsement of a candidate, which I think is unfortunate. The Louisiana Association of Business and Industry has made some headway in this area of guiding business interests in the state about where the candidates stand with respect to issues that concern them, but more room for improvement remains.

Some of these questionnaires are well thought out and carefully drafted. Some are contradictory or confusing. Others are just plain silly, but the candidate tries his level best to answer each one. It is absolutely essential that the candidate answer fully and consistently so he is not later put in the position of contradicting himself or appearing to try to be "all things to all people." The candidate himself may be the only person who actually knows his position on some of the questions that arise. The candidate will have to live with his responses to these queries; he is committing himself to support or to oppose projects which are very important to the people asking the questions. Finally, there are the endorsements of certain "political" organizations. When I first ran for office I could count these on one hand. Now they proliferate with every campaign. One might think that with the advent of television such organizations would become as extinct as the dodo bird, but such is not the case. When a candidate loses such endorsements, it is usually because of the political philosophy of those who actually make the choice. The group may claim membership in the hundreds or thousands, but the actual endorsement is decided by a much smaller clique; sometimes only one individual or a handful of people makes the decision.

These organizations have a definite role in the political process. Theirs are the foot soldiers who make certain the candidate's sample ballot and campaign literature get into the homes of the electorate. We candidates like to believe that the deathless prose we incorporate into our newspaper advertisements is read by every voter, but that's not so. Neither is it true that every voter carefully considers every candidate's television and radio commercials, no matter how profusely produced they may be. Nor are these endorsements without cost to the candidate. Like everything else in life, with endorsements there is no free lunch! Each endorsing organization asks for campaign literature to distribute, banners, bumper stickers, and the like. Much of this advertisement is useful. All of it is expensive. Nothing is quite so brutalizing to a candidate's psyche as entering a garage or warehouse somewhere, after the election is over, and finding stacks of unopened campaign material. Campaign posters are an excellent example. Posters are fine in a local campaign. In a statewide race, though, the cost of sticks to tack them to alone runs into the thousands. Every time it rains the process has to be repeated.

The cost of campaign material is only the beginning. Most such organizations also want to charge each candidate a "pro-rata" share of their campaign and electioneering expense. Those may be costs for telephone banks, election day transportation, research, voter canvassing, and advertising. Much of it is a duplication of the candidate's own organizational election expense. Much of it is wasted. None of it is free. Yet, it is next to impossible to determine precisely which costs are most valuable and most important. Consequently, each candidate tries, as best he can, to select those groups whose campaign expense is most appropriate to the kind of campaign he wants and needs to run. He looks for organizations with a good reputation, those with a track record for producing results, groups in an area of interest or a geographic region in which he may be weak or which has some other especially compelling attraction. In the final analysis, the candidate knows there is only so much money available for this kind of networking, and he has to pick and choose among the competing groups, knowing full well it is his personal responsibility to raise the contributions to keep the organization well oiled.

Inventing the Eight Day Week

All of this activity requires a tremendous investment of time by the candidate, at a time when he is often on the road, roaring from one stop to another. There were many times when I realized that a month had passed in which I had not eaten one meal in my own home—not a breakfast, lunch, or dinner. Campaigning is a tremendous sacrifice for a candidate and a harder one for his family. The logistics are impossible. Everyone expects the candidate to "dress for success," but that sometimes means he must change clothes three or four times a day, as in the case of going from a grimy factory to a formal dinner. Just getting his shirts done and suits cleaned is a major challenge. The process is physically demanding. It requires not just stamina but considerable self-control and character as well. Everywhere he goes, well-meaning people say, "Be a good ol' boy and have a couple of beers with us." They're just being friendly, of course, but if a candidate makes fifteen stops each day and has three drinks everywhere he stops, by the end of the month he'll end up in an alcohol treatment center. Over a lifetime in politics I have seen this happen to otherwise wonderful men and women on many occasions.

I set a personal rule that I have kept without exception. At one time I was concerned about offending someone by not drinking at a social event. It is, indeed, hard to be in public life in Louisiana without drinking, but even harder to survive if you do drink. You are tired when you get there and, a few drinks later, you make an innocent comment or you do something that may later be misconstrued. So I resolved not to drink. At one time I used to color my soft drinks, mixing Coca-Cola and 7-Up so it looked like a high-ball. Later, I decided that was ridiculous. If my friends had the right to choose to drink, I had an equal right to choose not to drink. I would respect their decision, and expect them to respect mine. I also learned to guard my time jealously. There are only so many hours in the day, no matter how thinly you slice them. So I learned to "make the room." I would work counterclockwise, shaking every hand in the room. And then I would leave. After the first conversation, there is absolutely nothing to be gained by lingering pointlessly.

Jim Comiskey, one of the grand old men in New Orleans politics of another era, used to say that I was the only man he knew who could enter a crowded room, walk through and meet every person in the hall, and leave through an alley without anyone knowing I was gone.

My days began then as they do now, at 6:30 A.M. or earlier, and ended well past midnight. Until I was lieutenant governor I could count on one hand the times I had taken an airplane. Now I spend much of my life in the clouds. I soon grew resigned to the inherent danger of air travel, although I never grew to like it. I happen to be a person of strong religious faith, and I learned to put my trust in the Lord when I entered each small airplane.

I am not, however, certain the Lord always knew the caliber of plane I was charging to His care. When you are depending on the kindness of volunteers for your air transportation, you do not always have the luxury of selecting the finest or best-maintained aircraft. One day we were in Lake Charles, on our way to some function at the race track in Vinton, and a friend volunteered his own small plane.

There was just enough room for me and the trooper in the back. We climbed in as the pilot said, "We have to hurry and leave before the fog sets in." I should have had second thoughts then because it was so clear we could see a hundred miles. But we left.

We were no sooner in the air than the pilot said, "The door won't stay closed. We have to land and close it." After several attempts he said, "It's no use. The door won't close. We'll just have to go with it open." And so we did. The door was open and the wind was whipping through the plane; it was like riding a tornado. As we returned we passed over Moisant Airport at New Orleans. I asked the pilot, who was also the owner, where he intended to land. "Moisant," he replied. "Didn't we just fly over Moisant?" I queried. His son, sitting in the copilot's seat, leaned out and allowed as how he thought that did, indeed, look a lot like Moisant. So we circled, returned, and landed. It was a sprightly little single-engine plane and I vowed to thank my friend for both trips, because I had privately decided I had just enjoyed both my first and last voyage in this small flying machine. It was the kind of trip you dare not mention when you get home. You wonder how you lived through it all. Generally, on such trips, I spent the entire time preparing for the next stop, reviewing the names of the people I was about to see. Nothing is more embarrassing than a candidate who arrives and looks at the assembled supporters with absolutely no idea who anybody is.

While air travel was essential in such a far-flung campaign, we spent thousands of miles on Louisiana highways too. I always tried to find the back roads and stop at service stations along the way. You meet absolutely no one on the interstates. I was accompanied by a state trooper, who is provided for the protection of the lieutenant governor and other elected officials, and a staff assistant or two. I tried always to travel light, in terms of both baggage and personnel. It was difficult to separate official travel for the lieutenant governor's office from political travel, but we always tried to have a private vehicle on hand when that leg of the trip was purely political. The troopers were invaluable. Billy

Booth, Eric Durel, Mike Sunseri, Steve Campbell, and Larry Antoine, among others, came to be like members of my family and are still dear and trusted friends. Many nights none of us was able to work in time for dinner. Somebody would pack the car with candy bars and we would simply forego dinner so we could see a few more people along the way. Sometimes we didn't even have the luxury of candy bars if nobody had exact change for the vending machine, so we would all go to bed hungry.

The opportunity to meet people on their own turf, in their home communities, was a great learning experience, invaluable and enjoyable to me. I remember campaigning one day in Lafayette. This was the heart of Mouton/Hardy country and very crucial to my campaign. I was campaigning door-to-door and met a barber named Mr. Francis. I told him I had a dear friend in New Orleans, Norman Francis, president of Xavier University. "That's my son," he said, and he became very helpful to me in the Lafayette area as time went on. My routine was personally to walk three or four blocks in different areas every place we went. Of course, I couldn't see everybody, and some were offended that I missed their home, but word did get around that I had been in town. Sometimes we used a recreational vehicle, loaned to our campaign by "Mr. Bill," the late Bill Bailey, owner of Bailey Lincoln-Mercury, whom I had met back in my railroad days. We stocked the recreational vehicle with typewriters and a telephone so it became a traveling headquarters, driven by former state trooper Jim Borgstede. We sent it ahead and it would be waiting when I got to a major city. We then had a base of operations as we worked within the radius of that city.

It was not unusual for our campaign to rely on recreational vehicles, cars, trucks, vans, airplanes, and occasionally boats just to accomplish one campaign swing across Louisiana. They were all necessary in our effort to compress as many stops as possible into one twenty-four-hour day. Sometimes we felt as though we had invented the eight day week! The campaign swing of July 20-21 was not particularly unusual, but it should give some indication of our travel demands.

That Friday, July 21, I left my home near New Orleans' lakefront in the FITZ Van at 7:30 A.M., bound for Covington, where I had a 9:00 A.M. meeting with Mayor Ernest Cooper, who had endorsed me. After that I was joined by FITZ Blitzers, local campaign workers like realtor Norwood Smith, Kay Fitzmorris, and others, and four reporters who were covering that day's campaign itinerary. At 9:15 we arrived at the St. Tammany Parish Courthouse where Chief Deputy Sheriff Wallace Legarde was to take us through the building. At 9:25 we met with Clerk of Court Lucy Reid Rausch and at 9:35 with Police Jury President Robert J. Innerarity. At 9:40 we arrived in the office of Assessor Wayne G. Wascom. This was an important meeting since the local assessor is a key figure and Wascom was reportedly leaning toward Lambert. At 10:00 I did a radio interview and was back on the interstate to Hammond by 10:15.

I walked into my Hammond headquarters at 10:45 and was met by campaign workers, two radio newscasters, and three newspaper reporters. We walked the streets and worked the businesses for an hour. The real reason for being in the neighborhood was to drop in on Ross Downing, a significant contributor to the Edwards campaign who had been leaning toward Treen but who we thought might be persuaded to join our campaign. As always, every trip had a financial motive. At 11:45 we went to lunch at Murphy's Restaurant on Highway 51 north where we were joined by another newspaper reporter. At 1:00 P.M. we were taken on a tour of Charter Marketing Company by manager Buddy Weir. At 1:30 we toured the Oliver Treatment Plant. We hurried across the street to Little Johnny's Restaurant where Johnny DeMarca was waiting. An enthusiastic supporter, he had supplied the sandwiches for the local headquarters opening and deserved a moment of personal appreciation. By 2:00 we were on our way to Ponchatoula for a 2:15 appointment with Mayor Collins Bonicard, S. Newman "Gramps" Fitzmorris—who managed that area for our campaign—and campaign workers.

At 2:30 we toured the Modern Maid Food Products Company. Roy Nelson and his son, Allen, owners of Elmer's Candy Corporation, took us on a tour of their plant at 3:00 and by 3:30 we were back on the road to Independence. Fifteen minutes later we were ln the office of Mayor John LaRock, who took us to the Kellwood Clothing Factory. By 4:15 we were on the road to Amite for a key reception in my honor. My friend, Dr. Dan Bryant, staged a successful gathering for me at city hall with virtually every public official in Amite, Kentwood mayor Nick Saladino, Tangipahoa police jury president Cade Williams, and Kentwood police chief Edsell Graham. We broke away from our own reception just in time to make my scheduled speech to the Amite Chamber of

Commerce Annual Banquet across town in the Jaycee Hall, where I shared the podium with Jerry Stovall, later LSU football coach. By 8:45 we were back on the road to New Orleans, which meant that I was home sometime after 10:00 P.M. Throughout the day, meticulous attention to the schedule was imperative because, like every day, the events were crowded together despite being miles apart.

The next morning I flew by private helicopter to Irwinville, where Chris Faser had arranged for me to meet Bill Lane of Big River Industries. We took the helicopter to Port Allen for an 11:00 A.M. speech to a thousand people, dedicating the new Port Allen Marine Service building, a $1.5 million barge building operation. By noon we were back in the air on our way to Independence. Supporters met me at the plane and drove me to the home of Joe E. Anzolne, Sr., and then to a 12:30 luncheon at Kluchin's Restaurant. Then we flew back to our Hammond headquarters for a meeting with area black leaders. At 3:45 we exchanged the helicopter for a private plane and flew to Ruston, where Jimmy Howard, retired businessman, community leader, and our Northeast Louisiana coordinator was waiting at the airport. At 5:30 I was the guest at a reception sponsored by Mr. and Mrs. John Williams, with some one hundred important local people on hand. I could only stay until 7:00 in order to make the curtain of the "Wild Wood Express," a three-hour Western music show. Howard had arranged for the night, which we sponsored. I delivered a few remarks before the show and, as soon as the entertainment got under way, left through a side door for the wedding reception of my friend Mickey McHale's son. By 8:30 I was back in the air and on my way home again.

That was my life, seven days a week, throughout the campaign. It was packed with receptions at which I could not drink even a cup of coffee, since it is physically impossible to shake hands while holding a coffee cup, luncheons and dinners at which I could not eat because I had to speak and run to the next affair. It was a hectic year, but it gave me an opportunity to meet thousands of wonderful people I would not otherwise have known, to hear their hopes and dreams—and even their fears and dislikes—for people told them all freely to a man they hoped would be able to do something about them as governor. It was also a daily opportunity to meet with our army of volunteers. A campaign attracts thousands of major and minor players, each of whom believes his own contribution, whatever form it may take, to be essential to your campaign. It is important, no matter how tired or distracted you may be, to remember that these people are helping not because they are paid to do so, but because they want to. Those wonderful people become a part of your life, and they stay part of your life forever.

Not a day goes by, no matter where I am, that I do not bump into someone from Eunice or Crowley or Mamou, Alexandria, Lake Charles, Shreveport, or Monroe, who brings up his memories of his own relationship to that campaign. There are a lot of heartaches in not winning; it is a major catastrophe in one's life. There are an equal number of compensating benefits that come from seeking public office, a great, lifelong relationship with thousands of people in every walk of life.

Awaiting the Edwards Endorsement

And so it went, the pace picking up each day as we aimed toward election day. We increased our campaign advertising daily in the final weeks as the large undecided category began reaching a decision. We stepped up the endorsement announcements and the personal appearances. In the final hours, we brought out all our biggest guns. There was no bigger gun than the sitting governor of Louisiana, Edwin Washington Edwards. I had served eight years under Edwards and had worked closely with him as presiding officer of the senate and as acting-governor in his absence. While he and I were very different in almost every way you could imagine, we had a mutual friendship and respect, forged through those eight years together.

I wanted and needed his help and his endorsement. The presence of George Fischer, an Edwards cabinet officer, did a lot to give us the appearance of having Edwards' support. Most important, it opened key financial doors. Not all of Edwards' people joined our team, to be sure. His commissioner of administration, Charles E. Roemer, had offered to meet with me early in the campaign. I did not want to make any kind of commitment to Roemer and declined to attend. Shortly thereafter, Roemer surfaced as campaign manager for Sonny Mouton, and I am sure he tried his best to arrange an Edwards endorsement for his candidate. Edwards faced "home pressures" for his endorsement from both Hardy and Mouton since the three shared the same geographic base of support. That made the goal of getting Edwards' endorsement for my campaign even more crucial. Louis Lambert had the active aid of Lafayette lawyer William Broadhurst, one of Edwards' closest personal friends. Broadhurst later gained national attention for his friendship with Sen. Gary Hart. Finally, in the waning days of the campaign, Edwards endorsed my candidacy. It was an offhanded, diffident endorsement and many people didn't even know he had taken a stand, but it was better than nothing. Every candidate but Treen had wanted, needed, and sought it, and I was pleased that Edwin Edwards' endorsement was mine.

The Day of Decision

Election eve at our headquarters was a beehive of activity. Every available volunteer was pressed into service for the most important day of my life. All our field workers, coordinators, and young volunteers had come into headquarters readying for this final push. My dear friend, Mary Pumilia, came by and saw that we were all working frenetically and that no one was stopping to eat. She went back home and literally cleaned out her freezer, returning with a huge banquet—a literal Italian feast for a small army. In minutes we had wiped it out; the tables looked like vultures had descended. Dinner was over by nine, but we all worked till past midnight; some workers never went to bed. It was past midnight when Bill Allerton came up with the idea of putting flyers on people's cars that read: "Good Morning. It's Election Day and We Need Your Help." We found an understanding printer and ran off hundreds of them, which our young people spent the post-dawn hours putting on cars in key precincts around the city.

A few hours later, Gloria and I were the first to vote in our precinct, the Twenty-Third Precinct of the Fourth Ward, at the East Lakeshore Fire Station. I had decided to remain in New Orleans, keeping close to headquarters and visiting polling places around the city. In between visits, I spent the day on the telephone talking to our headquarters operations in every city. Throughout the day, I toured polling places to make myself evident on the street. This kind of physical presence on the part of the candidate himself is important to reassure and invigorate the volunteers and to discourage opponents. I knew that I was a highly recognizable figure in New Orleans, and I thought it important to be seen, full of confidence and self-assurance, in as many parts of the city as possible. That kind of personal contact translates into extra votes, maybe only a few hundred, but I knew that this election might well depend on a few hundred votes of people who heard I was on the street, looking relaxed, confident, and in control.

My travels did raise some questions. The Lambert people and supporters of other candidates were offering large servings of food in some areas, a particular concern since this was my home base. I took particular note of this in some uptown precincts near the river and some downtown precincts in the lower Ninth Ward, areas where I thought I should have been stronger. If my strength at home was being diluted by these efforts, I needed to depend even more strongly on my volunteer forces elsewhere around the state.

Election day always represents a major expense, partly because of the high cost of providing transportation in rural areas where there is no other regular transportation to the polls. We had budgeted $100,000 for that day alone. That sum was a bargain basement amount because we depended on volunteers for most assignments. For example, we had a group of volunteers whose task it was to make "wake up" calls to our workers and poll watchers. We also had people spot-checking selected precincts to see how the vote was turning out, similar calls being made at each headquarters. Unlike the brilliant, sunny day when I announced, election day was less than perfect.

There was spotty rain throughout the day. Nevertheless, I had my driver take me to within a few blocks of each polling place, after which I would leave the car and walk to the polling place, shaking hands and accepting good wishes all the way, rejoining the car on the other side. The day spun by, a blur of faces and phone calls, until the evening arrived. Finally, there was no more to do. The television commercials had all run, the speeches had all been made, the hands all shaken, the issues all addressed. As I look back on the television commercials and speeches today, my emphasis on "jobs," "education," and "the environment" could just as easily have been run in the last campaign for governor—or the next. The problems confronting us are very much the same. So is the need for a strong leader to tackle them. But for better or worse, this Fitzmorris campaign was ended and the decision was in the hands of the people. So it was that, full of confidence, and knowing that I had done all I could do, I stopped by my house, gathered my family, and we walked down the long hallway of the Fairmont Hotel together, bound for Room 1216, the International Suite, and the longest, most important night of our lives.

Chapter 2

The Boyhood Years

My childhood neighborhood still exists but, like the rest of New Orleans and most of America, it has changed beyond recognition. The sights and sounds which pervaded the dusty streets of my boyhood now exist only as shadowy images of the past, fixed forever in the minds of a small and rapidly disappearing generation which grew up in the 1920s.

We lived in a raised, two-story home at 3830 General Taylor. The other side of the house was occupied by my maternal grandparents. It was a large but modest house, white with green trim, on the corner of the block. Directly across Dorgenois Street was St. Matthias Church and school, center of our education and religious instruction, site of one of our favorite playgrounds, and almost a second home in my youth. On the ground level of our house was a basement which served as a focal point for neighborhood gatherings. Political meetings and voting were held there, and bingo games for the church and school. For more than a decade, it was also home to the Edith Heslin School of Dancing. Throughout my childhood, there was always a clamor of activity around my home, for I grew up in a family and time in which one's home was the center of the universe. Ours was not a generation in which young people yearned to escape their homes and move out on their own. Indeed, until the day I married I lived happily at home and, after our marriage, my wife and I returned without exception for Sunday dinners with my parents and for every holiday.

The house and grounds were spotlessly maintained by my father, who had some kind of unfailing Irish radar which could sense the presence of even an abandoned Kleenex on the lawn. I inherited his emphasis on orderliness, to the occasional distress of my family and staff. My dad was terribly proud of his home. It was considered a "step up" from the Irish Channel of his youth. General Taylor Street was in the "Broadmoor Section," largely populated by Irish and Italians, usually only a generation or two removed from the "old country." We were situated between the Irish Channel and another Irish conclave known as "The Devil's Elbow." As was, even then, the pattern in New Orleans, ours was a mixed neighborhood with black families living in harmony only a few blocks away.

My Irish Roots

My dad's family lived first on Annunciation Street and later on Laurel. His father, Martin, a mattress maker, died when I was very young. He was waked at home and buried in St. Patrick's cemetery. His father, Martin Sr., had come to New Orleans from County Kerry, Ireland. I can remember many childhood visits to my grandmother, Catherine's, house. She was a tall, stately woman, deeply religious and very Irish.

Her father, John Cogan, had immigrated from Ireland and fought for the Confederacy. Her brother, James, had died as a young man while fighting for Sherman's army in Georgia. It was as a lineal descendant of Pvt. John Cogan, Company G of the Louisiana Infantry, First Regiment, that I was awarded the Cross of Military Service by the Daughters of the Confederacy in 1973, recognizing my own military service. There was, in my childhood, a stereotypical image of an Irish-American: loud, boisterous, given to cigars and strong drink. I knew many such Irish, but my father shared none of those traits, except, perhaps, his burning interest in politics and athletics. He never smoked or drank. I followed his example in never smoking. As a young man, I had an occasional social drink but never liked the taste of alcohol and soon stopped drinking entirely, although the world of politics and business is filled with people who enjoy both tobacco and alcohol, which never bothered me. My dad was an incredibly hard worker in those very difficult times. In fact, he was away working briefly in Texas when I was born.

My sister, Florence, had been born four years earlier and my arrival was a source of special joy to my father because my mother had a medical condition which was then thought to make it impossible for her to conceive male children. That was obviously not the case because, when I was ten, my brother Norris arrived. My parents, who were unfailingly private about such matters, had not even told Florence and me that they were expecting another child. Norris, like each of us, was born at home. Florence and I had been shuttled to a relative's house to stay overnight. We were told of Norris's birth just before going to a movie. Florence was so excited she pinched my arm black and blue during the movie; we couldn't wait to get home and see our new baby brother. Three children at home meant that my dad had to work even harder to provide for his growing family. He held a variety of jobs, sometimes several at once, to provide for us. He was a streetcar conductor, a deputy state fire marshal, a sales tax collector, and, for twenty years, a salesman and then city sales manager at the Falstaff Brewing Company. When I was young, he was a real estate salesman for L. P. Ganucheau, whose office was on Dryades Street. He dressed for work each day in a conservative suit and his trademark bow tie.

I was in grade school when the Great Depression hit New Orleans.

Life in the Great Depression

When Pres. Franklin Delano Roosevelt closed the banks in 1933, my father and his partners in the real estate venture lost everything, as did many others. Some prominent businessmen took their own lives; others simply walked away from their debts and began anew. For my dad, his business failure was a matter of personal honor; he would never declare bankruptcy. Instead, he worked long hours and extra jobs and paid every creditor his company owed, penny for penny. As a young boy, I remember the terrible disappointments and hardship that brought upon us, but I also remember his telling us that we must never, under any circumstances, do anything that would bring discredit upon ourselves or our family. I have followed his example all my life.

Seeing "The Kingfish"

Despite his long hours, Dad also managed to take an active, daily interest in politics, church, and community affairs. He was part of Gov. Huey P. Long's political organization and later active with the Regular Democratic Organization. He would often bundle Florence and me up and take us to hear Long speak in the big open field at Canal and Claiborne, where the Delta Towers building stands now.

These were the days before television when long, stemwinding political oratory was the order of the day. As a small boy, I was tremendously excited by the sense of energy, vitality, and power that surrounded Gov. Long and his organization. My father was deeply, quietly, but profoundly religious, and much of my own beliefs I inherited from his example. He headed the committee that raised $1.5 million to build the new Dominican High School and was honored by the St. Mary's Dominican Cooperative Association for a quarter-century of service. Florence was a Dominican graduate, as were her daughters. Dad remained active in Dominican affairs long after Florence was graduated, serving as Cooperative Club president four times and holding every other office as well. His love of the Jesuit High Blue Jays was legendary, and he spent decades raising funds for the school, from which both Norris and I were graduated. I have proudly continued his tradition, raising funds for Jesuit on many occasions. Dad was enshrined into the Jesuit Hall of Fame in recognition of his great support for the Jesuit Blue Jays. He was an avid worker in the Holy Name organization and the Ushers Society. He was long active in the Knights of Columbus; he and I were charter members of the Charles Carroll Council 2926 when it was built at 8300 Apple Street, some of our proudest moments together.

He was active in the building campaign of the new St. Matthias Church, where he was head usher at the 11:30 mass for twenty years. For forty years he was a division leader for the United Fund Drive, an interest which I also continued. He also took an active role in the Elks and was president of the Kiwanis Club.

Good Times with My Dad

Amidst all that, he made time for activities and adventures we could share together. He was an active supporter of Pelican Baseball in New Orleans during the years when minor league baseball flourished. We could be seen at each home game, proudly occupying his third-base box at the old Heineman Park, once the "White City" amusement park and later Pelican Stadium, where the Bayou Plaza Hotel now sits. The big event of each game for me

The 1939 CYO champion St. Matthias girls' softball team which I coached. Also shown is Rev. Harold Bru, assistant pastor. (Courtesy Charles L. Frank)

was a hot dog and a Coke, sometimes two or three. I later served as president of the "Grandstand Manager's Club," a group of business leaders joined together to promote the Pelicans. Larry Gilbert, Sr., was one of my favorite managers, and I later had the pleasure of sharing a personal friendship with his three fine sons, Larry Jr., Charlie, and Tookie—who later served as Orleans Parish civil sheriff. They were all fine baseball players in their own right. For many years Daddy was a member of the Pelicans board of directors. He helped lead the drive to send the local American Legion All-Stars to the International Legion series in Mexico City.

He would take me, in our old Chevrolet, to see boxing matches at the Coliseum Arena or St. Mary's Italian Church and to basketball games. I inherited his keen interest in sports. As a child, on the St. Matthias and the A. H. Wilson School playgrounds, I enjoyed softball, basketball, volleyball, and touch football. Later, in 1948-49, I coached a girls' softball team where the new St. Matthias Church extension now stands. I later coached at St. Stephens when we won the city championship two years in a row.

Daddy bore, quietly and without ever complaining, an extra burden in his life, for my mother was not well and, for many years, he did much of the work around our home. He always seemed so strong; I can remember him in pain only once. Part of keeping our home spotless involved frequent whitewashing of the trees around the house to fight the endless invasion of ants. Whitewash was a potent mixture, largely containing lye. One day Dad spilled some whitewash into his eyes, which could easily have caused permanent damage or even blindness. I was barely old enough to get him into our old car and rush him to Charity Hospital. I will never forget the wonderful, attentive care he received at Charity. He was just a common working man, but they cared for him as though he were an important civic figure and they saved his sight. I have always had a tender spot in my heart for Charity Hospital because of the wonderful care given my father.

Dad was a stern but loving father. Although he had little formal education, he could spell everything and had a wonderful gift for arithmetic. He believed deeply in the value of a good education and insisted that each of his children get as much schooling as possible. He was able to scrape together enough money to send Florence to college but by the time I was ready there was not sufficient money to do so for me; I went to night school at Loyola

University. Later, Norris was able to complete college and law school. Daddy was equally proud of each of us.

The Growing Fitzmorris Clan

The Irish are legendarily clannish and, in the Fitzmorris household of my youth, our little family was the whole world. Each of us children adored and supported the others, both as youngsters and as we made our own way as adults. Florence met George Rennyson Simno, Jr., when they were students at Loyola University. She was a freshman and he a sophomore. They were married at the old St. Matthias Church at Broad and General Pershing Streets on November 23, 1940.

I was their groomsman and Norris was their ringbearer. They marked their fiftieth anniversary in 1990 with a grand family gathering hosted by their five children and eight grandchildren. George worked for Greyhound Bus Lines when they were newlyweds. He retired as vice president of Kerr Steamship Company. Florence inherited my mother's wonderful musical talent and still teaches the piano, holding annual recitals with more than twenty-five students. Since our parents' death, she has assumed the central role of holding us together as a family, a very Southern tradition, and I talk with her each day as I once did my mother.

Norris Vernon, named after both maternal grandparents and our beloved uncles, was always an energetic, articulate, intelligent man. After graduation from Loyola University in business and law, he entered the army during the Korean Conflict. He served in Europe with the Judge Advocate General Corps. He retired after twenty-nine years with Pan American Life Insurance Company. He rose to become senior vice president in charge of its Medicare and public affairs activities. Norris also taught at Loyola and Dominican College night schools. He married Ann Marie Wadsworth on October 20, 1964. They adopted three children and had three of their own. He is now in the private practice of law.

Norris had a marvelous, natural talent in the arts and became quite well known throughout New Orleans for writing and narrating many carnival balls. He has been active in a wide variety of charitable and civic organizations, particularly Catholic Charities.

Daddy was a perfectionist, always urging me to do the very best I could at everything I attempted, and he was also my best friend. Among his proudest moments were my first election to the New

Orleans City Council in 1953, my re-election in 1958, and my election as councilman-at-large in 1962. He shared my deep disappointment in my unsuccessful campaigns for mayor in 1965 and 1969. When, on the heels of those defeats, I decided to seek the lieutenant governorship, many of my friends thought that was a very big step for a city boy from the Irish Channel, especially since I was out of office. My dad, however, approached that race as he approached every challenge in life: he urged me to do my best and put the outcome in the hands of the Lord. His religious beliefs were as real as they were deep; he lived his religion, quietly and daily. The example of his faith has sustained me through some of my darkest days.

It was one of the great thrills of my life to have Dad with me on the platform when I was sworn in as lieutenant governor of Louisiana. Daddy was very proud that an Irish Catholic from New Orleans could have gained the second highest office in our state. He was, throughout his life, profoundly proud of his heritage and deeply devoted to all things Irish. One of his special joys was Notre Dame's Fighting Irish football team. On the last day of his life, when he lay, desperately ill in the intensive care ward in Baptist Hospital, on the night Notre Dame played in the Sugar Bowl, his first question to me was, "How are the Irish doing?" Only one sad element was present at my inauguration, my dear mother was not alive to share the day. As I was about to step to the podium to take the oath of office, Daddy whispered, "How wonderful it would be if Mother were here to share this great victory with her 'big boy'." She was the center of his world and the one, great love of his life. Theirs was a deep and wonderful love which lasted from the moment they met until their deaths.

Remembering Mother

Mother was tall and beautiful, with long auburn hair. As a young woman she was much enamored of Louis Bordes, son of the operator of the Bordes Market in the Carrollton section—one of the early-day business leaders there. She and Louis had dated for some time and were a popular couple at the Saturday night "dairy dances" held at Robert Smith's dairy on South Carrollton and Washington, where the K&B Drugstore later stood. It was widely expected that Romolia Hanning would marry Louis Bordes, but he insisted on wearing his hair long, in the fashion of the day, and she preferred a more conservative style. While she was wrestling with her doubts, she met my father. Jim Fitzmorris was not the most handsome young man in town, but he was solid, ambitious, and decent. For his part, he was swept away from the moment they met. It was later said, her smile captured Jim, and he set out to win her heart. Finally, on July 5, 1916, at 5:00 P.M., in one of the worst rainstorms in the city's history, they were wed, at St. John's Catholic Church on Dryades Street, followed by a reception on an upstairs porch nearby. It was a marriage that would endure for more than half a century and a love that warmed the hearts of all who knew them.

Louis Bordes remained their friend for more than a half-century. Even as an older man, he made his way to my home each year, bringing me one of my favorite treats—figs from his own yard. Mother was a wonderful pianist, and Daddy was a lyrical Irish tenor. As a team, they were popular entertainers, spending countless hours doing charity work for the religious organizations and churches in which they both took such an interest. She was blessed with great beauty and a generous, outgoing personality, which won her instant friends everywhere she went. At home, she unquestionably ruled the roost. In later years, we affectionately called her the "Queen Mother," because we deeply respected and loved her. I cannot remember ever disobeying her or raising my voice to her. She was a constant source of inspiration and love to me and participated actively in my campaigns for councilman and my 1965 race for mayor. I called her every day and, in the months of her final illness in 1966, I went to see her at the end of every afternoon.

I would lie across the foot of her bed, hold her hand, and tell her every detail of the day's activities for she took such an interest in every aspect of my life. In our family, we children had no secrets from our parents and consulted them before making any important decision. When she died, it was a much harder burden for me to bear than losing the mayor's election months before. Politics seemed hardly to matter, in comparison to losing a central focus of my life. My father was to live another five years, but the years alone were incredibly sad and lonely for him—as they still are for me.

School Days

I take heart in remembering a wonderful, happy childhood. We were a normal family of only average means, but we did not feel deprived. Our favorite activities centered around church, school, and family. My mother's brothers, Vernon and Robert Norris Hanning, both worked for the Louisiana and Arkansas Railroad. They took a special interest in me as neither had sons of his own. I was later to take the same joyful interest in my sister's family before our daughter, Lisa, was born. From my uncles, I gained an early interest in the railroad, where I was later to spend a rewarding lifetime.

I was only an average student at St. Matthias School, across the street from my house. I could not have been a discipline problem, however, because my parents were closely connected with the school, would have known of it immediately, and would not have tolerated disrespect for the Dominican nuns who taught me. We were one of the first families in the parish. The church was then housed in a wooden frame building. Mother made breakfast and lunch for the nuns each day, for they were then forbidden to dine in public. The nuns had a deep influence on my life. I particularly remember Sisters Mary Gabriel, Mary Thomas, Mary Edwards, Mary Grace, Mary Dominic, and Mary Lewis—now all deceased.

I got off to a rather rough start in my formal education. Midway through the first day of school, I decided I had learned all that St. Matthias had to teach and I wanted to be home with Mother, so I simply left school and walked across the street to my house. I was rather abruptly returned to the school and firmly given to understand that there was much more I was expected to accomplish. That ended my brief truancy.

St. Matthias was the scene of one of my most embarrassing moments as well. We were all downstairs at a "penny party," at which each child paid a penny for cake and lemonade. The Sister asked me to mop the classroom, and I readily agreed. I went upstairs and found a mop and a bucket which was already full. I proceeded to mop the entire room and was nearly finished when someone came up to ask what had become of the bucket of lemonade—which, by then, I had carefully mopped over the whole floor. Sometimes, my youthful enthusiasm got several steps ahead of my actual knowledge as when we went to make ice cream

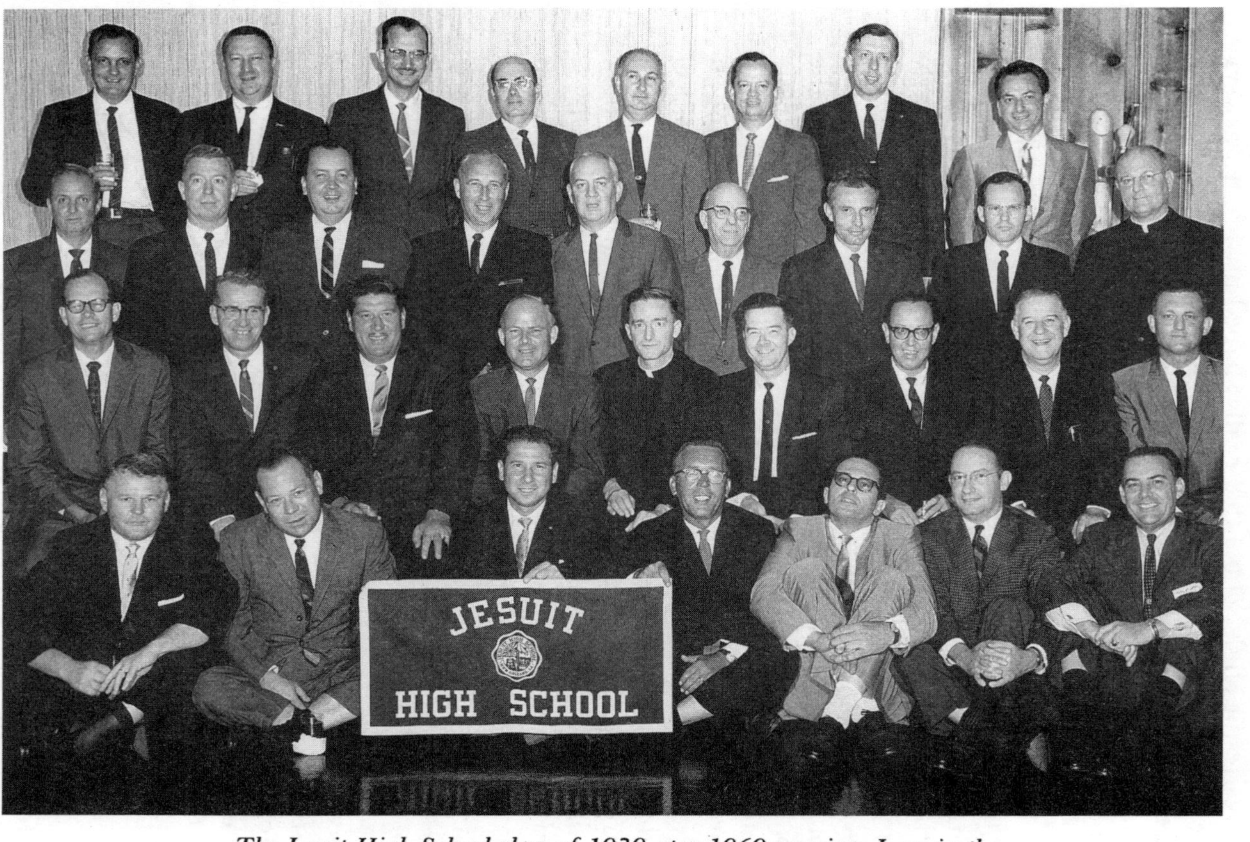

The Jesuit High School class of 1939 at a 1969 reunion. I am in the first row, far right, and Assessor Claude Mauberret, Jr., is in the top row, second from left. (Courtesy Town of Carrollton News photo)

at our friends, the Guidrys, and I added so much rock salt to the mixture we ended up throwing out the entire batch.

It was Jesuit High School that really shaped my life. I was very active at Jesuit, excelling in "speech" and other groups. Among my debating team partners were Roy Guste, of the Antoine's Restaurant family, and Russell Schonekas, now a New Orleans lawyer. Former attorney general Billy Guste was also a Jesuit classmate. More than any influence except my parents, the "Blue Jay spirit" of religious faith and determination guided me through the roughest times of my life.

Father Mulhearn, the principal of Jesuit, and Fr. Claude J. Stallworth, a teacher and later Jesuit principal, played a particularly important role in shaping my beliefs. We began each day with a prayer, both at St. Matthias and at Jesuit. That was a special part of our day, in which we asked for guidance, strength, and the inspiration to do our very best in every class. We were firmly encouraged to take a great sense of pride in our schoolwork, to regard it as important and as a source of personal accomplishment. I usually rode my bike to Jesuit or caught a ride with a neighbor. Being accepted into Jesuit was an honor. There were relatively few Catholic high schools and an applicant had to show a satisfactory report card to be accepted, plus come up with a hundred dollars per year tuition. I got fifteen cents for lunch: ten cents went for a sandwich and a nickel for a Barq's Root Beer. I was an altar boy for the 6:00 A.M. daily mass at St. Matthias. Monsignor Andre was the pastor and celebrated the Latin mass; it was a foolish boy who dared be late for his duties. I never was, for service at St. Matthias was also a profitable enterprise. Altar boys received fifty cents for participating in a wedding and a quarter for serving at a funeral.

Monsignor Andre had been the first pastor of St. Matthias, assigned when the parish was established January 6, 1920. The new church was already under construction when he died suddenly, after the six-thirty morning mass, June 22, 1941.

The Boys in the Neighborhood

Life was certainly not all school and church; my neighborhood was filled with friends and fun. I spent many hours playing with my dog, a wonderful, big collie named Boy. He was with us for many years and when he died, we buried him in our back yard. My friends and I formed an inseparable group consisting of Henry Briggs, Jr., Earl Bartley, Billy Walker, John Breslin, Harry and Jimmy Caire, L. J. Heroy, C. J. Green, Jimmy Smith, and me. We played "Light My Candle," "Simon Says" and, with the compliance of some of the neighborhood girls, "Spin the Bottle." In those days we had only dirt streets; we played ball on what is now the neutral ground and basketball in the Caire's back yard. I had a Duncan yo-yo, the great fad of that time, but my favorite gift of all was my very own red fire truck, a present for my sixth or seventh birthday. I had a brilliant white sailor suit in which mother dressed me for formal occasions, but my real ambition was to be a fireman or policeman.

I am happy to report that one member of our family made his dream come true: Daddy's sister, Genenieve, married William McCrossen and their son, Bill, rose to become New Orleans fire chief. He has now served for more than fifty years in that department with great distinction. His nephew, Mike, was recently elected recorder of mortgages. The Tivoli Theatre, now a Rhodes Funeral Home, was the big moving picture house in our neighborhood, a few blocks away on Washington Avenue. A big afternoon at the movies cost fifteen cents: ten cents for the ticket and a nickel for a candy bar or a soft drink. I don't think a youngster could attend a movie now with less than a ten-dollar bill without feeling disadvantaged. I loved the cowboy shows; I was a big Tom Mix fan. I also liked Jean Harlow, Clark Gable, James Cagney, Mickey Rooney, and others. We looked forward to the serials, and I developed an interest in the RKO news segments as well. The cartoons were called "colored comedy," not for any racial reason, but because they were the only colorized part of the day's entertainment. Nearby was Earhart's Drug Store, scene of my first and only venture into the dark world of gambling.

At the corner of Washington and Broad, Earhart's had a pinball machine that paid cash when someone won. I lost a quick fifty cents there one afternoon, dared not tell my parents, and never went back. That was the end of my gambling career. Aside from movies, these were strictly "radio days." No one had ever heard of television. We listened to Jack Benny, Edgar Bergen and Charlie McCarthy, the Lucky Strike Hit Parade, and—long before anyone had ever heard of "fireside chats," to Huey P. Long, to whom the radio was a great source of power. He would come on the radio and say, "This is Huey P. Long. I want you to call your friends and tell them I'm on the radio and please tune in. We're going to play a few musical numbers while you make those calls." The music would start and, sure enough, Mother and Daddy would commence to call their friends. There were vaudeville shows downtown at Loew's State, which opened in 1926, or the Orpheum, which opened in 1921, the year I was born. Bob Hope, Mickey Rooney, Harry Houdini, and Burns and Allen all played the Orpheum, but those shows were expensive so we children stayed with the neighborhood movies. Nor was I often able to go to the Strand, the two-thousand-seat theater which opened in 1917 at the corner of Baronne and Gravier Streets.

It was the first elaborate motion picture house in New Orleans, complete with a thirty-five-piece orchestra and a huge pipe organ. I did hear Ray McNamara play the massive organ at the Saenger Theatre and later became his friend when he played the organ at Pelican Stadium. One of the popular children's shows was Professor Schramm's radio show on WSMB, then located in the Maison Blanche building on Canal Street. He also taught elocution, which was considered an important part of any young man's education. My elocution teacher was Ed DeBryes, known as "Cousin Ed." He was a wonderful speaker but a demanding teacher, making me repeat phrases over and over again until I had the inflection and intonation precisely right. Lessons cost two dollars each week, which was a king's ransom in those days, but my mother scrimped so I could learn public speaking. After thirty years and several thousand speeches, I imagine it was a sound investment. Canal Street was like another city to us. Mother, like most of the women in our neighborhood, only shopped Canal Street on special occasions. When she went there, she wore her big, formal hat and gloves for an expedition to Canal Street was a serious social event. Mostly, she shopped on Dryades Street, which, at that time, was a marvelous street lined with beautiful and interesting stores.

My dad's real estate office was on Dryades, and we knew many of the merchants. We parked near his office each year and walked to St. Charles Avenue to watch the carnival parades. On Mardi Gras, we spent the whole day watching the parades, Mother made sandwiches for lunch. If we were particularly flush that season, we might get a stick of Roman Candy from the horse-drawn cart, a New Orleans fixture for generations.

Summers in the Country

During the summers, we sometimes took family outings. My uncle Loren Fitzmorris, his wife Larcie, and their five children lived in Bush. Before the construction of the causeway, that was a full day's drive. I remember one trip when our old car had three blowouts. The last two required that we jack the car up and roll the flat down the dusty road into Covington to be fixed and then back to the car. That trip took forever. Uncle Loren and his family had a real farm with chickens and cows. Their home was a country house with a small front porch, expansive grounds, an outdoor well, and no air-conditioning. We began each day with a big, country breakfast after which I rode horseback. We got to their farm by way of a dirt road which was deeply rutted after each rain.

Uncle Loren, who recently died, was one of my favorite relatives. He made certain that each of his five children got a college education—that emphasis on education seemed to run throughout our family. I enjoyed going with my friend Henry Briggs's family to visit their relatives in Thibodaux. That was an exhausting drive in their old car. I remember Henry and me falling in a mudhole up to our eyebrows. We went back to the house and spent the rest of the day huddled in sheets while our clothes dried. I also enjoyed outings to Slidell, along the old route before the Twin Span, which took an entire day each way.

Money of My Own

Before long I was big enough to work for part of my spending money. I delivered political circulars for the Huey P. Long organization. My assignment was the Seventeenth Precinct, Twelfth Ward. This territory was generally bounded by South Broad, South Galvez, Napoleon Avenue, and Toledano Streets. It was the home neighborhood of the famous local prizefighter, Jimmy Perrin. Sometimes I could get a glimpse of Perrin on my rounds. On other occasions, I saw the imposing figure of Congressman Paul Maloney on his massive front porch.

This was also the neighborhood of the Meyers family, who spawned three generations of riverboat captains, which I always thought sounded like an exciting life. Dr. Charles Menendez, Sr., a leader in the American Legion, and the Watsons, who are still in the automobile business, lived nearby.

One summer I worked for the Woolworth store downtown on Canal Street. This was long before the days of "child labor laws," and my shift lasted from 6:00 A.M. until nearly midnight at twenty-five cents per hour. My job consisted of catching the boxes being unloaded from the trucks. I came home bruised and sore each night. In those days, there were few "chain stores" in the area, and Woolworth was a treasure of exotic items from throughout the world we didn't see every day in our little neighborhood.

I had an easier, if more boring, time working as an usher at the Orpheum Theater. My shift lasted from 9:00 A.M. to almost midnight on weekends. This was a formal job; I wore black pants, a stiff white front that hooked in back, a black tie, and a white jacket. I soon knew the lines from each movie by heart. My job was to take a flashlight and guide patrons to their seats, allowing them to enter by unhooking the velvet rope which cordoned off the main theater from the lobby.

These were the days before integration; blacks bought tickets from a separate window and sat in a restricted section of the theater. For lunch and dinner I had a Lee's hamburger, purchased from the original Lee's stand next door and consumed in the basement of the theater. I became a fast friend of the head usher who let me work the main floor. We used to think that was a prime assignment because we thought we "saw more people." I made twenty-five cents per hour each weekend.

First Loves

It was sometime around these formative years that I first discovered girls. I think my first girlfriend was Gloria Napolitana. Later, I seriously dated Cupie Aucoin, who lived on South Claiborne Avenue.

A big date then consisted of taking a seven-cent streetcar ride downtown, going to a movie, and having a soda afterward in the K&B Drugstore on the way home. It was a largely uneventful evening unless some youthful prankster had "greased the track," in which case the streetcar would fail to stop. Those were simpler times. It is easy now to romanticize watching Mr. Guidry, the bread and milk man, making his door-to-door deliveries in the crime-free neighborhood where we grew up. Of course, they were harder times too.

We had an old washing machine with a wringer and a scrub board. We had no dryer, dishwasher, disposal, or microwave, things we would be hard pressed to live without today, but nobody we knew had anything like that, and we all did happily without. Communications in our home consisted of one old-fashioned telephone. When you picked it up, the operator came on the line and asked what number you wanted to call. I remember it as being a fine and relatively efficient system—party line and all.

Mr. Interlocutor

Yesterday's forms of entertainment would be out of place today as well. Mother and Daddy produced minstrel shows which they put on two or three times each year for churches, schools, Kiwanis club benefits, and the like. A minstrel show was a carefully crafted, choreographed, and scripted event featuring a long, half-circle of performers facing the audience. At each end of the line were the "end men," performers in black face. Nearer the middle of the stage were two groups of white face performers and in the center stood the interlocutor, my role. The end men were brightly dressed and had the verbal interplay with the interlocutor.

The men and women in white face near the middle provided most of the musical entertainment, although the end men sang as well. My father, and later, my brother Norris, served as director for the shows, and my mother and sister Florence played the piano. Mother, in true Sophie Tucker style, sang the finale, her signature piece called "A Good Man Nowadays Is Hard to Find," always bringing down the house with applause. Florence's husband, George Simno, did the scenery. This was a family production! It was a complicated show as well. We had a format of prepared jokes but no precise script, so the end men had to always be ready to "save the show" if the interlocutor somehow became stuck. The all-volunteer cast rehearsed for months prior to each show. These were major fund-raising efforts, very popular and extremely well attended. I probably performed in twenty-five to

The long-forgotten, once-popular "Minstrel Show" in 1950. I am at center stage as "Interlocatur," flanked by Mother and Dad.

thirty of them in my brief career as interlocutor. Nowadays such a performance would be roundly decried and probably downright dangerous to produce. Back then, no one meant anything derogatory by them, and the whole evening was a socially accepted community event. My experience was beneficial to my later political career because it taught me "stage presence," helped me overcome a fear of audiences, enabled me to speak extemporaneously, and taught me to think on my feet.

The War Years

The minstrel shows and much of the world to which we had become accustomed ended with the advent of World War II. My induction notice to the United States Army arrived with the first days of spring, and I was sworn in on June 5, 1942. The war, of course, had been raging on for several months by then so we were not entirely surprised. Everyone in my family was enthusiastically supportive of Pres. Franklin D. Roosevelt both in his conduct of the war and his leadership of the national recovery from the Great Depression which had so devastated New Orleans, along with the rest of the country. Nonetheless, getting my induction notice brought home the horror of war with a finality and emphasis. It was a particularly trying time for my parents. Except for occasional boyhood visits, I had never been away from home. As I packed and prepared to depart for Camp Beauregard, my father took me aside for a few words of advice. "Remember," he said, "the beliefs your mother and I have tried to instill in you. Have respect for other people. Be honest and aboveboard in all your dealings. Above all, be a good soldier." None of us knew what lay ahead for me or our family, but I promised sincerely to follow Dad's advice, and I tried always to do so.

I was profoundly homesick almost from the minute I arrived at Camp Beauregard in this, my first real experience away from home. There was little time and no sympathy for homesickness, however. I was soon classified to ship out and join the Combat Engineers at Fort Leonard Wood, Missouri. I was packed and sitting by the railroad tracks, waiting for the train to back in, to take me to Missouri, when Sergeant Major Wilson walked up and shouted, "Does any soldier here have experience in transportation?" My transportation experience consisted of being a messenger boy and ticket agent for the Kansas City Southern Railroad.

Nevertheless, this seemed an opportunity that had my name on it. Certainly it must be preferable to being in the Combat Engineers, I thought, so I promptly and enthusiastically volunteered. I was delighted to be assigned to remain at Camp Beauregard in the transportation section. While I still missed home, I made many lifelong, invaluable friends there, and those of us in the "Camp Beauregard Club" kept in touch throughout the years.

Many of those friends, like Sonny Briggs in Lake Charles, were immensely helpful later, when I ran my first statewide campaign for lieutenant governor. Other army buddies like E. L. "Ed" Stine, since retired from Lone Star Cement; Oliver Counce, now retired from Southern Specialties; the late Milton Gubler and John Shay, now retired from Crescent City Distributing Company, were my buddies as young men in the army and remained friends for life. So did Harry Caire, now a CPA, and the late James T. "Jim" Mehle, who had a successful career with the Kraft Company and who was my dear and devoted friend for life. My position also gave me the opportunity to meet some of the leaders in the war effort. One Sunday afternoon it was business pretty much as usual for me when there came a knock at the screen door to my transportation unit office. There stood colonels Dwight D. Eisenhower and Alfred M. Gruenther. They were in Louisiana observing military maneuvers and needed me to arrange transportation for them. No lowly sergeant ever moved more quickly than I, as I cut their orders. The only time I moved faster was when they had departed and I sprinted to the barracks to tell everyone who I had just met and served.

After the war, I met General Gruenther at an Industrial-Army Conference in New Orleans, which I chaired in 1950. Also in attendance were Army Chief of Staff, Gen. J. Lawton Collins; Assistant Chief of Naval Operations, Adm. Oscar Badger; Lt. Gen. Matthew B. Ridgeway, then deputy Army Chief of Staff, and Lt. Gen. LeRoy Lutes, commanding general of the Fourth Army. General Gruenther went on to serve with distinction as head of the International Red Cross. Years afterward, when I was on the New Orleans City Council, I had the pleasure of entertaining General Ridgeway and his new, young wife on a visit to the city. I asked Mrs. Ridgeway if there was anything special she would like to see or do while she was in town. It turned out that her great dream was to ride down Canal Street with the sirens blaring at 5:00 P.M. I saw to it that she got her wish!

The Quest for O.C.S.

I decided to make the best of my time in the military and immediately applied for Officer Candidate School. Months passed and I had risen to the rank of sergeant but still had no word about my application. I badgered my commanding officer, Maj. John Ryan, constantly about the status of my OCS application, and he assured me it was under consideration.

Finally, a year later in 1944, my friend, the late Ray Fleming, adjutant general of the Louisiana National Guard, stopped by to visit me. I explained my predicament to him, and he proceeded to ask Mayor Ryan about the matter. Major Ryan, it developed, spent as much time celebrating as soldiering, and my application had been misfiled in one of his desk drawers, where it had been for a year. With the intercession of General Fleming, it was submitted that same day and I was soon on my way to Camp Leroy Johnson for four months of Officer Candidate School. Assignment to Camp Leroy Johnson was a blessing for two reasons—one of which I knew in advance and the other which was soon to become evident. First, the camp was located near the present site of the University of New Orleans, on the lakefront outskirts of the city. That meant that I could occasionally get home to see my parents, which was a welcome event for me and my family.

Meeting Gloria

The second blessing came about by accident. As soon as I arrived at camp, early in the summer of 1944, I was instructed to report to the army hospital at Camp Plauche for my physical examination.

Camp Plauche is in Harahan where the offices of Canal Villere and the Coca-Cola bottling plant now stand. My blood test was done by a young, attractive, petite, blonde medical technician named Gloria Lopez. I had heard of "love at first sight," and this was just such a moment for me. I was taken by her beauty and her wonderful personality. Leaving the hospital after the tests, I asked for her telephone number and wasted no time in calling to ask for a date. I staged a more ardent campaign to win her hand than any political race I would ever run. It took better than a year of my very best efforts as suitor and salesman but, on September 15, 1945, we were wed. America was still at war, and wartime wed-

I was a captain in this photo and later rose to the rank of major. (Courtesy U.S. Army)

Our wedding day, September 15, 1945.

dings were brief and spartan affairs, without the luxury of a bachelor party or rehearsal dinner because the groom and all his attendants were on duty. Nobody had the money for an extravagant wedding in those days either. We were wed in a beautiful, simple ceremony at St. Matthias Church—which had been so much a part of my family's life.

The wedding was very much a family celebration. It seemed only natural to ask Daddy to be my best man, and I was thrilled when he agreed. My sister, Florence Simno, was matron of honor, and her little daughter, Florence Romolia Simno, was flower girl. Gloria's college friends from Loyola University, Elaine Villars, Marie (Mrs. Andre) Villere, and Marie (Mrs. Jules) Guidry, were bridesmaids. My attendants were my boyhood and army friend, Lt. Ed Little, and army friends, Lt. Steve Dupuis and Lt. John Walter. The Nuptial Mass was celebrated by Rev. Francis Baechle, our old family pastor and friend. As I looked once again at our wedding photograph in the process of writing this book, the years rushed in upon me with a pang, as I suddenly realized that every man in our wedding party except me is now deceased.

As we arrived at the church for the ceremony, the priest asked Daddy to make sure he was ready to hand us the rings. To his horror, he discovered that he had misplaced them. We rushed in a panic back across the street to search for them. We found that Daddy, in his lifelong habit of "cleaning up," had thrown the rings, along with papers and notes from his pocket, into the trash!

The rings rescued, we rushed back to the church, and the wedding proceeded. I could never remember being so happy and proud as I was that day, a feeling I would know again seventeen years later when our precious daughter, Lisa Marie, arrived to light my life. Lisa's arrival, on June 30, 1962, made that spring, and life for Gloria and me, complete. Like any proud father, I could write an entire volume about the joy of watching her careening through childhood and becoming a beautiful woman and a promising professional in her own right. There are some advantages to being the child of a father who is in public life. There are some terrible disadvantages, primarily the awful loss of privacy and the tremendous pressures. We have all read of the disappointments some such children have experienced in their personal and professional careers. Gloria did a marvelous job with Lisa during the years when politics demanded so much of my time, and I am happy to report that Lisa emerged unscathed from very real

Me, Gloria, and Lisa in a 1965 campaign photograph.

sacrifices she had to make growing up as my daughter. As she has grown into adulthood, she has developed great strength of character and a wonderful insight into the problems of others. In addition to being my daughter, she has become my most honest critic and most ardent champion and confidante.

Through the years, she kept her own scrapbook of a young girl's thoughts and impressions of my political campaigns, but one of my fondest possessions is a more recent note she sent, in which she quoted Martin Baxbaum who said, "You can use most any measure when you're speaking of success. You can measure it by a fancy home, expensive car or dress. But the measure of your real success is one you cannot spend. It's the way your child describes you when talking to a friend." Her note added, "If this is the measure of success, I guess you're the most successful man in the world." I feel very successful indeed when I think of Lisa and the accomplishments that really matter in life.

Of course, that was only a dream on our wedding day. Daddy had decorated our basement for the reception. I can still remember him Friday night, the evening before the ceremony, standing in his bare feet hosing down the basement as Mother stayed upstairs, convinced it would never dry in time.

My two-day pass allowed only enough time for a hurried honeymoon at a long-since demolished hotel on the beach in Biloxi, Mississippi. Our romantic view of the Gulf of Mexico consisted primarily of the parking lot and trash dump. We were so transported it might as well have been the Taj Mahal. Our brief honeymoon over, it was back to the harsh realities of life in wartime for Gloria and me. Since I was assigned to the barracks, we moved into her grandparents' home, where we were to stay for several years, until I was able to buy our first little home at 324 Homedale Avenue. It cost seventy-five hundred dollars, had a big window fan that blew dust into every niche and cranny of the house, and was, as I think back on it now, in deplorable shape. But Daddy and his friends came to fix it up and, to a young couple just starting out after the war, it seemed like a castle. The cost certainly seemed worthy of a castle in those modest times! As a newly commissioned second lieutenant, I was assigned as training officer at Camp Plauche. After the first four cycles of conducting training, it was about as exciting as watching grass grow. I pleaded with my commanding officer, Col. John Rogers, for a transfer to some more interesting and demanding position.

Colonel Rogers had been a state trooper in New Jersey before the war. He disliked Louisiana intensely and his position on my request was very simple: If he was forced to stay at Camp Plauche, I would remain there with him. On the day he was transferred, both our prayers were answered for I was also reassigned, as transportation officer and later, base transportation officer at Camp Plauche, where I spent the remainder of my military service handling post-war troop movements.

The War Ends

The war was winding down, but our lives would never be the same. Many of us had lost family members; all of us had lost close friends to this terrible war. Sometimes we were touched by the loss of people we had not even met. My longtime associate, Joe Willis, was a Navy coxswain, operating an LCPV landing craft in the invasion of Okinawa in April 1945. His job was to assist the medics on the beachhead with care of the wounded and identification of the casualties. On April 18, 1945, one of the last days of the war, Joe was on duty when the body of war correspondent Ernie Pyle, killed by enemy machine gun fire, was brought in from the front lines.

Pyle had a wonderful common touch; he brought the horror of war and the great bravery of our men home to each of us. His death was a terrible tragedy and a great shock. Finally the day for my discharge arrived, and I was sent to Camp Shelby, Mississippi, April 22, 1946, to complete the separation. I took a bus back to New Orleans that night and, at eight o'clock the following morning, I was at work at the Kansas City Southern Railroad—ready to put my transportation experience to work in the exciting new civilian world.

Chapter 3

View from the Siding: The Railroad Years

Ours was a railroad family. My maternal grandfather, Robert Norris "Papa" Hanning, worked for the Illinois Central Railroad and my uncles, Norris and Vernon, spent their lives working for the Kansas City Southern Railroad. At the time I was graduated from Jesuit, my father developed severe arthritis, which later disappeared as suddenly as it had struck, but for many months he was restricted to bed, unable to work. That meant that college for me was out of the question so at that time I needed a job.

My uncle Norris told me he had heard that a job was available as messenger boy for the Kansas City Southern Railroad. Uncle Norris had been with the railroad for years and he believed that this would be a good opportunity for me to begin my business career. More important than that, it was a paying job, at the attractive salary of twenty cents per hour. I wasted no time in hustling down to interview with Noah Shamlin, the railroad agent at 785 S. Liberty Street. To my delight, I was hired and stationed at the warehouse, where the freight office was located. Some of my earliest friends with the railroad were Jimmy and Emile Rausch, Mac True, Johnny Cook, who was later elected to the Louisiana House of Representatives where he served with distinction for many years, and Eddie Moore.

I worked seven days per week. My duties consisted primarily of delivering freight notices and picking up documents from the freight forwarders who were located at various sites along the Mississippi River and generally doing anything that needed to be done. Since there were few buses in service at that time, each week I was given a pocketful of "car fare tokens" so I could ride the streetcars where possible on my daily rounds.

An important turning point in my career came soon after I was hired. One day the Southern Belle came to New Orleans. It was the sleek, new streamlined train just put into service by the Kansas City Southern Railroad, offering comfortable, swift, direct rail service between Kansas City and New Orleans. I went to the station that Sunday to act as host and to take part in demonstrating the outstanding features of this modern, exciting, new passenger train. There, I met W. N. Deramus II, executive vice president of the Kansas City Southern Railroad. Something about my youthful enthusiasm apparently brought me to his attention, for he soon asked if I would be interested in accompanying the train on a one-week tour of the system. It was a wonderful, exciting opportunity for a lowly messenger boy, especially one who had never been away from home. Gaining my parents' permission, I eagerly agreed and soon, accompanied by the late J. B. C. Petativan, the local sales representative for the railroad and my dear friend, we departed for the tour. It ended in Kansas City, where I was told to arrange for pullman car accommodations for the return trip and put it on my expense account. The notion of an expense account was completely foreign to the daily duties of a messenger boy, and I had no idea how to accomplish the task.

I was too embarrassed to ask, so I simply made do, sleeping in a regular lounge car on the return trip to New Orleans. I later learned the intricacies of expense accounts rather well in my long railroad career.

Getting Ahead

It soon became obvious to me that the path to a rewarding career with the railroad lay somewhere other than in the warehouse and freight office. I needed to be closer to where the action was, where the passenger business was located. At about that time, I learned there was an opening in the ticket office, which was then located in the passenger station at the corner of Girod and Rampart Streets. I applied for the opening and was accepted. My job as the passenger station's ticket office began at five-thirty each morning, seven days per week. My first duty each day was to call the railroad telegraph office and speak with either Eddie Grappe or Wade Duffour to determine the actual arrival time for the incoming passenger train. My second call was to the terminal trainmaster, Sterling E. "Slim" Baskerville, to see if he had any special operating instructions. All these men began their service in 1917 and retired in 1971.

The new job was to become part of one of the most frightening experiences of my young life as well. At that time, there was one departing train in the morning and little other activity until the next train at night. It was early in my shift and I was alone in the office when a single, armed robber walked in. He pointed a revolver at my face and demanded the contents of my cash drawer. I quickly decided that discretion was the better part of valor and delivered what little cash was on hand without attempting any heroics. The robber stuffed the money into his pockets, ripped the telephone from the wall, and bound me hand and foot with the telephone cord. He then gagged me with a cloth rag, forced me onto the floor behind the ticket counter where I could not be seen from the street, and made his getaway.

It seemed like an eternity until my Uncle Vernon arrived. It was his habit to stop by about two-thirty each afternoon, on his way back to the freight office. He entered the office, freed me, and went nearby to call the police. I felt awful about the railroad's money, of course, but I was particularly depressed that the robber also took my wristwatch, a family heirloom given to me by my dad.

It was not terribly valuable; it was also uninsured, but it had been in my family for years, and I felt angry and violated by the loss. For weeks afterward, I searched the shadows as I made my way to work at five-thirty each morning. The whole thing was a shattering experience for a nineteen-year-old who had no previous exposure to crime or violence.

I recall the day the Japanese attacked Pearl Harbor. I was at work and heard the frightening news over the radio. Little did I suspect that in a short time I would be part of that great array of men and women serving in the armed forces of our country.

Choosing a Lifetime Career

My railroad career was interrupted by World War II, but I was taken back by Kansas City Southern when I returned from the service. Mr. Deramus, who, by that time, had been elected president and chairman of the board, had kept in touch with me during my military service, and I became somewhat of a protégé, when he named me assistant general passenger agent. I now worked in the railroad's main city office. It was located in the old

St. Charles Hotel, a handsome, historic New Orleans building which stood at the corner of St. Charles and Gravier Streets where the Place St. Charles office building is now located.

The position of assistant general passenger agent was essentially a public relations and sales position, soliciting business for the railroad throughout the metropolitan area. It was a wonderful, exciting job for a young man with a new wife. Here I learned, by experience, the rudiments and, eventually, the finer points of advertising, marketing, and public relations, skills which became central to my career both with the railroad and in politics. It was in this office that I renewed some friendships and began to build a group of professional friends, part of the "railroad family" with which I was to spend the next decades. I was quickly befriended again by Walter L. "Pat" Murray, ticket agent, who has since retired from the railroad. With him was Lester Muller, a ticket agent and later sales representative for the railroad, who has also retired, and ticket agent Elsie Salvaggio. I also worked with the late Earl Durio, who was also an assistant general passenger agent. My secretary was Lester's cousin Doris Kerner, who is now married with a wonderful family and lives in Jefferson Parish. These were exhilarating, "boom days" for the railroad in the rapidly expanding, post-war community. One of the best parts of my job was that I was outside, part of the business and professional community.

It was as a representative of the railroad that I subsequently became very active in the local Railroad Passenger Association, Traffic Club, Army Transportation Association, Young Men's Business Association, Lion's Club, Knights of Columbus, and a myriad of other civic endeavors. These groups, and the contacts I made with them, were to become essential elements in my early political ventures in New Orleans and later in my statewide campaigns. More important than that, scores of the people I met in those years became my lifelong friends. Many of them helped shape my life. I owe special gratitude to R. J. "Rome" Blair, who retired as vice president/general manager and recently died at the age of seventy-nine. Rome knew railroad employees, business people, and small town mayors throughout the state, and his contacts were invaluable in my campaigns for lieutenant governor and governor. T. S. Carter, who recently retired as chairman of the board and chief executive officer of Kansas City Southern Railroad, was very knowledgeable about engineering and rail-

My dear friends and Kansas City Southern Lines colleagues, the late Rome J. Blair, vice president and general manager, and T. S. Carter, who became chairman and CEO.

roading. Also a world traveler, he has a special place in my heart, as does Vice-President Robert L. "Bob" Haley.

Passenger traffic manager W. C. Clark, executive vice president Orval Frith, vice president/traffic J. W. Scott, and executive general agent in New Orleans Bill Burch were special friends. All of them are now deceased. I worked closely with retired vice president/traffic Bill Hill and with W. A. "Bill" Hardy, Joe Lee, Ed Mauterer, A. J. Perrault, Al Murphy, Earl Bordelon, Charlie Reinerth, and Stanley Gross and with the late Katherine "Katie" Sims, my railroad secretary who retired after more than forty years of service. It was my great pleasure to work with Irvine Hockaday, Jr., who was chief executive officer of the railroad before beginning a new career as president of Hallmark Cards. It was in my capacity as assistant general passenger agent that I had a chance encounter with New Orleans' newly elected mayor deLesseps "Chep" Morrison on the day he took office. It was a meeting which was to change my life. One of my earliest railroad friends was Jim McCall. Before the war, he and Bill Worden had started the D. H. Holmes Travel Agency, one of the early and few such businesses in our community.

The intervention of the war meant that there was little tourist or business travel activity, so Jim had taken a job as assistant general passenger agent with the Kansas City Southern Railroad during the years of the conflict. After the war, he went back to the travel business, and I assumed his position with the railroad.

The Fitzmorris Family Tour Enterprise

My friendship with McCall and Worden resulted in one of the most enjoyable experiences Gloria and I shared in our early marriage. The D. H. Holmes Travel Service arranged a series of guided tours each year, and they allowed us to select one to guide ourselves. I took one tour each year in lieu of a vacation. It was not only enjoyable but extremely educational. Lyndon Johnson used to tell the boyhood story of complaining to his father that his brother, Sam Houston Johnson, had been "two-wheres" and he had been "nowheres." Other than my youthful train tour to Kansas City, I had been nowhere either, and these tours represented a wonderful opportunity. We received no salary for conducting these tours, but we were paid our expenses, got to travel free, and met many wonderful people. Together, Gloria and I conducted tours to Seattle, Vancouver, Victoria, Montreal, the Grand Canyon, Banff and Lake Louise in Canada, California and Mexico.

These summer trips marked the beginning of the railroad's "scenic coaches," which carried our tour passengers to the destination, after which we took buses to see the sights. The railroads, specifically the Canadian Pacific, were also in the hotel businesses, operating big hotels in national parks, Sun Valley, Idaho, and other fascinating locations. The tour operation marked six of the happiest years of our lives, and I will always be grateful to Jim McCall and Bill Worden for the opportunity.

In this age of jet travel, it is sometimes difficult to remember that rail travel, in the 1950s, was the preferred means of transportation of America's business, entertainment, and social elite. My position allowed me to meet many motion picture stars. We ran a special train to Shreveport for Gov. Jimmie Davis and New Orleans-born entertainer June Preisser, who starred in his movie *Louisiana*, which was filmed there. I met Pat O'Brien, who arrived by train for a vaudeville appearance at the Saenger Theatre on Canal Street, as well as Bette Davis and Joan Crawford.

The major league baseball teams also traveled by rail. The teams had private cars, and the players slept on them when the trains stayed overnight in the city. Any messages for the players or coaches were called in to the ticket office where we would relay them to the private pullman cars. I remember the late Leo Durocher and his team on one such trip. He was then married to an actress and left a very firm message with me that if she called he was not to be found.

Bill Pohlmann's Grey Line Tours did a brisk sightseeing business with rail passengers who had layovers in New Orleans because there was little other daytime entertainment. George Toye's Yellow Cab Company was the preeminent taxi operation in the city although there were a number of small, competing "independent cabs" on the city streets as well. A. J. Nugon, Sr. and Jr. and two associates ran the New Orleans Transfer Company. It operated little shuttle buses which ferried railroad passengers and baggage among the five independent railroad stations in town. The Nugon's lucrative shuttle business was effectively ended when the New Orleans Union Passenger Terminal was completed in 1954.

Construction of the terminal was one of the most important developments in the long history of the New Orleans transportation industry. It was a long time coming. As early as 1882, attempts had been made to establish such a facility. The proposed structure was to replace the five small terminals scattered around the city and to eliminate more than a hundred dangerous, time-wasting grade crossings. The terminal crusade began in earnest in 1938, under the administration of New Orleans mayor Robert S. Maestri. With his support, and the leadership of public utilities commissioner Fred A. Earhart, Act 385 was adopted by the legislature, and the question then went to Louisiana voters in the form of a constitutional amendment. It is worth noting that terminal construction, like so many other issues which primarily concern New Orleans and which are to be locally funded, continue to require legislative endorsement and statewide electoral approval. So long as New Orleans city government must go hat in hand for such approval each time it seeks to meet a specific local need, its ability to govern effectively and responsively is hampered. Following voter approval, negotiations were begun with the nine affected railroads but were soon suspended with the commencement of World War II.

They began anew in 1945 when, in one of his last official acts, Mayor Maestri appointed the New Orleans Railroad Terminal Board to pursue the negotiations. He named a high-powered group of public-spirited citizens to the board including chairman William G. Zetzmann, Sr., George Bohn, Sr., Ralph P. Nolan, Joseph E. Haspel, Horace A. Sawyer, and Fred A. Earhart. When Chep Morrison was elected mayor, he continued the board's membership without change, enabling it to proceed in its work without interruption, and he voiced strong support for the terminal concept. In his view, a modern, centralized terminal was just one of the components of the contemporary city he intended to develop. Commissioner Earhart died in 1948 and Commissioner Sawyer resigned upon leaving New Orleans in 1952, succeeded by David R. McGuire, Jr., who would later be appointed the city's first chief administrative officer. The board soon concluded that closing and filling in the obsolete New Basin Canal was the first and most important priority in order to facilitate development of a site for the terminal and an affordable system of overpasses and underpasses. The logistics of combining the five individual terminals, with the necessary connecting tracks and track relocations, underpasses and overpasses, was a monumental job.

The Men Who Made It Happen

It was accomplished by a group of dedicated railroad representatives and outstanding civic leaders. G. C. Lundy, an elderly lawyer, represented the Kansas City Southern Railroad in preparing all the studies, requirements, and specifications into one huge document called *The Blue Book*. Lundy and the original members of the UPT Committee are almost forgotten now, but their personal dedication throughout the years of preparation this project demanded is directly responsible for the transportation infrastructure of modern New Orleans. Making the rather unwieldy project work also required tremendous community support and cooperation.

On October 22, 1947, the "Terminal Agreement," already approved by the city's commission-council, was signed by representatives of the nine railroads and Mayor Morrison. The terminal program provided that forty-four passenger trains would arrive or depart through the new terminal each day.

The facility would be used by the Illinois Central Railroad (The Panama Central, City of New Orleans, Creole and The Louisiana), The Louisiana and Arkansas-Kansas City Southern Lines (Southern Belle, No. 10), Louisville and Nashville Railroad (The Humming Bird, The Crescent, The Pan-American, Gulf Wind, Piedmont Limited, The Azalean, Commuters Special), Missouri Pacific Lines (The Orleanean, The Houstonian), Southern Railway System (The Southerner, The Pelican, No. 44), Southern Pacific Lines (Sunset Limited, Argonaut, Acadian), Texas and Pacific Railway, (Louisiana Eagle, Louisiana Daylight), and by the Gulf, Mobile and Ohio Railroad. With the new terminal, nine trunk-line railroads would connect New Orleans with vital centers to the North, East, and West. In conjunction with the Port of New Orleans and Moisant Field, this development brought New Orleans into the mainstream of national and international transportation.

Not only did the railroads derive a substantial benefit from the new terminal, they also undertook the cost. The $16 million terminal, while owned by the city, was built by the railroads and paid for by them through revenue bonds, issued through the Public Belt Railroad Commission. The Public Belt organization is one of the few municipally owned local railroad lines in the country. It serves local needs of marine and industrial operations.

Construction and day-to-day operation of the terminal was, as part of the agreement, the province of the new Union Passenger Terminal Committee. This group was composed of representatives of the city, the terminal board, the Public Belt Railroad Commission, and the individual railroads. Committee chairman was E. S. Pennebaker. Committee members were George Bohn, W. D. Burch, Paul D. Dorman, Clifton Ganus, Ed J. Garland, Olin Linn, H. C. Mauney, David R. McGuire, Jr., J. T. Moon, R. C. Parsons, C. H. Mottier, Ralph P. Nolan, B. S. Sines, Michael Prevosty, S. L. Wright, William G. Zetzmann, Sr., and Mayor Morrison. Two original UPT members died before the terminal was completed: C. D. Mackay, first chairman of the committee, and R. W. Barnes, who also served as chairman. Committee members W. T. Turner, G. C. Lundy, Col. L. L. Morton, and J. T. Suggs retired during the years the terminal was in planning and development. Terminal manager was C. J. Wallace. As chief engineer of the UPT committee, he also oversaw terminal construction. Harry McCall was chief counsel, assisted by Leonard B. Levy. George A. Heft was secretary and J. H. Marriott, auditor-treasurer.

Dedicating the Terminal

Dedication of the terminal was a big community event. Presidents of the participating railroads were on hand, along with the president of the Association of American Railroads and many Louisiana elected officials. Program chairman was William G. Zetzmann, Sr., who had done so much to make the terminal a reality, and New Orleans businessman Joseph M. Rault was general chairman of the arrangements committee. The station plaque was christened by Corinne Ann Morrison, the mayor's six-year-old daughter. She used a bottle of water drawn from the Atlantic and Pacific Oceans, the Great Lakes, the Gulf of Mexico, and the Mississippi, Missouri, Ohio, and Rio Grande rivers, the extremities of the passenger tracks which began at the New Orleans Terminal. There was much to see at the Saturday, May 1, 1954, dedication. This was the first air-conditioned passenger terminal in the country. The railroads had combined to create a special Exhibit Train for inspection at the terminal, displaying the latest in modern passenger equipment.

Inside the terminal were four brilliant fresco murals symbolizing Louisiana history over the preceding 435 years. The product of New Orleans artist Conrad Albrizio, a Louisiana State University faculty member, they were done in a rare fresco treatment which involved applying ground colors on wet plaster. The finished murals were resistant to deterioration and became even brighter with age. Now priceless, the murals depicted the ages of exploration, colonization, conflict, and the modern age. They are still a prominent feature of the terminal. The completed terminal looked much as it does today, except that those were the years of segregation. That meant that blacks had a separate waiting area and restaurant. Ours is a jet age which now considers passenger travel by rail almost an afterthought—although there remains a dedicated cadre of rail travel enthusiasts for reasons of both economy and aesthetics—and most of the passenger trains which served New Orleans are only a distant memory. Yet, in 1954, the opening of the terminal was a signal event in the life of our community, not to mention the scores of lives saved by eliminating the dangerous grade crossings which had blighted the city for generations.

There is a continuum between that time and this in the person of Ms Betty Foley. A rare and talented professional, she was on hand for the terminal dedication and served for years as secretary to the general manager. She is now secretary-treasurer of the UPT Committee, a tireless promoter of rail travel whose ability and enthusiasm has been an inspiration to decades of UPT committee members and the traveling public as well.

The exciting Union Terminal project occupied much of my time during my early years with the railroad after the war. Those were wonderful, rewarding years for me. In 1950, at age twenty-nine, I was selected as Outstanding Young Man of New Orleans by the Junior Chamber of Commerce, an honor which had previously gone to Mayor Morrison. I spent thirty-four years with the Kansas City Southern Railroad, rising to become general passenger agent, assistant to the president, and, finally, vice president of the railroad—one of the youngest transportation executives in the entire nation.

In conjunction with my administrative role, I tried to develop new marketing strategies which could both fill seats on the trail and broaden the exposure of New Orleans to residents of other parts of Louisiana.

Several of these innovative marketing programs were particularly popular: I persuaded the railroad to add a special, low-cost, commuter train between New Orleans and Baton Rouge. This special fare allowed Baton Rouge residents to take advantage of the larger selection of goods and services offered in New Orleans through a one-day shopping trip. It, and the other marketing programs we developed, proved to be good for both the railroad and the city.

Introducing Students to the City

I also developed a unique program allowing school children from around Louisiana to enjoy a special train trip and outing in New Orleans. Our strategy was to keep the ticket cost so low that even children from families of modest means could afford to participate. In addition, by scheduling the trip to New Orleans one night and the return trip the next, we eliminated the additional cost and complication of hotel accommodations for the children and their chaperons.

Shreveport sixth-grader Donna Phillips and her classmates from Arthur Circle Elementary School took one of those excursions. On Donna's trip, the class arrived in New Orleans early in the morning and spent the entire day touring the city. For most of the children, this trip marked their first—and sometimes only—childhood experiences in a "big city." It was a real adventure for which they prepared by studying New Orleans history for weeks before the trip.

After reaching the big, new terminal, something to see in itself, the children boarded buses to tour the city, seeing Lake Pontchartrain and Audubon Park. From the safety of their bus, they were driven in wide-eyed wonder down fabled Bourbon Street, where they visited the historic Cornstalk Hotel. This was the "Beatnik" period, the children were excited to see the quaint artists and poets in their turtleneck sweaters, beards, and berets.

In the afternoon, they enjoyed a short cruise on the Mississippi riverboat *President*, followed by a full-course dinner at Gluck's before boarding the train for that night's trip home. Later destroyed by fire, Gluck's was a world-famous, fancy French restaurant with gleaming china and silver and an elaborate menu.

Donna still remembers the special two-piece suit she wore on this trip. It was one of the first of the new polyester outfits, specially selected because it would not wrinkle during the train ride. For years she kept the twenty-five cent souvenir token she purchased from a machine on board the *President*. On this, her first visit to the city, she fell in love with New Orleans and told her schoolmates that she wanted to live there when she grew up. She eventually did move to New Orleans to live and now is the graphic designer at Ochsner Medical Institutions and a faculty member at the University of New Orleans.

The point is: We cannot know how many other young children chose to live in New Orleans as a result of their train ride, but I am sure that this experience touched many youthful lives and helped youngsters from all around Louisiana better understand New Orleans and its rich, colorful history.

In addition, we took a very active role in working with many of the schools along the route of the KCS to provide football special trains, picnic outings for employees, and educational trips between any two points on the railroad. One of our most active participants was Ms Sadye Hahn of Winnfield, Louisiana. Sadye was a well-respected schoolteacher and community leader. She was a great promoter of the educational tours and because of her interest she was greatly responsible for many trips between Winnfield and New Orleans.

As I moved up the ladder with the Kansas City and Southern, I went from the railroad passenger terminal at 701 South Rampart to the ground floor of the beautiful old St. Charles Hotel, then to the sales and executive offices in the United Fruit Building, later the Bank of Louisiana Building at 321 St. Charles Avenue, and finally to our modern, efficient, new sales, marketing, and executive building at 201 Airline Highway, adjacent to our massive yard operations. This facility, when completed, was one of the finest in the country. It was a thrill for me to work on the details of the structure during its construction and through the formal dedication, at which time Mr. W. N. Deramus III, members of our board of directors, and our many shipping friends honored us with their presence at another "ribbon cutting."

Leaving the Railroad

My active career with the railroad ended with my inauguration as lieutenant governor. My lifelong friend and campaign manager, the late William G. Helis, Jr.—a tremendously successful oil man in private life—had convinced me that I should run on the platform that I would be a "full-time lieutenant governor," a pledge never before advanced in any campaign for that office. Keeping that promise meant a significant financial sacrifice for the Fitzmorris family, for the lieutenant governorship offered a barely spartan salary. Nonetheless, I intended to keep my word, and I did, moving my belongings out of the railroad's new offices.

During the years when I combined my railroad position with service on the city council, I took no increase in salary. In fact, at the program marking my formal retirement from active service with the railroad, I was given only my regular final paycheck, with neither a bonus for thirty-four years service nor the traditional gold watch!

The Deramus Legacy

Throughout those years, it was my honor and good fortune to be associated with one of the legendary families in American railroad transportation, the Deramus dynasty. W. N. Deramus II was chairman of the board and president of the Kansas City Southern when I returned after military service, and he became my mentor, my professional inspiration, and my champion. When he died in 1961, he was succeeded by his son W. N. Deramus III, who inherited his distinguished father's foresight and executive ability. A Harvard graduate, he was assistant to the general manager when we first met in 1946 and was a true and valued friend throughout my career.

When he died in 1989, his post was assumed by W. N. Deramus IV. The passing of William N. Deramus III marked the end of an American era. He was a quiet, powerful, active, behind-the-scenes man who performed literally scores of good works in his community, always on the condition that they be kept anonymous.

He was wonderful to work for, that unique combination of executive focus which, on the one hand, required no fawning or flattery but, on the other hand, brooked no baloney from his employees. The Deramus family had a full measure of civic responsibility as well, allowing me to continue my railroad career working early mornings and late afternoons throughout the years when the middle portion of each day was consumed by my duties as a New Orleans city councilman, and I will forever be in the debt of these remarkable friends and associates for their years of understanding and support.

Chapter 4

The Morrison Years

My introduction to the Chep Morrison years in New Orleans politics came about quite by accident. It was May 6, 1946; I was out of the army and back working for the Kansas City Southern Railroad. It was also inauguration day for deLesseps "Chep" Morrison. I encountered him near my office as he was on his way to Gallier Hall to take the oath of office as the youngest mayor of a major American city. I had known Chep slightly when he was elected to the state legislature from New Orleans' Twelfth Ward and had admired his work as a floor leader for the reform administration of Gov. Sam Jones.

Morrison had led the fight for civil service protection for public workers and for voting machines to replace the notoriously corrupt paper ballot system that had been such a hallmark of shame in Louisiana politics. Apparently Morrison's constituents admired him too, for he had been re-elected while on active duty with the U.S. Army in Europe. Back from the war, supported by an enthusiastic personal following of similarly reform-minded private citizens who had not before been politically active, Morrison had unseated powerful incumbent mayor Robert Maestri by four thousand votes and, in the process, turned the mighty Regular Democratic Organization, which ran New Orleans, on its ear. "Come over and meet me at city hall, Jimmy," Chep said that morning, "I'd like to talk to you about getting involved with me in New Orleans politics." It was an idea that had been in my mind for several years, beginning with childhood excursions with my father to hear Gov. Huey P. Long. I thought the timing of Chep's offer was my signal to take the bull by the horns and get personally involved. In fact, I think Chep was surprised to discover that I beat him back to city hall and was waiting in his office when he arrived.

That chance conversation led to a close friendship with one of the most uniquely talented Louisiana leaders of this century and paved the way for my own thirty years in public life. Chep and I continued to visit in the following months. I worked hard for his re-election, which he won by the biggest landslide in our city's history. I was also an enthusiastic backer of Morrison's successful campaign to win voter approval of a new "home rule" charter. The charter change was one of those intimidating issues which most of the voting public barely understands. Who do you know who has actually ever read the New Orleans City Charter? The proposed new charter passed, as much in response to Chep's personal popularity and his enthusiasm for the plan as to voters' careful consideration of the complicated language it contained. The New Orleans political bosses knew what the charter was all about, though. They knew it forever changed city councilmen from full-time city administrators to part-time legislators. They knew it changed the mayor's role from ceremonial, "first among equals," to one of dominance and power. Most of the established political players in the city fought the proposal bitterly, and they lost.

The subsequent members of the city council, to be chosen in the 1954 city election, would no longer each have a city department to run as a personal fiefdom. They would be restricted to legislating from the sidelines, and the mayor would be firmly, personally in charge of running the city. In 1950, Gov. Robert Kennon asked me to run for lieutenant governor on his ticket. I discussed the matter with my dad and Chep Morrison. Both urged me to delay making a statewide race. Chep thought that, while I would provide a useful geographic, religious, and philosophical balance for Kennon, it might seem hasty for me to make my first race a bid for the second highest post in the state. In addition, he wanted my help in establishing a new direction for New Orleans city politics.

Seeking the Council Seat

Chep wanted a new council which shared his reformist and activist goals, and he urged me to consider running from District C. The change to a part-time council would work well into my personal agenda only if I could maintain my railroad career. In those days, independent professionals, owners of businesses, or retired persons of wealth were about the only citizens who could afford to seek public office.

Persons who worked for large companies were virtually shut out of public service and the political process. Chep thought that was wrong and he spoke, in my behalf, to W. N. Deramus II, telling him how important he thought it was that businessmen at all levels be encouraged and allowed to participate in government. Mr. Deramus agreed and allowed me to seek election to the council and continue my full-time responsibilities with the railroad at the same time. As Chep and I talked about the possibilities of my making the race, it began to appear that the timing might be right. Under the old system, there had been seven council members, each elected from a district. Only the mayor was elected city wide, serving as the eighth member of the council. The new charter changed all that. Now, district councilmen would be elected from five districts, with another two being elected at large, running city wide. The mayor would continue to be elected city wide but would no longer sit as a member of the council. I lived at 900 Chapelle Street in Lakeview, which was in the new District C. The district comprised Wards 2, 3, 4, and 15 including the lakefront area, part of the Irish Channel, the French Quarter, and all of Algiers.

Also living in that district were incumbent councilmen Victor Schiro and Glen P. Clasen. This was the first time that Clasen's Algiers constituency had been lumped together with precincts on the New Orleans side of the river into a new, larger district. Both men were well-established political figures and would have been very difficult for a newcomer like me to defeat. Fortunately for me, both men were interested in holding one of the two new "at-large" council seats. The Schiro candidacy posed a problem which threatened to split Morrison's carefully constructed personal political organization.

The Cold Water Committee

Chep's path to power, in his first race for mayor, had been paved by the enthusiastic efforts of his unique personal organization, known as the "Cold Water Committee." The committee was composed of outstanding business and civic leaders, most of whom had not previously been politically active. In fact, the committee was the forerunner of the New Orleans Business Council of today. It originally had no name and was dedicated primarily to the defeat of Huey Long.

It was a brilliant, brave, and sometimes contentious group of men and women who were, for the most part, sufficiently personally wealthy and independent to dare to confront the powerful, entrenched political machine of Mayor Maestri. The group had such local luminaries as Edgar and Edith Stern, owners of WDSU Television, Cliff Ganus, founder of the A&G Cafeteria chain, Cliff Favrot, who had real estate and other holdings, investment figures Herman Kohlmeyer, Darwin Fenner, and Arthur Waters, and developer Lester Kabacoff. Original members had included Fenner's father, Charles, A. B. Freeman and his son Dick, Esmond Phelps, and Monte Lemon whose son, Steve, later participated. They met in offices on the top floor of the United Fruit Building at 321 St. Charles Avenue. Herman Kohlmeyer was the group's first and only treasurer. Only Kabacoff and Kohlmeyer remain of the original group which became the Cold Water Committee and forever changed the face of New Orleans politics. Fiercely independent, sometimes the Cold Water Committee pursued its own agenda, at cross purposes with Morrison, the committee's founder and titular leader. This was one such instance. The Cold Water Committee decided to back local activist and committee member Mrs. Martha G. Robinson. She was a respected power in her own right, one of the framers of the new charter.

The committee asked Schiro to withdraw from the at-large race and run, instead, for the council from District C, which would have posed a real problem for my candidacy. Schiro refused to withdraw and was supported in his decision by the other source of Chep Morrison's power, the Crescent City Democratic Association. The CCDA was composed mostly of political figures and elected officials. Morrison firmly exerted his considerable political influence in the maneuvering for that race, engineering the CCDA endorsement of Schiro and convincing the Cold Water Committee to endorse only Clasen for one at-large position and to make no endorsement in the Schiro-Robinson race. The outcome of the internal bloodletting within the Morrison organization meant that there was room for me as the candidate of the CCDA and the Cold Water Committee for the new District C position. It also forced Mrs. Robinson into a rather unlikely alliance. She emerged as the candidate of the RDO, on the same ticket with

Councilman Thomas M. Brahney, Jr., who was opposing her friend Chep Morrison for mayor. I faced spirited, well-funded opposition in this, my first political race. Francis Clesi, a respected businessman, sought the post. So did Algiers lawyer George O'Dowd. O'Dowd's candidacy in Algiers, used to having its very own council member, posed a particular challenge.

To round out the field there was lawyer Guy Deano, who now lives in St. Tammany Parish. Deano was the choice of the powerful Regular Democratic Organization, led by Assessor Jim Comiskey, one of the most colorful, brilliant political strategists I have ever known. The RDO operated from the Choctaw Club, a musty, antique-filled headquarters near the intersection of Poydras and St. Charles Avenue, where what we later called the Amoco Building or Lupo Building now stands. A three-story townhouse with two balconies, it had once been a private mansion. This was a private club of a totally different sort from the genteel Boston Club and others in its social strata. The RDO was the second oldest political organization in America, anteceded only by New York's Tammany Hall. The Choctaw Club and the RDO were fueled by raw political power, the spoils system, including "deducts," the monthly dues automatically taken from its members on the public payroll. The RDO even maintained an active ladies' auxiliary. The Club had no dining room or bar, although food and liquor frequently appeared within the hall. Local cynics used to suggest that its location was no doubt selected so the membership could keep a watchful eye on the goings-on at city hall, then located in Gallier Hall across St. Charles Avenue.

The "Old Regulars" also had a perfect vantage point from which to view the city's two daily newspapers, the *Times-Picayune*, then located down the street, and the *States-Item*, a few blocks away. All the old locales in this corridor of power are gone now, the Times-Picayune Building demolished in the mid-sixties and the *States-Item* merged with it in a sprawling, new complex on the edge of the city. City hall moved to the new government complex on Loyola Avenue, and the Choctaw Club became only a memory shared by a rapidly diminishing circle of old-time politicians. Also gone is the Marble Hall, a sandwich shop and oyster bar just out the side door of Gallier Hall on Lafayette Street. The Marble Hall, now almost completely forgotten, was a singular temple of intrigue where reporters rubbed elbows with politicians of all kinds. Chep used to utilize Marble Hall as a handy source of political

The Choctaw Club, headquarters of the Regular Democratic Association, once stood at the corner of St. Charles and Poydras Streets. (Courtesy New Orleans *Times-Picayune*)

rumors, for the latest "inside stories" were readily available there, along with scores of unfounded, unreliable rumors—some of which I probably started myself! The Choctaw Club was the preeminent, but by no means the only, political headquarters in the city. Morrison's CCDA met either in the mayor's office, on Orleans Avenue, or in Constable Clyde Bel's awning shop.

Each of the city's five powerful assessors had his own political establishment as well. Orleans Parish is the only one in the state to have more than one assessor. These political kingdoms have survived to this day, a quaint anachronism. In their day, however, the assessors, Henry Heaton, Sam Boylan, Claude Mauberret, Sr., Charlie Degan, and Jim Comiskey ran political organizations of unquestioned power and independence.

Losing the Assessor's Race

The worst political defeat of my life came in 1960 when, at Chep's urging and against my own inclinations and best judgment, I challenged Dr. Claude Mauberret, Jr., for assessor. Chep wanted to break up the assessors' powerful block, and when Claude Mauberret, Sr., died in office no one thought his son would run for the job. It seemed to Chep like the perfect opening for me. I had never experienced any desire to be an assessor, but I ran. Mauberret's son, Dr. Claude Mauberret, Jr., sought the seat. The assessors' positions, in those days, stayed in the same family through several generations. Although I had Chep's support, endorsements from the newspapers and the unions, I lost every precinct.

Mr. Jim

No assessor wielded such power as Jim Comiskey. Tall, muscular, white-haired, a florid-faced Irish orator and political infighter without parallel in the city's history, Comiskey ran his district with an iron hand. He was a highly successful businessman as well, operating The Comiskey Company, a liquor distributorship. Comiskey spent every waking hour practicing the art of politics from his home, the assessor's office, his business, or his own personal political headquarters at 118 S. Broad Street. When he closed his own headquarters, "Mr. Jim" drove a short distance to the Larry and Katz Bar, operated by Larry Reynolds, behind the present ODECO building on Canal Street. This was a sawdust-floor

"Mr. Jim," James E. Comiskey, legendary assessor and RDO leader, and I meet the press.

operation, a favorite of interns from Tulane Hospital in those days. The bar even provided separate window service, through which black customers could purchase half-pints. Behind the bar itself was a huge warehouse, for Larry and Katz was the biggest liquor seller in town. Every Sunday afternoon an eighteen-wheeler, operated by the sheriff of Hancock County, Mississippi, backed up to Larry and Katz to load up the week's transport of liquor for the dry, Mississippi county.

It was here that Jim Comiskey operated late into the evenings, dispensing patronage, finding jobs, helping constituents who had problems with city hall or the court system. It was all part of perpetuating Comiskey's sprawling, well-oiled political machine which was closely allied with the Regular Democratic Organization, of which he was probably the leading figure. Times in New Orleans have changed so in the past quarter-century that it seems impossible to remember the influence "Mr. Jim" wielded in the city and the skill with which he exercised it. He was the last of the old breed of politician, a colorful figure who could be a great friend and awesome adversary. I admired and respected Mr. Jim although we were frequently at odds during the Morrison years. His son Jim, my dear friend, inherited his father's legacy and sense of political loyalty. He went on to serve with me on the city council. I ran for councilman-at-large on his ticket when he ran for mayor. He was a distinguished federal judge before retiring from the bench to a successful banking career.

As the campaign opened, arrayed against Deano and the history and power of the RDO—including three powerful assessors within the district—seeking election to the new District C council post were candidates Clesi, O'Dowd, and James E. Fitzmorris, Jr., not yet thirty-three, politically untried but long on enthusiasm. I ran that race on less than twenty thousand dollars, spent mostly on handbills, flyers, and bumper stickers. I spent little money on radio, even less on New Orleans' sole television station, WDSU, and absolutely none on items which would today be considered essential: polls, political consultants, direct mail, and the like. Mine was essentially a neighborhood campaign, going door-to-door talking to friends and former classmates, asking them to elect me as part of the Chep Morrison team. Morrison's own organization, as was the custom, paid most of the expenses related to the ticket as a whole, sample ballots and such. A campaign for the same district today would cost at least a quarter of a million dollars. Of course, there was not yet the proliferation of political groups, each demanding expenses for its own electioneering. In those days only the RDO and the CCDA were major players. There was only one major black organization in the city, that of the late Rev. A. L. Davis, who later became a member of the city council himself.

When the votes from the first primary were counted, Chep Morrison had been overwhelmingly elected. Clasen also won a first primary victory, and there was a runoff between Schiro and Mrs. Robinson, which Schiro was to win. I ran ahead of Deano, beating him by some two thousand votes. In the runoff, endorsed by Clesi, who ran third, I won a convincing victory, receiving 13,391 votes. It was that campaign which first established my long pattern of maintaining friendly relationships with my opponents. Clesi, Deano, and O'Dowd became valued friends after the election and remained so through the years. I tried to run without personal attacks or mudslinging and continued to do so in subsequent campaigns which spanned the fifties, sixties, seventies, and eighties. Sam Rayburn, that year temporarily displaced as Speaker of the House in one of the two occasions in modern history in which Republicans controlled the U.S. House of Representatives, was the speaker at our inauguration. Rayburn was feted at a hundred-dollar-per-plate dinner at the Loyola Field House, long since demolished. While that event made a significant dent in the Fitzmorris family budget, I bought a hundred-dollar ticket for Gloria and for myself.

I was shocked and dismayed to find out that the hundred-dollar dinner consisted of cold cuts and soft drinks; we had planned to live on that menu ourselves the next week to afford the price of admission! Rayburn was also the guest of honor at a private reception, hosted by Edith Stern at her palatial home, Longue Vue Gardens on Bamboo Road. As a newly-elected councilman, I was invited. As I approached the beautiful, manicured grounds of the home in my rattletrap old car, I saw the lines of limos and beautiful vehicles in the drive. I elected to park my car on the street, away from the limos. As I walked up to the house, a taxi arrived and out stepped a tall, distinguished-looking man I had not met. In a burst of hospitality I said, "Hello, I'm Councilman Jimmy Fitzmorris." "Nice to see you," the stranger replied, "I'm Averell

New Orleans City Council inauguration day, May 1, 1954, after my first election, l-r: Councilmen Paul Burke, Fred Cassibry, me, and Walter Douffour, Mayor deLesseps "Chep" Morrison, Councilmen Victor Schiro and Glen Clasen. (Courtesy Leon Trice Collection, Howard-Tilton Library of Tulane University)

Harriman." So I walked into the Sterns' home with Harriman, trusted advisor of presidents Roosevelt and Truman. He would later become governor of New York, and would make an indelible mark on the international affairs of this nation. No two men could have been so different as the elegant Harriman and the short, blunt Texan, "Mr. Sam," but their friendship endured until Rayburn's death from cancer a decade later. Mrs. Stern was a gracious hostess, and it was a wonderful, memorable evening.

The first big issue to confront the new council was also one of the silliest: the question of providing city cars for councilmen. The holdover incumbents from the former council already had cars from the departments they had managed under the old system. The proposal really only affected those of us who were newly elected. The issue proved to be incendiary and incredibly controversial. Harry McCall, Sr., distinguished community leader and head of the charter committee, publicly derided the notion of cars for councilmen, saying it was unnecessary for the city to provide eight-cylinder automobiles so each councilman could ride in style from his home to city hall and back. McCall said that we should form a car pool or take a taxi. I wonder what he would think about the current system in which councilmen not only have cars but each has an assigned driver from the police department as well. In the face of such public pressure we had to ask Morrison to veto the authorization for cars and we new councilmen had to wait until the incumbents turned in their old vehicles, after which they were quietly given new ones and we inherited their hand-me-downs. In the meantime, I used my railroad car for city business, a star-crossed vehicle as it turned out.

One day I took that car to the French Market where I bought a hamper of fresh shrimp, which I put into the trunk. Apparently some of them spilled out, underneath the spare, where they remained unnoticed, turning particularly rancid in the steamy New Orleans summer. The decomposing shrimp were not in plain view, and no one could discover the source of the rather acrid odor emanating from my vehicle. One day I parked it under a window at city hall where the window fans drew the awful smell throughout the building, and some of the secretaries went home sick. I finally found the remains, but I never could get the smell out. After numerous unsuccessful cleanings, I finally traded the car in, taking special care not to reveal to the railroad the real necessity for this transaction!

The Riverfront Expressway Battle

The benefit of historical perspective and hindsight is valuable in thinking about two other issues that arose before the council. The first was the proposal for an elevated riverfront expressway. The idea was to alleviate New Orleans' growing central business district traffic congestion by providing a new roadway along the riverfront.

You must realize that the riverfront in those days had no resemblance to the picturesque area today. Then, it was mostly marked by garbage dumps, dilapidated wharves, and railroad tracks. I supported the expressway concept and, except for one last piece of federal approval, it was a virtual *fait accompli.* Then came Mrs. Martha G. Robinson, the same woman recently defeated for the council by Vic Schiro. Mrs. Robinson was no oddball addict to wild causes. She was a respected civic and cultural leader, a preservationist before any of us knew what that term really meant. The expressway proponents attempted to compromise with those who thought it would ruin what city councilman Mike Early was later to call the "tout ensemble" of the Vieux Carré. They even provided for the expressway to dip when it came to the area near St. Louis Cathedral so parishioners' view of the river from the cathedral steps would not be obscured. No amount of conciliation or persuasion swayed Mrs. Robinson and the opponents though. She was a tireless adversary, marshaling her facts and her forces, unrelenting in her contention that there was another, better future for the riverfront than as a superhighway. She managed to stop federal approval of the plan, and the project died. In retrospect, she was absolutely right.

Although we had no way of knowing the future and had the very best intentions at the time, if we had succeeded in building the riverfront expressway, we could never have built the Moon Walk, the Aquarium of the Americas, Woldenberg Park, or the Convention Center—which have provided the basis for our critically important tourist industry.

Public Housing: How a Good Idea Goes Wrong

Another issue from which we have learned was the construction of the public housing projects. They replaced some really ghettolike enclaves and provided the first decent housing for a whole generation. Two of the projects provided some of the nation's first senior citizen public housing. At the time we thought they were wonderful, and New Orleans was celebrated across the country for our foresight in providing these projects. We now have come to realize that they also grew to become havens for criminals and locked successive generations into a cycle of poverty, humiliation, and despair. Given the lack of available land for scattered site housing, I am not sure that anything other than what we built would have been possible. Nonetheless, the projects did not serve the grand public purpose we intended, and their present condition is shameful and unacceptable.

I won re-election in 1958 in the primary. Against my RDO opponent, former Tulane All-American Lou Thomas, I received 15,533 votes. Once again, Thomas and I became close, lifelong friends after the election. This was the first inauguration held in the newly constructed city hall. Chep Morrison had just lost the 1956 race for governor to Earl K. Long. Morrison ran well in the city, as always, but "Uncle Earl" took special pleasure in humiliating him in the rural parishes, poking fun at his cosmopolitan wardrobe and speech. I always thought that Chep was hurt by his results in the country; he was proud of his own rural roots as a native of New Roads. The fact was, Chep's rather sheltered childhood on a rice plantation in Point Coupee Parish did not sufficiently establish him as a "country boy" against a homespun candidate like Long. In the 1958 race, Chep Morrison was handily re-elected to a fourth term as mayor.

The Charter Change: Breaking with Chep

He began immediately to put together a coalition to change the city charter to allow him to seek re-election after that term. The existing charter, which he had sponsored, had already exempted him from the two-term limitation, which made him the last mayor to be able to serve four terms.

I disagreed profoundly with his effort and opposed him. There were also some lingering bad feelings from his efforts in pushing me into the disastrous race for assessor. Then I clashed with him and Schiro over an ill-considered plan to build a monorail from Moisant Field to downtown New Orleans. No city in the country had successfully built such a long-distance monorail, and I saw serious safety problems with the project as well. A key Schiro

New Orleans City Council at its 1960 inauguration, l-r: Councilmen Walter Douffour, me, Glen Clasen, Mayor Chep Morrison, Councilmen Victor Schiro, Paul Burke, Henry Curtis, and Fred Cassibry. (Courtesy Leon Trice Collection, Howard-Tilton Library of Tulane University)

supporter, Thomas Lupo, created "Monorail of Louisiana" to facilitate the project, and the political pressure for me to endorse the scheme was oppressive and unpleasant. The combination of those events caused a rift between me and Chep which damaged our formerly close relationship. Morrison lost the 1960 governor's election to Jimmie Davis and, one year later, his referendum to allow him to run again for mayor failed as well. A few months later, he resigned the mayor's position to become United States ambassador to the Organization of American States. He was succeeded as mayor by council president Vic Schiro.

The Kennedy Campaign

I supported Morrison in that governor's race, as I always did. I spent much of 1960 working enthusiastically for the election of John F. Kennedy for president of the United States.

My introduction to Kennedy had come about in a strange way. One night I received a call at home from someone identifying himself as "Jack Kennedy." Thinking it was some prank, I said, "Sure, Jack, what can I do for you?" It turned out, to my considerable embarrassment, to actually be Senator Kennedy. We had a mutual friend in Kansas City, businessman Don Hewitt, who had recommended that Kennedy call me for help in the Louisiana election. I wound up speaking for Kennedy throughout the state. As a Roman Catholic, I was particularly sensitive to some of the outrageous religious slurs I encountered speaking on his behalf in some small, rural Louisiana communities. I took pride in pointedly telling these audiences that, in my years in public office, the archbishop had never once called me to ask for a political favor. My experience with President Kennedy taught me the importance of actually *asking* for someone's help. I don't know that I would ever have become that involved in the Kennedy campaign had he not taken the time to ask. I was very much impressed by his intellect, wit, and industrious campaign and thrilled that I was able to have some small part in helping him win election to the nation's highest office.

On November 22, 1963, I was eating at a lunch counter across from the St. Charles Hotel when word came of the president's assassination in Dallas. I went immediately back to city hall. My deepest memory of the following days, beyond my personal sense of loss, is of the terrible, anguished silence on the streets of the city. You could sense the painful sadness throughout the city as New Orleans went into mourning for a brilliant young man we had grown to respect and to love.

The Mayor's Race I Should Have Run

I wanted to run for mayor in the following election, 1961, and asked Morrison for his help. Our relations at the time were sufficiently damaged that he declined to support me, choosing, rather, to endorse an able but not well known state senator and former first assistant district attorney, Adrian Duplantier. A new member of the Morrison ticket that year was Maurice "Moon" Landrieu. Morrison's curious logic was that I would be a weak candidate because I had just lost the race for assessor, conveniently forgetting that I had only run for that job as an accommodation to his own wishes and against my own. Councilmen Jim Comiskey and Paul Burke had also opposed his charter change proposal.

Relations between Chep and me had sunk to such a level I wound up running against his ticket, as a candidate for councilman-at-large on the RDO ticket with Jim Comiskey, the Old Regulars' choice for mayor. The late Robert Ziblich ran for the other at-large seat. Despite the support of Morrison's old nemesis, Gov. Jimmie Davis, Comiskey lost in the primary; I received twice as many votes as he. The *Times-Picayune* endorsed Duplantier, me, Landrieu, and a fresh, new face in New Orleans politics, Jim Garrison, for district attorney. This was the year of the famous "Boat House Deal," a phrase concocted by Councilman Paul Burke, who finished fourth in the primary election for mayor. The "deal" was an arrangement in which the CCDA joined with the RDO to jointly support the candidacy of Jim Comiskey for mayor. The following year, I helped to engineer a formal merger of the two political organizations, which had long been bitter rivals. I finished in first place for councilman-at-large, followed by the late Eddie Price, another All-American from Tulane University, Landrieu, and Joseph DiRosa. Duplantier led interim mayor Vic Schiro by 4,225 votes.

DiRosa and I were the candidates of the RDO, but since our mayoral candidate, Jim Comiskey, had lost in the primary, we had no ticket on which to run. Consequently, we had to join forces with mayoral candidate Schiro for the runoff. Councilman Paul Burke, who had run as an independent candidate for mayor that

Qualifying for assessor in 1960, my worst political defeat, l-r: Victor Wogan, CCDA ward leader, later U.S. marshall and my 1965 campaign manager; Mac Casse, CCDA and CRD ward leader, later state senate sergeant-at-arms; me; my dad; John Caswell, vice chairman, CCDA; and Morey Sear, later federal judge. (Courtesy Mayor's Office, photo by Ann Blaize)

A New Orleans Chamber of Commerce business development tour to Minnesota, August 1956. Pictured at a stop at Breezy Point, Minnesota, front row, l-r: Joe Shelton, our Minnesota host; Warren Smith, Lone Star Cement Company; me; Harold Mouney, vice president, Southern Railroad; Louis Schwartz, Traffic and Transportation Bureau director; Adm. Whittaker F. Riggs, chamber executive director; and George Schneider, chamber development director. Standing, fifth from left, is Clay Shaw, then executive director, International Trade Mart.

year, also endorsed Schiro, as did councilmen Dan Kelly and Guy Deano. In the runoff, Schiro relied heavily on the late Willard Robertson, a local automobile dealer and extraordinary fund-raiser, and Clem Sehrt, attorney and powerful leader of the RDO, skilled designer of the citywide political coalition for his candidate. This was not to be the last time Schiro managed to come from behind in a campaign; he won over Duplantier by twenty thousand votes. Duplantier had been an effective state senator and is now a federal judge. His campaign manager in the mayor's race was former councilman Glen Clasen, who was later named the city's chief administrative officer, upon the death of David McGuire. I was swept into office with 111,588 votes, carrying sixteen of seventeen wards and losing only Ward 2 by an eyelash.

Nineteen sixty-one was also the year unknown Jim Garrison toppled the incumbent district attorney, Richard Dowling, a capable official tainted by the air of "machine politics." Almost as the votes were being counted, a lonely, twisted figure named Lee Harvey Oswald and a sordid group of lunatic associates were promoting the "Fair Play for Cuba" committee. We will never know what would have happened had Dowling been New Orleans district attorney in the aftermath of the assassination, two years later, of Pres. John Fitzgerald Kennedy ln Dallas. For that matter, what if the third-place finisher, famed defense attorney F. Irvin Dymond, had won? We do, of course, know that Garrison won, developed a controversial, convoluted conspiracy theory, and prosecuted New Orleans businessman Clay Shaw, managing director of the International Trade Mart, for his supposed role in the conspiracy. The embattled Shaw hired Dymond who destroyed Garrison's case and set in motion the forces which eventually destroyed the DA's public support. He was defeated in the next election by Harry Connick who remains in office to this day.

Chep Morrison as Internationalist

Morrison loved his work as ambassador to the Organization of American States. His interest in Latin America was legendary; he was a highly effective salesman for the Port of New Orleans.

During the Morrison years we called the port "Gateway to the Americas." As mayor, he made more than two dozen trade trips to Central and South America. They were very productive, and he was always extremely well received there, a popular and respected figure. Contrast that situation with the riot which took place when then vice president Richard Nixon visited Caracas, Venezuela, in 1958, in which his very life was in danger.

Dr. Alton Ochsner: A Man Like None Other

Morrison's interest in Latin America paralleled the rise of one of America's legendary medical institutions, Ochsner Hospital. Its guiding spirit and namesake, the late Dr. Alton Ochsner, was one of the most gifted and respected pioneering researchers and physicians in the world. I first met him in the home of my dear friend, William G. Helis, Jr., and later in Los Angeles, when I was in California as lieutenant governor, on a trade mission to that state. I was having breakfast at six-thirty one morning in the same hotel as he. Dr. Ochsner was in Los Angeles to testify in an asbestos case, he being one of the first to point out the cancer-causing properties of this then-popular product. It was he who first found the relationship between smoking and lung cancer, and he campaigned tirelessly against smoking.

Ochsner Hospital was one of the first New Orleans medical institutions to completely ban smoking from its facility. Dr. Ochsner was a man of many parts. He was not a New Orleanian by birth. He moved to the city from South Dakota in 1927 and was something of a celebrated trumpet player in his youth. Once in New Orleans, he developed a deep interest in Latin America, and Ochsner Foundation Hospital treated scores of both powerful leaders and common folk from throughout that region. Ochsner still advertises heavily in markets below our border. Dr. Ochsner was alarmed by what he saw as the rise of communism throughout Latin America. For many years he was the main financial support behind a vigorous anti-communist group called INCA, managed by Ed Butler, which worked to resist the communist influence in the hemisphere. Dr. Ochsner, despite his international interests and the considerable task of building one of the nation's most prestigious hospital and research facilities, maintained a huge personal medical practice. He had much of the "old country doctor" in his medical approach, balancing sophisticated testing and diagnostic procedures with an old-fashioned ability to really listen to his patients.

I believe that there are a good many impersonal physicians who could benefit from studying his style. He was a particularly close

A 1973 press conference for the Information Council of the Americas. The late Alton Ochsner, Sr., Gen. William Westmoreland, and me.

friend of my dearest political ally and longtime campaign manager, Bill Helis. The Helis Foundation contributed mightily to the development of Ochsner's enterprise through the Ochsner Foundation. Those who missed knowing Alton Ochsner missed a rare opportunity, for his kind appears seldom in this life.

Chep's Final Campaign

In September of 1963, Morrison resigned the OAS position to make one last run for governor of Louisiana. Earlier that year I had been approached by supporters of the late Rep. Gillis Long to see if I might run for lieutenant governor. Long had a keen desire to serve as governor. He was certainly not the only congressman to feel that way for congressmen Hale Boggs, Edwin Edwards, David Treen, Billy Tauzin, Bob Livingston, Buddy Roemer, Clyde Holloway, and others all sought the governorship. I like to think that they shared my feeling that state service was really where the most rewarding political action was, closer to the people, where a person's actions could really make a difference in daily lives.

Once Morrison decided to run for governor again, I was committed to support him. That also meant that I would not be a candidate for lieutenant governor, since Morrison would need a ticket mate from somewhere else in Louisiana. Chep chose the late state senator Claude Duvall from Houma, a highly decorated Marine and one of the most conservative members of the Louisiana senate. Morrison's chief opponent was Public Service commissioner John J. McKeithen, seeking to replicate Huey Long's own vault from the commission to the governorship decades earlier. McKeithen was a shrewd, single-minded politician. He promptly gained the support of "Miss Blanche," Earl Long's widow, and the visible endorsement of key Long operative, J. M. "Pete" Menafee, who became his finance chairman. McKeithen came to call on me several times. I was unable to help him because of my commitment to Chep, but I did introduce him to key New Orleans political figures like Dr. Claude Mauberret, Jr., Clarence Dupuy, Walter Marcus, and others. I told them, as I introduced McKeithen, that I was personally backing Morrison but thought McKeithen was someone they ought to meet.

Of course, after the election, they became the leaders of his New Orleans organization, the "people to see" if you wanted something done by the governor, and my role in facilitating that relationship seemed mostly forgotten. Chep thought that Louisiana had matured and modernized sufficiently that his 1964 race for governor had a real chance. I traveled the state speaking on his behalf. I also worked particularly hard in the metropolitan New Orleans area for we knew we had to win big at home to offset McKeithen's support in some rural parishes. On one average day, I traveled throughout the state and returned that night to appear for Chep at a Donolon-Cronvich-Mollere rally at the Arrow Room on Jefferson Highway in Metairie and a huge Morrison rally at the Fountainbleau Hotel on Tulane Avenue. Chep led by 142,000 votes in the primary, but then the McKeithen campaign pulled out all the stops. Running an essentially racist campaign in the rural parishes, McKeithen claimed that Chep had a "secret agreement" with the National Association for the Advancement of Colored People (NAACP) to place negroes in high administration positions. The truth was, blacks did support Chep overwhelmingly.

He had proven his compassion, sensitivity, and sense of justice, but to my knowledge, there was no "secret agreement." The Duke-Edwards campaign for governor in 1991 proved once again that the strategy of linking one's opponents to the NAACP never goes out of style. The rumor hurt Chep in the country parishes, for feelings about integration ran high in Louisiana and throughout the South. In New Orleans, McKeithen was backed by the Regular Democratic Organization, Morrison's old nemesis, and by District Attorney Jim Garrison. But McKeithen found a more potent weapon. He erected billboards near the Mississippi River Bridge promising that, if elected, he would remove the tolls on the span. Morrison, unwisely, was drawn into the debate. He responded that bridge tolls were a necessity, particularly if future bridge expansion was ever to become a reality. It was a phony, self-serving issue; tolls were later returned to the bridge and commerce between the two banks did not cease—indeed a new bridge expansion was constructed, using the tolls, which alleviated the considerable congestion that had plagued the bridge for decades.

Nonetheless, the toll debate was a mortal blow to Morrison in the metropolitan area, teaching us the political value of being in favor of services and against any means of paying for them. I also refused to promise to keep tolls off the bridge when I ran for governor in 1979, for the same reasons as Morrison, and I am sure that my decision damaged my candidacy as well. McKeithen's strategy worked; he won by 46,000 votes out of 935,000 total votes cast. He went on to defeat handily the Republican nominee, Shreveport oil man, the late Charlton H. Lyons, Sr., the late lieutenant governor Taddy Aycock having easily defeated Duvall in the primary. Chep resigned as U.S. ambassador to the OAS to make the race. He had been appointed by President Kennedy on June 13, 1961, and resigned September 13, 1963, at which time he was probably the best-known United States citizen in Latin America. Upon his resignation, Kennedy said, "You have performed most capably and with tremendous devotion and enthusiasm for the cause of our nation in Latin America. After twenty-six months of extensive duty, you leave the government with the respect, admiration, and friendship of your fellow U.S. officials, as well as the deep affection of your Latin American colleagues. You have been truly an able diplomat and champion for the cause of democracy and freedom in this hemisphere."

We who were his personal friends, of course, knew the human side of Chep, in addition to his towering international reputation. Chep was a wonderfully witty and incredibly energetic man, a great dancer and avid water skier, who thought nothing of skiing around Lake Pontchartrain and back on a Sunday afternoon—back when one could still safely do so. Morrison's talent in the international arena was unsurpassed and unquestioned; McKeithen drew upon it by naming Chep as special ambassador for economic development. Then, in February 1964, Morrison was named executive vice president of the Bank of New Orleans, a position arranged by bank president, the late Larry Merrigan. He offered me the same position after my defeat for mayor in 1969, but I declined, knowing I intended to seek statewide office soon. I never thought Chep was very happy in the bank position, although he had accumulated few financial resources during his years in public life, and I am sure he appreciated the position. Chep's problem was just that, after managing the city administration and budget and being deeply involved in international affairs, it was a psychological letdown to sit in a bank office and deal with the daily affairs of business and commerce.

Chep telephoned me, calling me out of a council meeting, one Thursday to tell me that he was about to go to Mexico to look at a cattle purchase he was attempting to broker through the bank. He urged me to go along. I didn't have much interest in the cattle business, and I really didn't have time to make the trip, so I thanked him but declined. It was on that trip, May 23, 1963, that his small plane crashed into a mountainside near Ciudad Victoria in rural Mexico, and the man who changed New Orleans in profound and enduring ways was gone.

His City Says Goodbye

At the request of the Morrison family, I handled arrangements for the state funeral of Chep Morrison. This was a time of deep, personal grief on my part; the incessant public contact required by this sad duty was not a role I would have sought. It was a time when I would have preferred to be in seclusion, encircled only by my family and closest friends who knew what a painful, personal loss Chep's death was to me. Yet, perhaps the round-the-clock pressure of coordinating the largest funeral in our city's history was therapeutic for me, in some awful way, for the hours literally whirled past.

To better coordinate the intricate details surrounding this outpouring of admiration and respect for our city's "first citizen," I took over an office on the second floor of Gallier Hall, where the Cultural Centre Commission was then located. I was aided immeasurably by Chep's secretary, the late Rosalie Grad, and the late Phyllis Dennery, a wonderful, civic-minded woman.

We began by preparing a detailed rendering of every foot of Gallier Hall, where the bodies of Chep and his young son, Randy, would lie in state, and of St. Louis Cathedral, where the funeral mass would be celebrated. In every instance, I was guided by my desire to sense what Chep's wishes would have been. I wanted to plan a funeral which combined the essential spirit of the city he served so long with a religious ceremony reflecting his own deeply held spiritual beliefs. Representatives of the city and state government, the police and fire departments, the Louisiana National Guard, under the capable leadership of Brig. Gen. Karl N. Smith, and the Catholic church were wonderfully understanding and accommodating. They sensed how shattered I was by this entire experience, and they sustained and supported me in coordinating the two-day ceremony.

For the first day, May 25, 1964, we removed all furniture except for the piano from the traditional "Mayor's Parlor" in Gallier Hall, where Chep Morrison had taken his first oath of office fifteen years earlier. We established a catafalque for the caskets, installed two kneeling rails, and provided a dozen chairs. We designated a private room off the chamber for use of the family, Chep's mother, son, Toni, and daughter, Corinne. Chep's beautiful wife, Corinne, had died earlier at the age of thirty-seven. The American flag and General's Colors were placed in stands, for Chep had risen to the rank of general in the post-war Army Reserve. At seven o'clock that morning, a contingent of city police was on duty at the Morrison home on Coliseum Street, over which an American flag flew at half-mast. The massive banks of flowers, which had been arriving from throughout the nation, were removed to Metairie Cemetery, the cards retained so we could later respond. By ten o'clock, the exterior of Gallier Hall was draped by the city's designer, Betty Finnan, and the military units, commanded by Col. F. X. Armiger, were in place, with an honor guard posted in front of the hall. At that hour, five police cars for the use of the family rolled to a stop in front of the Morrison home.

Another five were on duty at police headquarters to transport the dignitaries, who were arriving from throughout the world—for Chep had become an international figure. At precisely 10:15 A.M., the caskets arrived from Sontheimer's Funeral Home, Chep's draped with an American flag and Randy's covered with a blanket of flowers. We proceeded quickly past the honor guard at the St. Charles Avenue entrance to the Mayor's Parlor, where Msgr. Henry Bezou was waiting. We then closed the parlor to all but the family and close friends, protected by a Military Death Guard which would stand at alert for the next twenty-four hours—a unit composed of one policeman, one fireman, and five military men. After about an hour in private, the family departed Gallier Hall through the Lafayette Street entrance, where the police cars were waiting to return them to Chep's home. The chairs and kneeling rails were removed, the Military Death Guard was positioned around the caskets, and, at noon, the massive doors to Gallier Hall were opened and the mortal remains of Chep Morrison were ready to receive one last, great outpouring of respect and affection from the people of the city he loved so well, and who so loved him in return.

Huge lines formed before the marble stairs to Gallier Hall, yet there was a profound silence and sadness, all along St. Charles Avenue and throughout the hall. The privileged and the powerful, who had been Chep's friends and supporters, stood side by side in line with the common people of our city, men in working clothes, women in simple, cotton dresses whose only connection with Chep Morrison had been that they loved and respected him and shared his vision for the city. Some had voted for him in nine elections: two legislative races, four times for mayor, and three for governor. Now they were with him one last time, to say goodbye. All day, into the night, and beginning at dawn the next day they came, thousands of them passing the funeral bier under the watchful eyes of the New Orleans police detail, led by Capt., and later Chief, the late Henry Morris. Shortly after dawn Tuesday, the line was halted to allow Chep's father-in-law, Jack Waterman, a brief, private visit. At 9:45, Lt. Gov. Taddy Aycock arrived, and at 10:30 I received Governor and Mrs. McKeithen and Judge and Mrs. Carlos Spaht at the foot of the steps to Gallier Hall. Even as we entered the hall, six limousines arrived at 1805 Coliseum Street, the Morrison home, to bear Chep's family and close personal friends to Gallier Hall again.

A separate limousine brought Monsignor Bezou from St. Patrick's Church, at 724 Camp Street, arriving at Gallier Hall at the same time as the military pallbearers, upon which the public line into the hall was interrupted. After the hall cleared, the family, a close circle of friends, Monsignor Bezou and the pallbearers entered the Mayor's Parlor for a brief, five-minute service.

Then the caskets were removed, preceded by the general's two-star flag, down the steps of the hall, past the Armed Forces honor guard which lined each side of the steps, and the procession to St. Louis Cathedral began. I had the entourage drive past city hall one last time to give Chep a final farewell.

The cathedral was already filled with mourners, who had been issued entrance tickets in order to control the size of the crowd. City firemen guarded all five entrances with Fourth Degree Knights of Columbus members forming an honor guard for Archbishop Cody, who met the procession at the cathedral entrance and escorted it up the aisle to the altar. After the one-hour funeral mass, the procession left the cathedral for Metairie Cemetery. The entourage was made up of city and state motorcycles, twenty-seven vehicles, and scores of private cars.

Monsignor Bezou conducted a brief, ten-minute graveside service, and the flag from Chep Morrison's casket was folded, military style, and presented to his son, deLesseps S. "Toni" Morrison, and daughter, Corinne.

There remained only three rifle volleys, the bugling of Taps, and a thirteen-gun salute. That consumed only three minutes,

One of the saddest days of my life. Mayor Victor Schiro, Chep Morrison's daughter Corinne, his son Toni, his mother, and me leaving their home for Chep's funeral.

and a singular, important chapter in the life of this city and in my personal life was over.

In the days following the ceremony, I saw to the responding to hundreds of pieces of mail. Some were letters of appreciation to the several hundred volunteers and officials who participated in the intricate scheduling of events for the funeral ceremony. We tried to thank each person who took part in the arrangements, for Chep would have expected and insisted upon that kind of personal expression of appreciation. There were formal letters from business and government leaders from throughout the nation to be answered.

I was most touched by the scores of letters from private citizens. Many of them were like the handwritten note from David and Gae Kleinberger, which read: "Dear Mr. and Mrs. Fitzmorris: Both Gae and I wish to express our sympathy to you for the loss of Chep Morrison, your good friend. Although we never met him, we both liked him. It's our feeling that this state, indeed this country, has lost a good man. . . ." I was touched, as was the Morrison family, by the powerful need, on the part of people Chep had served, to somehow say "goodbye." It was as though Chep's magical hold on the people of the city was so strong that they were unwilling to simply let his legend fade away. Thus was born our quest to create a lasting, physical memorial to Chep, a substantive symbol of our love, honor, and affection that could last through the generations to keep his memory alive among us. It took six long years, but finally, on Monday, January 18, 1971, Capt. Neville Levy, chairman of the Louisiana Morrison Memorial Committee, I, as chairman of the executive committee, and a host of Morrison's friends dedicated the Morrison Memorial to his memory. We chose January 18 because it was the day of Chep's birth and close to the twenty-fifth anniversary of his first election as mayor.

We chose Duncan Plaza at the New Orleans Civic Center as site of the statue because it was there that many of us most clearly felt his presence.

The dedication was preceded by a solemn memorial mass at St. Patrick's Church. Principal speaker was Gov. John J. McKeithen. The forty-foot statue portrayed Chep as we remembered him best, informal and energetic. Three sides of the statue bore inscriptions to his career as politician, army officer, and ambassador.

Architects for the statue were the firms of Mathes, Bergman and Associates, Inc., August Perez and Associates, and Parham and Labouisse, longtime friends of Chep and the same firms which designed the civic center. Local sculptress Lin Emery designed the sculpture.

Other committee members were the late Louisiana secretary of state, Wade O. Martin, Jr., former mayor Victor Schiro, state senator Michael O'Keefe, state representatives Edward LeBreton, Jr., and Thomas Casey, state public works director Leon Gary, state AFL-CIO president Victor Bussie, and city public relations director Winston Lill, a former Morrison assistant. The late John Tims, president of the Times-Picayune Publishing Corporation had, before his death, also served as a committee member. The committee was authorized by the Louisiana legislature and appointed by Governor McKeithen.

Phil Johnson, editorial writer for WWL Television in New Orleans, best captured the spirit of the memorial when he said, "It . . . stand(s) today as this city's promise to always remember Chep Morrison. Remember him for what he did, and even more basically, for what he was. What he did we see all around us . . . the modern face of New Orleans is Chep Morrison's face. He took this city after World War II and thrust us into the jet age with quality and class. That's a good word for Chep Morrison, quality. He had quality, and a certain kind of intuitive charm that made him a consummate politician . . . and one of this city's most effective leaders. And what he was as a man is what we miss most of all. He was one of the most original, truly professional politicians that we ever knew. He was one of a kind, a man who thrived on doing, a man who needed challenge, a man who was truly able to lead. His loss was a great loss for this city . . . a loss that grows as the years go by."

I often remember the words of poet George Barker, who said, "He is a procession no one can follow, but be like a little dog following a brass band."

The change from Mayor Chep Morrison to Mayor Vic Schiro was massive. They were very different in tone, stature, temperament, and training. Schiro lacked Morrison's charisma. In the following months, the CCDA was racked by internal dissention and lack of leadership. Key CCDA figures, like Richard Burke, simply resigned. On the council, we set about trying to continue Morrison's legacy under Schiro, but it was difficult. Schiro and I had both been key Morrison lieutenants; Chep often called upon us to represent him before civic and business groups or at the regular Thursday bus tours Morrison scheduled around the city to show such groups the city's construction and progress in action. Schiro and I soon parted company on several key issues. He wanted to raise from 2 percent to 5 percent the street-use franchise fee the city received from New Orleans Public Service, Incorporated and Louisiana Power and Light. Schiro contended that his tax would raise $2 million and that the city would be $3.5 million in the red without it. I questioned his rather casual math, but my disagreement was more basic.

I thought that if the utilities had indeed been overcharging consumers (Schiro's justification for the increase), the excess collections should be rebated to the consumers from whom they had been taken, rather than simply being added to the city's coffers. I called for a public hearing and the *Times-Picayune* agreed. The strident differences between Schiro and me continued to grow and appear during his term, and it became obvious to most of us involved in city government that if I really believed what I said, I needed to challenge Schiro's approach at the next election for mayor. We would then let the people decide.

Remembering the Progressive Years

During those years after Chep, I took great comfort and pride in the accomplishments that he and I and fellow members of the city council had been able to bring to New Orleans. These were the "Progressive Years" in New Orleans, and they made possible most of the improvements that have followed in the years since that time. I had been particularly involved in plans for the Union Passenger Terminal, because of my own railroad career. The Union Terminal was a $57 million project which eliminated 144 dangerous and time-consuming crossings in the city. It added twenty-four new overpasses and underpasses, which made possible the infrastructure that still serves our traffic needs today.

The project had languished since the time of Mayor Maestri, and it took Chep Morrison's leadership to bring it to fruition and construction. I spoke forcefully for the bond issue that made it possible at meetings throughout the city. We worked very hard to rebuild the central business district, long before attention to the core of American cities was recognized as a national problem.

Businesses located downtown were facing an increasing challenge from the suburban shopping malls. In the Morrison years, we rebuilt Canal Street, added economical bus transportation to and from Canal Street, and began an aggressive campaign urging people to "come downtown and shop." It was our dream to have all city government agencies and much of the judiciary located together, where they would be accessible to citizens. Most people think of a "civic center" as a sports arena or a convention and entertainment complex. Our concept was different and larger. To accomplish our end, the city purchased a seven-square-block slum that had long been an eyesore in the core of the central business district.

The tenements were an intractable impediment to the growth and development of the downtown business corridor, but only government had the resources to acquire such a vast plot of land and to bring about such a large-scale development. Had the city's progress been required to wait for individual developers to acquire the land, on a patchwork, piecemeal, building-by-building basis, I suspect that this slum would have endured until well into the next century. Surely, the entire Poydras corridor of office buildings, the New Orleans Centre, Superdome, Hyatt Regency Hotel, and the other towering, impressive structures which now ring the civic center and which so revitalized downtown New Orleans would never have been built had they faced the prospect of adjoining the crime and poverty-infested slum which stood adjacent.

It required the mayor's leadership and a council of considerable courage and foresight to undertake this ambitious project. It immediately became a local political issue; my chief opponent in the 1954 council race stridently opposed the project.

We persevered and the civic center complex came into being, comprising:

The main library, a $3 million structure which doubled the size of the old library. Its design was well ahead of its time, featuring interior patios, meeting rooms, and an auditorium.

The eleven-story, $8 million city hall, encompassing 431,000 square feet, which consolidated city departments formerly spread throughout ten scattered downtown locations.

The State Building, a $4 million, 179,000 square-foot building, which brought together state agencies from seventeen previous, scattered locations.

The $2.5 million Civil Courts Building, a 117,000 square-foot structure which provided a modern, centralized home for many court and related government offices.

The $1.8 State Supreme Court Building, which provided a courtroom, judges' chambers for the seven justices, conference rooms, a modern state law library, and offices for the attorney general.

A decade later, while I was council president, we cleared another slum near South Broad Street to make way for a $9 million police/courts complex, space for police department administration, central lockup, and the municipal and traffic courts.

The fact remains, however, that no city administration can revitalize and energize a municipality just through public construction. A year-by-year review of the years of progress, the Morrison years, reveals a creative cavalcade—the most unique public/private partnership in any Southern state. With city government leading the way, encouraging and facilitating private development, we sailed through a period of progress that has been unprecedented, before or since.

1953

In 1953, the first Pan American Life Building, now an adjunct to city hall, was under construction on Canal Street. So was the American Cyanamid plant at Avondale and the Ideal Cement property. Much of city government's attention was focused on the New Orleans Recreational Department, NORD. It was a special favorite of Morrison's and mine, and we used to take weekly trips through each of the NORD projects to watch and encourage their development. In this year, NORD sponsored "The Recreation Story," in conjunction with the New Orleans Symphony at City Park Auditorium and entertained ten thousand persons. NORD also began "Golden Age Clubs" to provide services and activities for senior citizens.

Newsweek magazine praised NORD in a national survey of cities fighting juvenile crime. Following his election, Chep had seen the need for an active recreation department and had been able to attract the services of longtime Warren Easton coach Johnny Brechtel, loved and respected by all who knew him. He took over the leadership of what would become a shining light in city government. His daughter, Councilwoman Jackie Clarkson, serves with great distinction in city government today, and I am pleased to see a renewed interest in the NORD program by the New Orleans business community, led by Jim Bob Moffett and Councilwoman Clarkson.

The year 1953 also saw Pres. Dwight D. Eisenhower visiting New Orleans to sign a replica of the Louisiana Purchase document. I was honored to serve as civilian aide to the president during this visit. Speaking at Jackson Square, Eisenhower said, "Here, in the Port of New Orleans, we see reflected America's strength, her vitality, her confidence, her irrepressible desire for improvement, her magnificent ability to meet resourcefully the demands of changing times and conditions."

1954

This was the year I was sworn in as a member of the new council form of government. We all wore white suits from Haspels—a garment Chep grew to love so much he wore his until it was frayed and shiny.

Nineteen fifty-four was marked by the opening of the Union Passenger Terminal. In addition, we completed the Earhart Expressway underpass on a street formerly named Calliope. It was dedicated to the memory of the late commission-council member Fred A. Earhart. We covered the New Basin Canal, resulting in the opening of twenty previously dead-end streets. We unveiled plans for the massive Pontchartrain Expressway. The giant South Claiborne Overpass was constructed and dedicated to the late Gen. Allison Owen, president of the Parkway Commission. NORD sponsored the Community Ballet and the "Traveling Theatre" which took dramatics into neighborhoods.

1955

In 1955, the Port of New Orleans was second in the nation in dollar volume, with its twenty-six-mile waterfront. That year we unveiled plans for a new assembly center to the left of the municipal auditorium and a new sports arena on the right. Under the guidance of the city's decorator, Betty Finnan, we renovated the Municipal Auditorium.

She is worthy of special recognition. Ours was one of the only cities in the nation with an official city decorator. Her work de-

A City Council paving hearing, May 1, 1955, when we were still headquartered at the historic Gallier Hall. At the council table, l-r: Councilmen Henry B. Curtis, Fred Cassibry, me, A. Brown Moore, two unknown persons, and Walter Douffour. At the administration table holding glasses, CAO David R. McGuire. Speaking is Albert Wyler, director of streets. To his right, Robert Deville, director of finance. At the press table, veteran New Orleans Times-Picayune *reporter, Jim Gillis.* (Courtesy New Orleans *Times-Picayune*, photo by F. H. Methe)

signing street decorations for Mardi Gras and Christmas contributed much to the "look" of progressive New Orleans. I have recently seen the renovations to the municipal auditorium, and it is once again a very attractive facility. Had I been elected mayor, I had intended to construct a secure, well-lighted parking garage with a covered skyway to the auditorium which, in my view, would have avoided the long period of decline in use of the auditorium. The sports arena, of course, was superseded by the Superdome, but we did complete an attractive Theatre for the Performing Arts in later years. Nineteen-fifty-five was also the year that ground was broken for the new Mississippi River Bridge, built at a cost of $65 million, which was completed in July 1958. Chep Morrison, in those years, was the first mayor to begin holding regular staff sessions with city department heads. He also named a uniquely talented genius, the late David R. McGuire, as the city's first chief administrative officer. McGuire was literate and brilliant, an incredibly hard worker. He was also the conscience of Chep Morrison and his alter ago. His death left a massive void that was never successfully filled.

Morrison also attracted the services of wonderful volunteer citizens like Gervais Favrot, who served for years as chairman of the City Planning Commission in those challenging times. We then enjoyed one of the best credit ratings of any city in the nation. Nineteen-fifty-five also saw the opening of our first Office of International Relations, under the leadership of Mario Bermudez, which operated in conjunction with International House. By that year we were the South's largest city with 765,000 people, third largest in geographic area with 363 square miles. Downtown New Orleans began to be revitalized that year with the construction of the large office building at 1010 Common and similar projects. That year we were the first city in America to win an Urban Renewal grant. Our goal was to bring forty-five thousand sub-standard housing units into compliance within a decade. By the end of the year, four thousand badly blighted housing units in the controlled area and another ten thousand units outside the area had been brought up to minimum housing law standards. By the following year, the Housing Rehabilitation Program, a unique public-private partnership, was operating in five of the neediest districts of the city.

In 1955 we began a house of detention farm, which provided fresh vegetables. Sixty men volunteered to live in barracks on the farm to relieve prison overcrowding. That year the port commissioners constructed new steel and concrete wharves. The Foreign Trade Zone business increased by 25 percent. We completed design of the new Moisant Terminal, planned to accommodate 700,000 passengers per year. The $17 million expansion began with the east-west runway, with terminal expansion and north-south runway work to follow in a four-year construction program. We also opened the city's fourth neighborhood health center. The city's health department included a milk testing program, praised by the U.S. Public Health Service as one of the nation's best, and an active school inoculation program. The city's traffic safety department operated a driving school. The city's bus line increased by the purchase of new fifty-one-passenger, air-conditioned buses, operated by New Orleans Public Service, later assumed by the Regional Transit Authority.

In the preceding decade, NORD had gone from a mere dream to one of America's most praised programs. Five million persons participated in NORD programs that year alone. Beautified neutral grounds had doubled to 120 in that same ten-year period. In 1955 alone, the city parks commission planted thirty thousand shade and flowering trees and thirty-nine thousand flowers. In that same decade, library circulation had doubled; the number of borrowers increased 116 percent. During that period we had constructed a new main library, part of the civic center complex, and five new branch libraries.

1956

In 1956, in a three-year program, Pontchartrain Park, in New Orleans East, went from a wilderness to an eighteen-hole golf course, basketball park, with stocked lagoons, a playground, and clubhouse. At City Park we opened Story Land, which is still a favorite attraction. The Civic Symphony was planning a Latin American concert tour, and a million people visited the Municipal Auditorium.

This was the year we occupied the new city hall. We also laid eighteen miles of new sewerage mains, closed the city landfill dump, and opened a $750,000 odorless, nearly smokeless incinerator, widened Camp Street, renovated Canal Street, and paved neighborhood streets all over the city. The private sector was booming as well. In 1956 $32 million in new single-family homes was expended, the new NBC Bank building cost $3 million, the Fountainbleau Hotel, now the Bayou Plaza, was announced for the old Pelican Stadium site, with four hundred rooms at a cost of $5 million, and Loyola University began a $15 million, six-year building program. The Baptist Theological Seminary added $6 million in new construction, and the $2 million Gentilly Woods Shopping Center was under way. Callender Field on the West Bank was converted to a naval air station. Phase 1 of this project cost $30 million. In 1958 we announced the new Juvenile Detention Center, first of its kind in the nation. The following year, in 1959, the new $7.5 Moisant passenger terminal opened, and the $15 million post office and federal complex was announced.

The first five miles of the seventy-seven-mile, $100 million Tidewater Ship Channel were completed, a faster, more efficient route to the port which cut forty miles off the Mississippi River trip for commercial shippers, and the New Orleans East Interstate highway project began. A total of $35 million in new homes was achieved that year. Commercial construction was everywhere in the city including the 350-room Royal Orleans Hotel—first major new downtown hotel in thirty years—the $8 million, twenty-eight-story 225 Baronne Building, the $2 million Oil and Gas Building on Tulane Avenue, and the $10 million Hancock Building on Lee Circle. Plans for the International Trade Mart were unveiled, and a ten-story addition to the YMCA on Lee Circle was completed.

Full Speed into the Sixties

The decade of the sixties began with the death of David R. McGuire, the city's first chief administrative officer and perhaps the single most vital component of Chep Morrison's record of achievement. Chep could bask in his role as visionary, catalyst, and chief advocate and architect of the New Orleans revitalization.

The fact is, it remained for David McGuire to make all the pieces fit, to make the numbers work, and to factor in the human equation, the humanity and morality in all these plans. He was a valued friend to all of us and an absolutely indispensable ally and resource to Chep, moving almost always behind the scenes. In his quiet, unassuming way, he shared a large portion of the credit for the unparalleled progress of the previous decade. The following year, on July 14, 1961, Morrison resigned to accept the appointment as U.S. ambassador to the Organization of American States.

Council president Vic Schiro succeeded him until the next election. Such was the mighty momentum of the Morrison years that the city's forward progress continued even after his departure. By the time Chep resigned, NORD, which he had created from a mere idea, was serving seven million people per year. It was managed with great effectiveness by Lester J. Lautenschlager, who worked for one dollar a year. He was assisted by G. Gernon Brown, and, after his death, by Ernest H. Gould. The three of them were loyal, dedicated, and exceptional in the way in which they took a good idea and helped it become the standard against which all such programs in the nation were judged.

President John F. Kennedy came to New Orleans on May 4, 1962, to dedicate the Nashville Avenue Wharf. There was a huge throng on hand for his address at city hall. This year also marked the 150th year of Louisiana statehood. Seven days after Kennedy's speech, I was sworn in as councilman-at-large. One of our first tasks was to review plans for the Riverfront Expressway, which I favored. The proposal had first been advanced as part of a 1946 Arterial Study, conducted for the city by legendary New York planner Robert Moses. The construction agreement for the International Trade Mart was signed on February 7, 1962. It was one of the last acts completed by the late William G. Zetzmann, Sr., a public-spirited citizen whose name appears, in quiet dedication, on a whole spectrum of boards, commissions, committees, and community organizations. He was a remarkably talented, generous leader who played a big role in helping New Orleans through this period of growth and development. Managing director of the ITM was Clay Shaw, soon to be part of history because of the Kennedy assassination and subsequent trial brought by District Attorney Jim Garrison.

That was also the year of the Cuban Missile Crisis. Because of our proximity to the Gulf of Mexico we were particularly sensitive to the question of missile attack from Cuba. Mayor Schiro met with department heads to prepare them for the crisis and swore in new Air Force volunteers. More than 110 fallout shelters were opened, which would accommodate 23,800 persons. President Kennedy congratulated the city on its response to the crisis. The NASA project at Michoud was going full speed ahead developing booster rockets. That year's budget was $32 million, with $169 million planned for 1963 and $250 million for 1964. A $4 million Federal Reserve Building replaced the former Sewerage and Water Board headquarters at St. Charles and Poydras. The $1 million cinerama on Tulane Avenue, now a catering hall, was the first in the South. Schiro's confidant, the late Willard E. Robertson, as chairman of the Housing Authority of New Orleans, announced plans for the Fischer Homes project on the West Bank, which the council approved. The Jewish Home for Aged also opened on the West Bank.

In 1963, the Regional Planning Commission was created, under the chairmanship of Schiro's supporter, Thomas J. Lupo. In 1959, he had sought an exclusive franchise to operate a monorail system from outlying areas into the city. The city planning commission and the bureau of governmental research, an independent agency, opposed granting the franchise. Morrison's CAO, David McGuire, recommended six months of additional study. Morrison appeared before the council, in his brigadier general's uniform—on leave from training duty at Camp Leroy Johnson—to ask for immediate approval of the franchise, which he said he would sign without delay. I moved to declare the monorail "unfeasible and contrary to the public interest," My motion carried, and the monorail scheme was dead, but it made me powerful enemies in the future. Downtown, the Solari Building was renovated and Le Petit Theatre reconstructed in the Vieux Carré. Attention was focused on education in 1963. There was new construction at the LSU Medical School and LSUNO. The largest construction project ever at Tulane University, a $2 million, twelve-story mens' dormitory, was begun.

There was work under way at Loyola, Dillard, Southern, and Xavier as well, not to mention an $11 million building program by the Orleans Parish School Board and four new Catholic high schools built by the archdiocese. Transportation and tourism continued major roles as well. The New Orleans port led the nation in rail cargo unloaded. One-fourth of all exported American grain went from metropolitan New Orleans elevators. The entire seventy-six-mile Tidewater Outlet opened, and the Committee of International Relations, headed by Dr. Alton Ochsner, was formed. The Spanish government contributed $350,000 to build Spanish Plaza as part of the ITM complex. Some 138,000 visitors came to the city that year, spending $19 million. Among them was Pablo Casals, virtuoso cellist. We completed renovation of the Presbytere for $700,000, and Guste Homes, a housing project a few blocks away from the Union Passenger Terminal, for $13 million. I became council president when the new council took office in 1964. We were sworn in following a luncheon which honored the second year of the Schiro administration. Luncheon speaker was John J. McKeithen.

Taking the oath of office, that May 4, in addition to me, were councilmen Joseph DiRosa, Henry B. Curtis, Walter F. Marcus, Jr., Clarence O. Dupuy, John J. Petre, and Daniel Kelly. During the following two years I remained on the council, and despite heated but genuine disagreements, these men were to become my lifelong friends. I still host an annual luncheon each fall for those of us who remain, and it is wonderful to meet with them again and share old memories. In 1964, the first Saturn booster rocket, part of the Apollo manned lunar landing program, was produced at the NASA Michoud plant and shipped that April. Using our city's unique transportation hub to its best advantage, the barge which transported the booster rocket to the George C. Marshall Space Center in Huntsville, Alabama, for testing navigated the Mississippi, Ohio, and Tennessee Rivers. Poydras Plaza, a $3.5 million dollar, twenty-story office structure across from the civic center complex, was begun. Seven new fire department facilities were underway.

This was the year of the proposed "West End Land Swap," a Schiro administration switch which would have resulted in private land developers receiving invaluable "neutral ground" at the West End near Lake Pontchartrain. It was a bad deal for the city and a terrible deal for our future for once this land is gone it can never be reclaimed for the people, to whom it really belongs. I fought the measure vigorously, bringing the governor and the attorney general into the fray. Once again I earned powerful enemies, but I fought the proposal to a standstill, and eventually a compromise was crafted that retained the public's priceless West End land as beautiful boulevards, not commercial projects to enrich some private developer. Jackson Brewing Company, since closed, was actually expanding that year. By 1965, the West End Boulevard Interchange and the $11 million high-rise bridge, which spanned the Inner-Harbor Navigation Canal, were completed, as was the Plaza Tower—at that time New Orleans' most imposing skyscraper.

Most of these public projects are now taken completely for granted, but when they were proposed we encountered a literal fire storm of criticism and controversy. A councilman put his career on the line each time he stood up to take a position, either

Former City Council members at a Thanksgiving 1990 reunion I sponsored. Front row, l-r: Moon Landrieu, me, Victor Schiro, and Ted Hickey. Second row, l-r: Peter Beer, Clarence Dupuy, Philip Ciaccio, Dan Kelly, James A. Comiskey, Fred Cassibry, Joseph DiRosa, Walter Marcus, Paul Burke, and John Lambert.

for or against, one of the intimidating issues that seemed to come before the council almost weekly throughout the Morrison years. For example, there was violent opposition within the council to the civic center concept. Morrison was in Peru when the matter came up for vote, and I managed his side of the debate, against the virulent opposition of Councilman Fred Cassibry. I managed to win council approval and then led a citywide campaign to pass the necessary bond issues to construct the center. When we constructed a $65 million bridge over the Mississippi River we had the courage to put on the tolls necessary to pay for it. I led the battle before the Young Men's Business Club and other key civic groups. Many were opposed to the bridge's location; an equal number were opposed to building a bridge at all. One of our great backers in this crusade to gain passage was the late Capt. Neville Levy, owner of Equitable Equipment Company. He was a tireless champion of the bridge with a highly personal management style.

Levy operated from his suit coat pocket, rather than his office, and always seemed to have at least fifty letters tucked away so he could do business throughout the day from wherever he was. A plaque commemorating Levy's efforts is still in place on the original bridge. The expansion and modernization of Moisant Field, now New Orleans International Airport, was also highly controversial. These were the Eisenhower years, and many people were content to mark time and drift in the economic tide. Chep Morrison and most of us on the council were builders who believed that we must prepare the city for the growth and economic development which was sure to come—even to sedate, sleepy New Orleans. Despite criticism from some about the cost, the New Orleans Recreational Department grew to 142 playgrounds and seventeen free wading or swimming pools. At its peak, NORD served 150,000 children per day, offering football, basketball, baseball (with Dr. A. L. "Dutch" Legett, former major league catcher, as the first volunteer chairman), track, archery, fencing, golf, tennis, marbles, dramatics, ballet, arts and crafts, music, cooking, and sewing.

We were aided in these efforts by former Tulane football player Lester Lautenschlaeger and Jesuit coach G. Gernon Brown. NORD was perhaps the project closest to the heart of both Chep Morrison and me during those years. We simply believed that, in order to provide the quality of life which qualified as a "great American city," we had to give children something to do, and we withstood considerable criticism in funding and enlarging NORD. It has since fallen on hard times and barely survives, a pitiable parody of its former glory, saved only by the public spirit of the city's business leaders, led by Jim Bob Moffett. In our day, it was recognized as the best recreation program in America. Roundy Coughlin, nationally syndicated sports columnist, said, "When I was in New Orleans, I looked into the recreational programs rather well. I have seen most of the programs in the big cities, but I must say New Orleans has the best set up in the United States."

Much of the public and some of the press questioned the timing and the expense when we began drainage of outlying areas for residential and industrial development, particularly in the Lakeview and New Orleans East areas. I worked very hard to get petitions signed for the closing of many of the city's disease-infested and dangerous canals. For years children routinely drowned in those canals. That task has not yet been effectively completed.

Progress Requires Courage

A good deal of what we accomplished was not brick and mortar; it was invisible to the naked eye. For example, we built a modern, efficient city government, beginning with the home rule charter and cutbacks in unnecessary city personnel. We restructured the police department and provided meaningful training for existing and new police personnel, ending the old days when a new policeman was simply issued a uniform and a gun and sent out to the streets. We built a new police academy, several fire stations, five neighborhood health centers, a youth study center for delinquent children, and neighborhood public branch libraries.

Many of these were pioneering ideas in the nation; most had a direct benefit to the citizens. Business benefitted from the improved fire and police training and the new facilities through their relationship to their insurance rates as well as the security factor. We tried to awaken the city's interest in and support for untapped areas of economic development—the port is a prime example. Chep Morrison had a genuine interest in and love for the Port of New Orleans, and he was the first mayor to feel this interest so deeply. As a lieutenant colonel during World War II, he had built ports in England and France for handling troops and supplies. He had been chief of staff at the Bremen Port

Command—essentially the acting mayor of that German city—and he translated much of what he had learned about running a great port into his work in New Orleans. In that connection, he was a fearless spokesman for New Orleans' growing involvement in world trade, calling us the "Gateway to the Americas." I shared his dedication to international trade and development and supported our activities such as the World Trade Center and similar hemispheric efforts.

In later years, our commitment lagged and the major airlines, import businesses, the consular corps, and a part of the mainstay of our economy were lured to more aggressive cities like Miami, Atlanta, and Houston—to our continuing discredit. Morrison was the city's best salesman, and much of what I know about industrial development I learned by his side. He almost singlehandedly established such a close relationship with visionary Henry J. Kaiser that Kaiser Aluminum chose Chalmette as site of its $177 million plant after earlier rejecting us. During those years, we brought a billion dollars in new or expanded facilities to the metropolitan area.

Learning to Live Together

Perhaps our great accomplishment was in the area of race relations. The South of the 1950s and 1960s was seething and simmering, a boiling pool of black resentment and white resistance. Beginning with the U.S. Supreme Court's decision against segregated schools in 1954—striking down the "separate but equal" rule which had existed since the *Plessy v. Ferguson* decision of the 1890s, civil rights became the single most rabidly debated issue in New Orleans and throughout the South.

These were the years of the 1956 Montgomery, Alabama, bus boycott, the 1957 violence in Little Rock, Arkansas, the 1960 sit-in in Greensboro, North Carolina, the Freedom Riders in 1961, James Meredith's integration of Ole Miss in 1962, Birmingham and Bull Connor, Gov. George Wallace in the school house door, the massive March on Washington, and the 1964 civil rights murders in Mississippi. In the face of the virulence, the violence, and the viciousness between the races, New Orleans quietly but firmly integrated its public facilities. We integrated city buses over one weekend, without fanfare or racial foment, simply by taking down the signs of segregation inside the buses. We were aided by many unsung heroes like Dr. Albert Dent, president of Dillard University, and A. P. Tureaud, an influential black lawyer—both of whom were my dear friends. Together, we believed that if our real goal was effective integration and not just violent confrontation, the best way to accomplish it was to work quietly together. It was always my personal goal to bring people together, and we did so with considerable and crucial support from the black community.

In later years I faced some criticism from younger, more radical black figures for not being sufficiently committed to their goals, but I always enjoyed, and appreciated, the total support of the older black leadership. They knew what a terrible danger we faced in those years and how, working together, we had kept New Orleans from becoming another Watts. That was not accomplished without dissent and sometimes bitter disagreement. My point is that, through the willingness of all parties to communicate and cooperate, it was accomplished without the destruction that marked so many American cities. It was in this spirit, as the rightful heir to the Chep Morrison legacy, that I determined to keep the "Progressive Years" alive by seeking the office of mayor myself.

Chapter 5

The Campaigns for Mayor

1965: The Fitzmorris-Schiro Race

Victor Hugo Schiro was inaugurated as mayor on the same day I became councilman-at-large in 1962. Schiro was a colorful, often controversial figure, in many ways the exact opposite of me. His style of government was often diametrically opposed to my beliefs about the standard of city government the people deserved. He had won by defeating a capable candidate, state senator Adrian Duplantier. It was a race I had wanted to run, for I was confident I could have won.

However, Chep Morrison and some of the political leadership had selected Duplantier, and that effectively closed my options. Vic Schiro and I first met in September of 1946 when my good friend, Dr. Larry LeBon, now deceased—and what a great person he was—asked me to join the Young Mens Business Club. As Larry put it, "Jimmy, the YMBC is really making things happen; that's where the action is." And how right he was! From the very beginning, Vic and I developed a warm friendship, working side by side in the YMBC on many major civic projects. As time went on, we were together politically on many occasions, but every once in awhile Vic had his political agenda and I had mine. Regardless of our political differences, until this very day Vic and I share a warm and wonderful friendship which I value greatly. I was never one to hold a political grudge; when the election was over it was over, win or lose, and I would always put the campaign, its political attacks, rumors, and tension behind me and move on. After four years of the Schiro administration, I was even more certain that

The Fitzmorris family in the 1965 campaign. In front, l-r: Mother, Dad, my sister Florence and her husband George Simno. Standing, l-r: my brother Norris, his wife Ann, me, and Gloria.

running for mayor was the right thing to do and that 1965 was the right time to do it.

It is one of the cruel ironies of politics that on many occasions the timing of a campaign is out of the candidate's hands. You simply have to run when the race is available; otherwise time passes you by. In this case, the political realities meant that if I wanted to seek that office, I would need to defeat a sitting mayor—no small task regardless of who the incumbent may be. I had been around the business of city politics long enough to know full well the demanding task I had established for myself. Vic Schiro was a tireless campaigner, a feisty little figure with an interesting past that sounded as though it had been written by a Hollywood press agent. He was the son of an Italian immigrant, fluent in six languages, who had become a self-made banker. Along the way Schiro had been a scuba diver, a Colorado gold miner, a Hollywood actor, a movie director, a radio announcer, a Coast Guard officer, an advertising man, a civic leader, and an insurance executive. There is a thin line in the public's perception between a man who is seen as a gallant, heroic Horatio Alger figure and a man of the same background who is seen as an opportunist. In politics, it all depends on the momentary view of a transitory and often fickle public.

A candidate may lose one race because the public somehow decides that he isn't experienced enough for the job, and then lose the next because the same public concludes that he is now too old to perform effectively. In short, running for office demands that the candidate have a thick hide, the willingness to lay his background and record out for everyone to judge, and the courage to accept the election-day decision.

The Schiro Style

And so it would be with the Schiro race. We knew, going into the campaign, that Vic would try to put the best possible face on his background. It is a process now called "spin control"; it requires talented media managers and vast amounts of money. We were painfully aware that an incumbent mayor, in particular one not bothered by the niceties of fund-raising among people who did business with the city, would have no difficulty in the money area. In fact, thirty-one Schiro administration insiders each gave five thousand dollars to his campaign—by the standards of that time, a very significant war chest. Schiro had other assets beside a potentially bulging campaign bank account. The powers of incumbency are very broad and are not limited to the ability to raise money.

There are thousands of city workers, their families, friends and people they do business with—each of whom can be made to feel that his future will only be secure if the incumbent is re-elected. There are hundreds of people who come to city hall for licenses and permits, and the Schiro people were not shy about giving them to understand that the fate of their request was at least indirectly tied to their position in the mayoral campaign. It is a process accomplished subtly, without brass knuckles or overt coercion, but it is very effective. The same concerns hold true for the hundreds of citizens from all walks of life who serve on the myriad city boards, bureaus, and commissions. Some have never really met the mayor, but their appointment often provides the major source of prestige and influence in their lives. It takes very little time at all for them to develop the feeling that their continuation in that appointed position is directly related to the depth of their commitment to the incumbent mayor's campaign. Schiro was also in an enviable position in terms of his relationship to the really astounding accomplishments of the Morrison administration which preceded his own. A great many of the monumental public projects begun by Morrison were actually completed after Schiro assumed office, and he was not shy about taking full credit for each of them.

He was thus able to benefit from the visible Morrison legacy; he called his term the "Years of Fulfillment." At the same time, he was able to undo, in an entirely invisible way, many of the "good government" controls and safeguards Morrison had instituted. One had only to look at the quality and caliber of key appointees to city positions to discern the difference between the two administrations. Morrison had been the first mayor to name a full-time chief administrative officer. His had been the brilliant David R. McGuire, a creative, literate, highly moral executive. After McGuire's death, that role was filled by former councilman-at-large Glenn P. Clasen, a gifted and dedicated public servant with a keen knowledge of every aspect of city government. Schiro, by contrast, chose Thomas J. Heier, Jr., a city employee, basically a good man and good friend, but Tommy was more politically oriented and understood the importance of using the CAO's office to its full political potential. Those of us involved in the daily administration of the city could see the difference in caliber and commitment, but it was a subtle shift the public and even most of the press was unable to easily discern.

Finally, Vic Schiro, as the incumbent mayor, would be able to absolutely dominate the media. Any mayor has the constant opportunity to speak at as many civic organization breakfasts, luncheons, and dinners as his waistline can withstand and, to his credit, Vic made them all. The ability to capture the headlines would later be used to devastating advantage by Schiro during Hurricane Betsy, which occurred during the crucial final weeks of the campaign. In fact, the Schiro campaign organization's use of city hall as a virtual campaign headquarters came dangerously close to violating the political code of ethics. My campaign was very careful to avoid such appearances of impropriety. We rented a campaign headquarters separate and distinct from my council office, first in the Delta Building, located on Baronne Street, just a short distance from city hall, later in a two-floor complex next to the Fairmont Hotel. Public criticism of Schiro's blatant use of the mayor's office from which to run the campaign grew so strident that he eventually opened a purported "headquarters" on Baronne. His was a storefront operation with a few tables and chairs that could be seen through the window from the street. The rest of the room was draped off and without any action most of the time.

From the outset of the campaign, we knew we had to capitalize on Schiro's perceived shortcomings and liabilities in order to level the playing field and compensate for the advantage of his incumbency. His verbal gaffes were legendary, probably unchallenged for hilarity until the advent of Vice Pres. J. Danforth Quayle, who managed to empathize with an important black audience that "a mind is a terrible thing to lose." Schiro, for example, once appeared on radio during Hurricane Betsy to reassure listeners, "Don't believe any false rumors unless you hear them from me." Asked for clarification he simply shrugged, "That's the way the cookie bounces." He once boasted, "We in New Orleans are sitting on some of the greatest assets in the world." Complimenting the wife of the governor of Louisiana at a testimonial dinner for her husband, Schiro gushed, "And we have Mrs. McKeithen with us tonight. When she smiles, every wrinkle in her face glows." Vic had great "off the cuff" remarks and, frankly, I loved them all.

The Fitzmorris Issues

The dynamics of our own campaign, however, did not provide for us to simply paint Schiro as incompetent. First, in thirty years in public life, I never traded in personal attacks or demeaning, humiliating, or belittling remarks about another candidate. As you will see in the Landrieu race, I am not comfortable with "attack politics"; I don't do it very well, and I feel terrible about it afterward—the result, I suppose, of my Jesuit upbringing. So we probably wasted some of our best opportunities to heap ridicule on Schiro while I was busy sticking to the issues and raising questions of substance. Second, the New Orleans press in those years was much more docile than today. A contemporary candidate who constantly misspoke or showed such lack of comprehension or sensitivity would suffer the same damage to his public image as Vice President Quayle has, perhaps rightly so. Those kinds of frontal assaults on public leaders did not occur so frequently back then. Third, New Orleans had just experienced four terms of leadership under the tall, urbane, sophisticated Chep Morrison. I was consistently on various "best dressed" lists, but in this year, that was not necessarily what the people were looking for.

Finally, one had to be terribly careful about ridiculing Schiro. The book on him, with many average New Orleanians, was that he was aggressive and sincere. How many people do you know who have never accidently said something that came out the wrong way? There was a real danger of creating sympathy for Schiro if we played too strongly upon his rhetorical weaknesses, so we largely avoided the subject. We decided, instead, to concentrate on the more substantive shortcomings most people in New Orleans could sense in Schiro. He frequently spoke on every side of any given issue, trying always to manage the politics of the issue rather than to do what was obviously in the best long-term interests of the city. This vacillation and his general lack of candor and specifics came to the fore in many media discussions of the difference between the two major candidates. The inconsistency permeated all the way through his administration. For example, shortly after Schiro pledged "no new taxes," his chief administrative officer

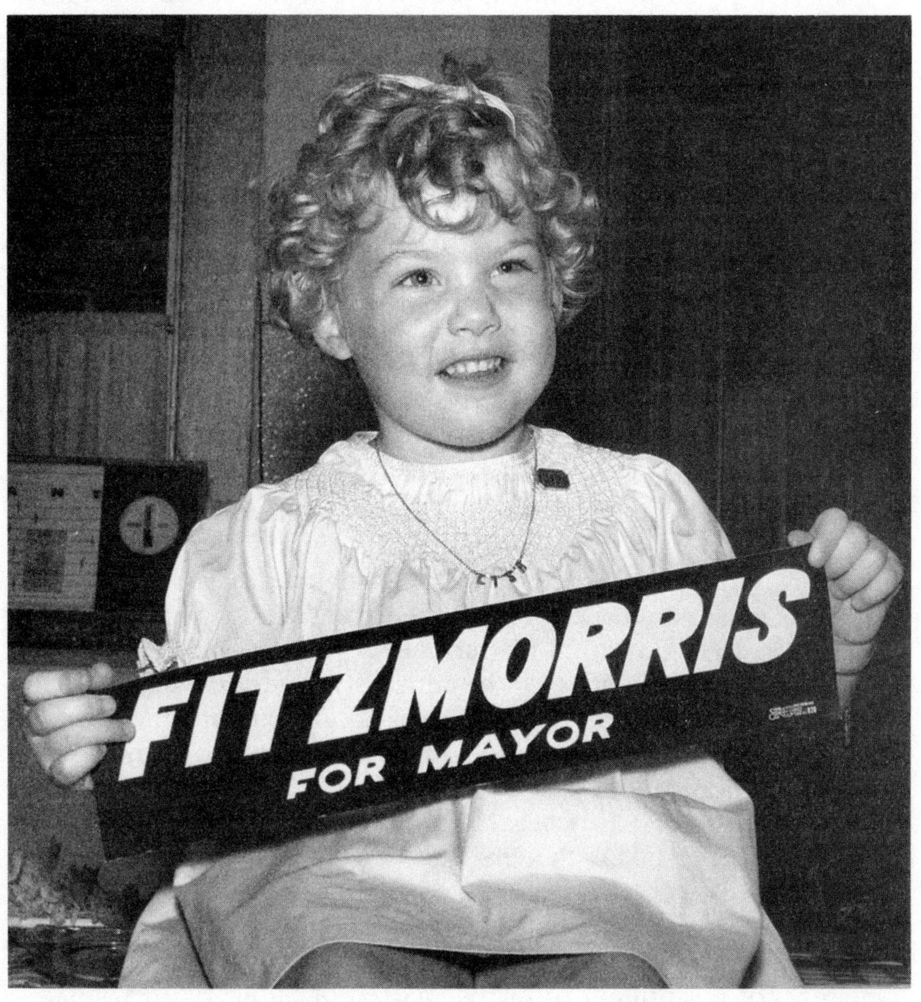

Lisa was my youngest and most enthusiastic supporter in 1965.
(Courtesy Fulcran F. Randon, Jr.)

told the press that the city absolutely needed to reconsider additional bond issues.

Our campaign was evenly divided between those who thought that such statements were made by design, allowing the mayor to run as an "anti-tax" candidate while permitting his principal assistant to send the signal that, in reality, the growing city did require additional revenue, and those who simply thought that no one was in charge of the Schiro team. We made the leadership issue a strong plank in our campaign platform. Finally, the Schiro entourage had been historically marked by some persons who were unquestionably insensitive to and unsympathetic with the special needs of our black citizens, who were just beginning to be an electoral force in New Orleans politics. With this campaign coming only one year after the Civil Rights Act, which caused such tension and anxiety throughout the South, I chose not to make race an issue—although, in retrospect, I could have benefitted from doing so. I did, however, take every opportunity to reach out to the black community, where I had always enjoyed considerable support.

In 1965, as in every election, I ran the kind of race I am most comfortable with: a thoughtful, issue-oriented, fast-moving campaign. I must admit, however, the race got off to a frustratingly slow start. To begin with, I was virtually a full-time councilman-at-large with responsibilities for the entire city in addition to my full-time executive position with the railroad. When combined with the campaign, this meant that I had almost no time to spend with my family, particularly with my young daughter Lisa, who was still asleep when I left before breakfast each morning and back in bed when I returned late each night. It is one of the few regrets of my life that the career I chose exacted such a terrible price on my family, and it is a particular tribute to Gloria that our daughter was able to grow up positive and well-adjusted without the deep currents of resentment so many children of public figures show. In addition, at the beginning of the campaign there was the candidacy of levee board president Gerald Gallinghouse. Later to become a distinguished United States Attorney, Gallinghouse shared many of the same friends, contributors, and supporters as I, and his candidacy complicated the process of putting my own campaign organization together. He later abandoned his own candidacy and became a vital and valued supporter of mine, but the weeks of delay damaged our early effort.

The Fitzmorris Blueprint for Progress

Finally, our campaign was hampered by our own dedication to comprehensive planning and substantive issues. Schiro could grandly say, "If it's good for New Orleans, I'm for it," but I was committed to spelling out the specific challenges I saw ahead for our city. To this day, I believe that our platform was the most detailed and comprehensive of any candidate for mayor in this century. When we talked about streets, we didn't just say that we were for better streets; we identified the potholes by particular location on specific streets. The same was true of playground improvements, housing rehabilitation needs, and all the rest. And I didn't get these proposals from a windshield survey conducted by some campaign aide, either. I personally visited every one of the hundreds of specific locations I identified as needing improvement. The process consumed hundreds of hours which, in retrospect, might have been more profitably spent in raising money and delivering banal, generality ridden, "safe" speeches. Ours was the first mayor's race to target specific neighborhoods for special mailings. For example, in my campaign letter to West Bank residents, I pointed out:

The field near Elmire would be ideal for a ball park.

Swings and seesaws near Behrman were broken, and there was an overgrown jungle at the rear of Behrman Memorial Park which had become a breeding ground for mosquitoes.

Bristol Park needed cleaning, drainage, and playground equipment.

The drains in the 600-700 block of Pelican were stopped up, and there was no drainage in the 700-1000 blocks of Wagner.

Collins Avenue, Numa Avenue, Odeon Street, 3100-3300 Lamarque, DeArmas, Diana, Wagner, and Brooklyn needed repairing and paving.

More police protection was needed throughout Algiers.

There was excessive speeding along Pacific, Atlantic, Hendee, General Meyer and Behrman Avenues, and Shirley Drive. Youngsters in the Walnut Bend were speeding, and motorbikes often used the walkways in that subdivision.

Magellan Canal was filled with snakes. Rats and mosquitoes bred in the high grass near 2200 Halsey and in the high grass on vacant lots near 1500 Odeon. The same was true of an empty lot in the 3100 block of Lamarque Street and in the old Southern Pacific Railroad yard.

I also proposed construction of a major hospital on the West Bank, which years later resulted in Jo Ellen Smith Hospital—a project I would have made a priority in the first months of my administration. We went into similar, exhaustive detail in mailings targeted to each of the city's major areas and also included a "suggestion section" on the back of each mailer so individual citizens could voice their own concerns. It was a time-consuming and expensive approach to running for mayor, but it symbolized our commitment to responsiveness and dialogue with every neighborhood, and I am proud that we took the time to care. We thought it important to illustrate emphatically our concern for every area of the city, a priority I had pointedly tried to emphasize throughout my term as councilman-at-large. Ours may have been the last of the old-time campaigns to refer to "downtown, uptown, back-of-town and front-of-town." Most New Orleanians today have a good idea what "uptown" and "downtown" mean, but only natives with several generations behind them will recall that "back-of-town" meant the Lakeview and Third and Fourth Ward areas, and "front-of-town" meant the Canal Street, Claiborne, mid-city area extending to the Mississippi River.

Our Campaign Promises

Our campaign platform, when finally produced, ran to a hundred very specific goals and proposals. Some were designed to point up the stark contrast between me and the mayor. For example, I pledged to take a leave of absence from my railroad position while serving as mayor, unlike the present mayor, whose private insurance business was able to move forward while he was in office. I promised to appoint the best-qualified chief administrative officer available and to remove him from partisan politics. I promised to make appointments to city boards and commissions without regard to candidates' personal or political affiliations. I promised to reduce the appropriation for the mayor's office, a plan which I would have implemented by eliminating some "make work" positions for political friends. I promised an immediate raise for city employees, many of whom worked at sub-standard salaries with deplorable benefits. The Civil Service Commission had proposed a reclassification and pay plan which I endorsed. The mayor followed suit and promised a similar raise but, when elected, reneged and offered to put it into effect only in little bits and pieces spread over a number of years.

The cornerstone of my platform was, without question, the leadership issue, but I tried, throughout the campaign, to get New Orleanians to think and walk into the future. I emphasized planning and long-range goalsetting in a series of specific proposals which were, unfortunately for my campaign and political career, many years ahead of their time: I called, in 1965, for creation of a regional Lake Pontchartrain Development Commission. I said that without immediate and aggressive action against residential, rural, and industrial pollution, major portions of Lake Pontchartrain would die. I also said that we had been lax in developing a water recreation-based economy as the Mississippi Gulf Coast had done successfully. I proposed that all four parishes bordering the lake join in an orderly, careful and environmentally sound development providing for sandy beaches, golf courses, riding trails, protected homesites in selected areas, fishing lodges, and water recreation areas. I suggested that such a development, in combination with the New Orleans' Vieux Carré, would make ours a tourist destination with unlimited potential. Unfortunately, these pleas fell on largely deaf ears. Much of the lake did die, and only recently did we realize what we had lost.

The Lake Pontchartrain Commission and the "Save Our Lake" movement took another quarter-century to become a reality, and the lake has yet to be effectively utilized to its full potential.

I proposed a five-parish task force to speak with one voice in promoting the growth and development of the Louisiana State University at New Orleans (LSUNO). I was joined in this effort by the late Col. James Moreau, then a state representative and candidate on my ticket for the city council. I wanted LSUNO to become independent of the LSU system because I believed that was the only way it could ever fully develop. It did finally become UNO and operates as kind of a quasi-independent institution, although still formally controlled by the LSU system. I proposed that UNO develop into a residential institution with dormitories, rather than just a commuter school, which took place years later. I proposed aggressive development and adequate funding of a Gulf Coast Research Institute, centered on the UNO campus, which would combine technological and educational resources into a facility similar to the Triangle Park project in North Carolina. I saw this as a tremendous opportunity for business/education partnership.

Unfortunately, it must be remembered that these were the years before public-spirited, far-sighted business leaders like Jim Bob Moffett and Pat Taylor and groups such as the New Orleans Business Council. So, for the most part, my vision was considered novel but unrealistic and far-fetched. Such an institute was eventually created, but a venture like this required aggressive support and nurturing, and it eventually died for lack of funding. Just this year, a quarter-century later, the state legislature finally got around to approving a bill that would give tax credits to medical and scientific research parks throughout Louisiana including the proposal for one such project at UNO, which had languished since my campaign of 1965. I called tourism the "Sleeping Giant" of the New Orleans economy and proposed a New Orleans Convention Center, a Latin American Free Trade Zone, and the opening of a trade and business development office in Latin America. While the mayor gave some lip service to Latin American trade relations and to tourism in general, it would be decades before the city would gain state support for the convention center, which now, finally, brings millions of dollars to the city's economy and which almost singlehandedly saved the city from ruin after the oil slump.

At the time I proposed greater attentiveness to the Latin American market, the New Orleans "experts" were still concentrating their efforts on Europe, whose importance to our region I knew was waning. Similarly, a decade later, by the time Louisiana had come to recognize the economic importance of Latin American trade relations, I suggested, as lieutenant governor, in 1972, that it was now time to engage in trade efforts with Japan and Far Eastern trading partners. Had we undertaken an aggressive development effort then, we would have been at the forefront of such activities. Unfortunately, we waited to get into the Japanese trade quest until the market was saturated by many other states and finally shut down our Japanese trade mission in failure and discouragement, turning our attention once again to Latin America. My position was simply that leadership meant we needed to be on the cutting edge of such marketing trends—not lagging behind to pick up the economic "leavings" from other states' more far-sighted programs. The mayor and I clashed, throughout the campaign, about a number of significant issues. I proposed that the city council retain its own independent audit staff, similar to the function the General Accounting Office performs for Congress.

At that time, the council was forced to simply accept the economic projections and reports furnished by the city's administration, even though we suspected them to be inaccurate and inadequate. Years later, the council adopted such modern management tools for itself, and the council's research staff has served the public effectively. When New Orleans Public Service, Inc. (NOPSI) realized increased income through a reduction in federal income taxes, I proposed that the additional income be passed through in the form of rate reductions to New Orleans consumers, rather than simply being pocketed by NOPSI shareholders. I was joined in this request by Councilman Clarence Dupuy. Similarly, the mayor charged that NOPSI had been levying excessive charges on New Orleans customers and asked for a $2 million franchise tax increase to be paid by NOPSI to the city. I suggested that if our consumers had, indeed, been overcharged by NOPSI, those amounts should properly be rebated to the consumers through rate reduction rather than simply poured into the city's tax coffers. I called for a public hearing on the entire matter, in which I was joined by the *Times-Picayune*.

I continued efforts I had begun the preceding year to block the infamous "West End Land Swap." This was a dark-of-night scheme, hatched in the closing hours of the Jimmie Davis administration, under which the state would grant invaluable neutral ground between Robert E. Lee Boulevard and Polk Avenue to private developers. The developers would then give the city land the city already believed it owned, on which the civil defense center was constructed. It was a terrible deal for the city and highly questionable. At my insistence, Gov. John McKeithen and the state attorney general instituted an investigation and the city filed suit to block the deal, which would have meant untold millions to the developers. City councilman Joseph V. DiRosa introduced a measure dropping the suit and agreeing to a compromise settlement of the dispute. He introduced it "by request," but steadfastly refused to say who had requested the plan. Along with other alarmed councilmen, I fought this scheme to a standstill, arguing that the neutral ground should be used for public benefit as green areas, not for private developers' profit. More than two decades later, the state finally gave the disputed land to the Orleans Levee Board thus assuring that it will remain green and untouched.

The mayor, who professed to have been completely unaware that this "private developers' relief act" was about to be foisted on the unsuspecting citizens of the city, was particularly ineffective in our fight to save the neutral ground at West End. He and I clashed again over two proposals before the state legislature to finance sewerage and water installations in new developments in New Orleans through establishment of sewerage districts backed by sale of revenue certificates to the public. A companion bill would have covered paving in a similar way. The certificates would have been guaranteed by a first mortgage lien on the property, which would have been paid by the individual homeowner. The bills were carefully crafted so they would only have benefitted three developers, Aurora in Algiers, LaKratt, operated by key Schiro supporter Marvin Kratter, and New Orleans East, a project of Texas developer Clint Murchison and Toddy Lee Wynn. In addition to this hidden burden to homeowners, the bonds would have resulted in weakening the city's position in issuing subsequent general obligation bonds, so the city would have had to pay a higher interest rate on such later issues—in effect making every citizen bear the burden for these developers' relief.

As an appointed member of the Sewerage and Water Board, I scheduled a special meeting to take action opposing the bills. The mayor's reaction was simply to remove me from the Sewerage and Water Board's drainage committee. Fortunately, by that time, the public uproar had grown so pronounced that the bills were allowed to die quietly in Baton Rouge. As the campaign continued, I stressed my major themes: better public health and sanitation programs, improved mosquito control, recreation programs for all age groups, coordination of recreation programs for the elderly, improved vocational education through Delgado Trades School, major street improvement, paving and sub-surface drainage, housing improvement without a massive urban renewal program, increased police and fire protection, and improved public education. My ticket, the Crescent City Democratic Association slate, was filled and looked promising. I had endorsed Moon Landrieu and Paul Burke for councilmen-at-large, council candidates Henry B. Curtis, Walter F. Marcus, Jr., Clarence O. Dupuy, Robert Ziblich, and Philip C. Ciaccio.

I backed Harold "Tookie" Gilbert for civil sheriff, Louis E. Thomas, Jr., for criminal sheriff, Lawrence LaMarca for recorder of mortgages, and Ernest J. Hessler for register of conveyances, along with Rep. Edward L. Boesch for clerk of first city court, and Clyde F. Bel, Sr., for constable of first city court. Bel, Curtis, Marcus, and Dupuy were also endorsed by the Schiro slate. The problem with joint endorsements is that they effectively remove those persons from the campaign and force them to remain neutral in the mayor's campaign—depriving both candidates of much-needed organizational support in those districts. My campaign enjoyed most of the major media endorsements: The *Times-Picayune* said ". . . During his three terms on the council, Mr. Fitzmorris usually has been outspoken on critical issues. Some five years back he opposed the city charter change to allow the mayor more than two terms in office despite its sponsorship by his strong political friends. He was in the same position with respect to his opposition to the monorail plan. Right or wrong, he took a stand against the tax increase three years ago and stuck with it. . . . The mayor says he'll say 'tomorrow' how he'll propose a municipal sports arena . . . next spring how he'll arrange to reopen NORD swimming pools. In brief, he's long on promise and sometimes short on performance."

The editorial pointed out that Schiro's platform was full of generalities while mine was specific, and labeled ridiculous his claims that the city started running off and leaving other Southern municipalities behind when he took office. The *States-Item* editorial pointed out that Schiro had ordered a study of the city's streets department and then, when it turned out to be highly critical of department inefficiency, lack of initiative, and subjection to political pressures, had hidden the report for a year. The editorial criticized Schiro's plan to award a sweetheart garbage composting contract without calling for bids, his proposed settlement of the West End Land Swap, and his lack of leadership in stopping Lake Pontchartrain pollution and in interparish planning. The editorial concluded, "If New Orleans is to achieve its capabilities, it needs a fresh approach, a new verve for tackling community problems. . . . Mr. Fitzmorris' election . . . will supply these qualities to the mayor's office."

Hurricane Betsy

So our campaign was proceeding positively, sitting well in order, when two events intervened that turned the tide against us. The first was Hurricane Betsy, which struck Thursday night, September 9, 1965, bringing torrential rains and hundred-mile-per-hour winds. The storm forced fifty thousand persons to flee their homes; twenty thousand were housed in city shelters. Some thirteen thousand persons were immunized for diphtheria. The death toll in the city was near fifty, with a similar loss of life in other portions of the state including St. Bernard and Plaquemines Parishes. Scores more were reported missing. Damage and loss were in the hundreds of millions of dollars. In the days following the hurricane, Mayor Schiro was everywhere in evidence on television and on the streets, wearing his raincoat and hard hat. He dominated the news coverage of the hurricane and became the most quoted source of news and information. On September 15, 1965, Rep. Hale Boggs brought Pres. Lyndon B. Johnson to New Orleans to inspect the damage and tour the Lower Ninth Ward, hardest hit by the disaster. Mayor Schiro was seated prominently next to the president in the lead car of the entourage. Dressed in my work clothes, in which I had been helping at a shelter in New Orleans East, I had to fight for a lowly spot on the press bus.

To everyone who watched the evening news—and that was everyone who could get his television set to work, it was Lyndon Johnson and Vic Schiro, in charge of hurricane relief. Jimmy Fitzmorris, "the challenger," was nowhere to be seen. But such is politics! And, after it's over, you learn to laugh it off, which I did.

Of course, the mayor did not get entirely high marks for his administration's preparedness and conduct before and after the disaster. Levee board president Gerald Gallinghouse reminded people that one year earlier, on June 7, 1964, the mayor had said that the prospect of a severe hurricane in New Orleans was a "bugaboo." Dr. Edward Teller, renowned nuclear physicist and father of the atomic bomb, charged that adequate civil defense preparations before Betsy could have prevented much damage and loss of life. Dr. Teller criticized the city for not carrying out a timely mass evacuation. Governor McKeithen responded by quoting President Johnson as saying that Teller was "a scientific nut." Channel Six News went into the Almonaster, South Gentilly, and other badly flooded areas well back from the lakefront. Residents there consistently charged that they had been given no warning prior to the hurricane and no rescue assistance by the city afterwards.

Tulane engineering professor, Dr. Chester Peyronnin, said that a 1962 Corps of Engineers report had accurately predicted such heavy flooding. Asked about the mayor's assertion that such heavy flooding could never have been predicted, Dr. Peyronnin said, "It has already been predicted. It has been predicted and shown where you could get this damage. Now whether these men would understand it or whether they took the trouble to find out, whether they could comprehend it, this is not mine to say." It was made known that there were serious defaults in the shelter run by Dr. John Charles Rosen, a consultant in that campaign who is now involved in employee testing. In this shelter, which was across the street from the one President Johnson visited: no representative of the mayor showed up until three days after the hurricane, no police protection was on hand for the five thousand shelter residents, no coordination was done for medical personnel and supplies, no patrolling was carried out to prevent looting of residences, no food and clothing were distributed, no organization of communications or transportation facilities was provided, no garbage collection and no federal assistance was made available until finally requested by Rep. Hale Boggs.

Nonetheless, every person who suffered a hurricane loss received a personal letter from the mayor offering his assistance and promising better efforts in the future. To them and many other New Orleanians, Victor Schiro had been their father-figure throughout the terrible hours of death and destruction.

The Last-Minute Superdome Proposal

Then, hours before the election, and trailing in the polls, Schiro turned one last miracle. His public relations man, David Kleck, also represented Dave Dixon, who was promoting the idea of a giant domed stadium for a proposed professional football team in New Orleans. Schiro seized upon the idea and made it his own. With Schiro recently recovered from an appendectomy, the public relations team held a news conference at his home with him dressed in a bathrobe and slippers and filmed a "sick bed spot" in which Schiro "announced" the plan, which had actually been floating around New Orleans for months. A Schiro ally, Marvin

Kratter, who would have been one of the beneficiaries of the land development bond scheme I had earlier opposed, promised to donate land in New Orleans East on which to build the stadium.

We were in an impossible position. To point out that a superdome stadium in New Orleans East made no economic sense would seem like sour grapes. To remind voters that this innovative Schiro breakthrough had been someone else's idea and had been discussed around town for months would have seemed small-minded obstructionism. The best I could do was say half-heartedly that I hoped it would come to pass so I could throw out the first ball.

Sportscaster Hap Glaudi, now deceased, a longtime friend, hit the nail on the head. "That's going to cost you the election," he said, the night the story aired. And Hap, as usual, was absolutely right on target. New Orleanians love their sports; they wanted a professional football team, and Mayor Vic Schiro was promising them one.

When the votes were counted, I missed the runoff by 256 votes. Had rabid segregationist A. Roswell Thompson—a cab driver (Jim Comiskey delighted in calling him a "transportation executive") drawn his customary vote, as in his previous races for mayor, that would have been enough to put me in the runoff. But this year the segregationists deserted Thompson to back Schiro.

Schiro and Segregation

Many blacks believed that the segregationists' confidence in Schiro was well-founded. They felt left out of the administration, partly because he had previously been endorsed by the segregationist Citizens' Council of New Orleans, which some called the White Citizens' Council. One of his first acts as mayor had been to fire Chep Morrison's black city race relations director, the late Rev. A. L. Davis. To show how much the city has changed, Rev. Davis later became a respected and productive member of the city council. The Citizens' Council had been a powerful presence in local politics during the years of white control. Each candidate was routinely given a questionnaire asking if he favored continuing segregation in the city, whether he would support additional pro-segregation laws, whether he belonged to any organization which favored integration of the schools, public transportation, or parks, whether he supported use of the Armed Forces to enforce racial integration, and how he would work to make segregation continue and prosper in the city. The council was then located in Room 323 of the Balter Building, where the Hotel InterContinental now stands.

Schiro had seemed insensitive and sometimes adversarial to the concerns of black citizens. On December 18, 1961, 290 black students were arrested at a demonstration without being given an opportunity to disperse peacefully. The next day, a dozen marchers, led by Rev. Avery Alexander, who is now a state representative, were arrested on their way to city hall to protest denial of voter registration rights. Rev. Alexander had requested a permit for this march but his request was denied, so the group was marching without a permit. Two years later, blacks did successfully march on city hall, but Schiro refused to meet with them, although he did meet with George Singleman of the White Citizens' Council to discuss a white voter registration drive. Later that same month, October 31, 1963, Rev. Alexander and some supporters were refused service in the city hall cafeteria; he was arrested and dragged from the building by his feet. When he returned the following day to present a petition protesting such treatment, he was arrested again, this time in the mayor's reception parlor.

The Schiro administration denied use of the Municipal Auditorium to the Rev. Dr. Martin Luther King, claiming that King's presence "would tend to incite someone to violence," a particularly ludicrous charge against the man who would later receive the Nobel Prize for Peace! The Citizens' Council, closely allied with the Ku Klux Klan and other extremist organizations, had no such difficulty gaining a permit to use the auditorium. In fact, Mayor Schiro was on the podium as his director of safety and permits presented the speaker honorary New Orleans citizenship and the keys to the city. Outside, peaceful black pickets were chased away by the city police. To his credit, Schiro did appoint Mr. Philip Baptiste, the first black aide of his administration. However, the Schiro administration closed the city's pools to avoid desegregating them, claiming lack of funds to run them. NORD, however, failed to request any city funds for pool operation in 1966-70, and Schiro declined an offer of private donations sufficient to operate all the pools.

As a member of the council, I voted, on November 3, 1960, for a resolution requesting the legislature not to close the schools during the desegregation crisis. Then a council member, Schiro left the chamber hurriedly before the vote and was the only member failing to take a stand on the issue as we passed the resolution. In his race for mayor against state senator Adrian Duplantier, Schiro claimed that a machine had been organized against him consisting of the *Times-Picayune*, the *States-Item*, Mrs. Edith Stern and her television station WDSU, Ambassador Morrison, his Cold Water Committee, and the NAACP. In analyzing the results of the first primary, in which he trailed Duplantier, Schiro said, "The history of the communist satellite countries proves that a well-organized minority can easily usurp the prerogatives of the majority." Given the recent history of the mayor's administration, I thought that blacks had good reason to be concerned and resentful. I shared their concern and sympathized with them. I tried to show my support, however, in ways that did not further inflame racial tensions and escalate the potential for violence. I believed that a city on fire could not be a city of progress—a position amply proved in other major American cities during those years.

Had I been able to make the runoff, in the coming weeks when cooler heads prevailed and people began asking questions about the super-dome scheme, I believe I would have been able to win. But that's not how politics works, and my election was not to be. In fact, I later served, in my private capacity as a railroad executive, to put together the necessary railroad land to make possible construction of the Superdome where it now stands. In the meantime, I had learned once again that when the polls say you're winning, it only takes one big event to turn those polls on their ear. In the final analysis, the only poll that really counts is the one on election day—and then only if you can keep that result honest, as I would learn fourteen years later in the race for governor.

1969: The Fitzmorris-Landrieu Race

When the mayor and the new city council took their oaths of office in 1966, it marked a major transition in my life. For the first time in twelve years, I was off the council and out of public life.

Unlike some who leave public life, I was forced to confront neither boredom not financial hardship. I moved, without hesitation, back into the daily work of representing the KCS railroad, a career I had maintained on a full-time basis even while I served on the council and ran for mayor. I was still busily involved with scores of civic, professional, and religious organizations throughout the city, and I kept in touch with hundreds of people who had been actively involved in my campaign. For the first time in her childhood, I was often able to see my daughter, Lisa, in the mornings and evenings, a special joy I had missed during the long days campaigning and serving on the council. Nonetheless, I missed being on the council. To be honest, I must admit that I missed the personal staff I had assembled at city hall and the various perquisites that go along with being a member of the council.

But I missed more than that, the action of city government and the wonderful, if sometimes harried, relationship I had established with other councilmen and city administrators. Most of all, I missed the opportunity to serve and to work with people on a day-to-day basis. I had always believed that local government was the government closest to the people. I tried to put those feelings into words in my last council meeting, April 28, 1966, when I told the council and the audience in the chamber, "These have been happy years for me, and I want to express my grateful appreciation to the people of New Orleans who have honored me by affording me this opportunity to serve them on the city council for twelve wonderful and exciting years.

"On every one of the thousands of important issues that have come before this council, I have always placed the public interest first and foremost, supporting what I believed to be right and opposing what I believed to be wrong, without regard for personal or partisan considerations, as a true representative of the people of our city."

I closed by telling my friends on the council, "To me, public service is, and shall always be, a noble profession and sacred trust, and I hope and pray that in the years ahead I shall again be allowed to serve the people of New Orleans in an elected office. Meanwhile, I shall devote a large part of my energies and time to our community's civic and charitable institutions."

In a sense, I had "come of age" in public life, growing and maturing in the turbulent years of the Morrison administration. As I walked out of city hall, a private citizen for the first time in twelve years, I could sense the presence of Chep Morrison and the feeling of action and purpose he brought to those chambers. It was a bitter disappointment that I had not been selected to continue his legacy, but I knew I would return to do battle on another day and, in my heart, I knew that day would be the next election for mayor of New Orleans. Under the terms of the city charter, Mayor Schiro was required to step down at the end of his second term; there would be a new election—this time without a powerful incumbent. Encouraged by the support of my friends and hundreds of private citizens I encountered throughout the city during the next three years out of public life, I decided to seek the office of mayor one more time.

To be honest, I had spent every moment preparing myself for the important role of political leadership. On Thursday, April 10, 1969, I announced my candidacy, saying, "During the past three years, I have made careful, thorough, and objective comparative studies of New Orleans and several other leading cities, and municipal government administration, from my private citizen viewpoint in light of my years of experience in government and civic affairs." I said, "I will submit our comprehensive program of specific measures for the future growth and development of our city, and the progress, prosperity, and welfare of our people based on these studies and advice. I will present detailed position papers to explain my exact stand on the many issues that confront our city." I called for a clean, positive and vigorous campaign featuring full and candid public discussions of the issues and the candidates' proposed programs. I pointed to my combination of government service and private business, saying, "Only a man with extensive practical experience in private enterprise can be expected to provide the administrative competence and managerial ability that is urgently needed in our public affairs."

I stressed the need for economic development and jobs as well as sound fiscal management and urged a creative private/public partnership to move New Orleans forward. Way back then, I called for transfer of taxing power from the state to the cities and for standardization of statewide assessments on a uniform and equitable basis for different kinds of property. Nearly a quarter-century later, those two proposals are still the most important unmet goals of city governments throughout Louisiana. The lack of cities' ability to raise revenue and independently administer those revenues still cripples city governments all over the state, and the failure to fully equalize statewide assessments still results in some wealthy parishes benefitting at the expense of poorer, usually urban, parishes with greater needs and fewer resources.

No New Orleans mayor has been able to effectively forge the

kind of statewide municipal lobby to bring about these important reforms. Indeed, some New Orleans mayors have been unable even to achieve consensus and cooperation within the New Orleans legislative delegation when it comes to supporting vital municipal legislation.

I called for modernization of our port facilities to achieve competitive advantage over other ports and formulation of resourceful plans and promotional programs for commercial and industrial development. However, to the contrary, in the following twenty-five years we have seen our port's competitive advantage slip away, and New Orleans has been significantly surpassed by the aggressive economic development promotions of other cities in the South. I am proud to say that we are now back on track and moving forward in a positive, aggressive manner. With the help and support of the Transportation Trust Fund, our port will grow and prosper. I called for a better-paid, better-equipped law enforcement program at all levels with an all-out crusade against crime and vice of all kinds. I believed that if city government did not launch such an effort in 1969, within our lifetime New Orleans might become one of the murder and crime capitals of America—and I was right! I wanted to involve every element and aspect of the city in this program, saying, "Government is a decision-making business. We must have at the helm men who can and will act decisively for the best interest of the majority of our people and for the good of local civic and governmental progress."

Under the leadership of my old friend and campaign chairman, William G. Helis, Jr., and finance chairmen, the late T. Sterling Dunn, Edward M. Rowley, and the late Richard "Dick" Montgomery, we opened a campaign office at 1801 American Bank Building. As usual, our campaign depended primarily on volunteer workers. The generous contribution of time and talent by people from every walk of life had been my secret weapon in every past campaign, and it would be needed in increasing numbers for this race. We would utilize paid media advertising and all the other costly trappings of modern political campaigning as well. Soon, I opened a larger central headquarters in the Gateway Building, which stood at the corner of Camp and Common at 124 Camp Street, which operated in high gear eighteen hours each day, seven days per week. U.S. marshal Vic Wogan, a veteran political operative from past campaigns, resigned his position to become co-chairman of my campaign along with Henri Wolbrette, a former Tulane football great, newspaper editor, and business leader.

In the early weeks of the campaign, I put together a creative, balanced ticket with the best city leadership I could find. For councilmen-at-large I endorsed Councilman James A. Moreau, now deceased, and former U.S. commissioner Fritz H. Windhorst, later a distinguished state senator. For district council positions, I backed Peter H. Beer, now a federal judge, Harwood "Woody" Koppel, now a member of the Orleans Parish School Board, incumbent councilman Clarence Dupuy, attorney Peter J. Compagno, and incumbent councilman Philip C. Ciaccio, now a district judge. I supported civil district judge Thomas A. Early, Jr., and Edward G. Gillin for juvenile court judge. I endorsed all incumbent assessors and Algiers assessor candidate James W. Smith and all other incumbents except for district attorney.

The Fitzmorris Team

Ruth McCabe, Kathy Vick, and Helen Mervis lead a giant effort to recruit volunteer workers in every precinct of the city. We had an active and aggressive youth volunteer movement, with Chuck Zatarain, Bill Allerton, Mickey Russell, and George Simno in charge. Mrs. Mitty Terral coordinated coffee parties and other important activities of the Fitzmorris Ladies' Group.

Each councilman district had its own field headquarters, and we assembled an impressive leadership team to run them. This group included John Hainkel, then a state representative—who went on to become Speaker of the House and is now a state senator, Mrs. George Kussman, Childs Dunbar, Miss Ellen Reaney, then-senator Fritz Eagan, Leo Happel, Mrs. Roy Amedee, Mrs. Allan Conners, Mrs. James Mayer, George Schreiber, Mrs. Lee Kirchem, Col. Ed Christiansen, and Mrs. Jerry Komerech.

Developing this kind of depth of support in a comprehensive campaign organization was a real accomplishment for a person who was out of office. I knew, however, that every last vote would be crucial because, as the qualifying for mayor continued, it became obvious that there would be a large and exceedingly well-qualified group of candidates for mayor in 1969. In fact, I think this race attracted more high-profile candidates for mayor than New Orleans had seen in many years before or has seen since.

The Opposition

In addition to me, five other very capable major candidates emerged:

Judge David Gertler had strong support from the Jewish community and was extremely well financed. He had been active in the Shrine and served as its Potentate and had a very effective personal organization throughout the city. State senator William J. Guste, Jr., now retired as Louisiana's attorney general, had served as the state deputy of the Knights of Columbus and had a strong business and personal following. His was one of the best-known families in New Orleans and he came extremely close to making the runoff election. City councilman Maurice "Moon" Landrieu had started his political career as part of my ticket when I ran for mayor against Vic Schiro in 1965, when he sought the position of councilman-at-large. My friendship with him went back many years to when he was first elected to the house of representatives from the Twelfth Ward on the CCDA ticket. He and Verna and their young family were living in the Broadmoor section and became close friends of the Fitzmorris family. Verna was a great asset to his campaign. While I was disappointed that he chose to run for mayor at this time, I understood his decision. As a councilman he had been in the public eye almost daily the previous three years, and I believed, correctly, that he would be my strongest opponent.

The Landrieu Promises

Landrieu proposed enactment of a one-cent earnings tax on every worker in the city. While his plan was of dubious constitutionality and has since been advanced on numerous occasions without success, the notion of taxing persons living in neighboring parishes but working in New Orleans was a very attractive proposal for local consumption. He also made a tentative gesture to compensate for that new tax by reducing the city's sales tax by one cent. This was an attractive proposal for business owners, since we were at a competitive disadvantage with the neighboring parishes because of our higher sales tax rate. It was also attractive to poor people who would not have been touched by the earnings tax but would have enjoyed the sales tax savings. Of course, neither of these plans stood a snowball's chance of ever becoming reality, but they were difficult to speak against, and they made for good politics to propose. Landrieu was an active city councilman who made many new, young friends and built up some strong support, and he had influential friends like his law partner, Pascal Calogero, now chief justice of the Louisiana State Supreme Court. Pas and I had also been close friends; he had campaigned door-to-door for me in the Eighteenth Ward in the 1965 campaign for mayor. Now we found ourselves on opposite sides, but we remained friends.

John J. Petre was a strong candidate. A councilman-at-large, he was also a former district councilman and state legislator. An insurance man by profession, he had a common-sense approach to financing city government, pointing out that Landrieu's proposed earnings tax was illegal and that so-called "economizing" in city government would not result in the millions some other candidates liked to promise. Finally, the late Lloyd J. Rittner, then school board president, was running. He had been a capable and courageous board member during the school desegregation crisis and had many admirers. He also had a comprehensive ten-point program he said would bring $12 million in new city revenue the first year.

In all our debates, I stressed that the proper role for the mayor was that of a catalyst and leader—the man who could hold things together, create a consensus, and make events take place. I said that the mayor should be more effective in bringing together the city's twenty-representative, eight-senator Baton Rouge legislative delegation. I also thought that he should work more closely with the state's congressional delegation to squeeze every dollar in federal revenue sharing possible. I felt that the mayor should play the key leadership role in economic development and tourist promotion; he should be the star salesman for the city.

I proposed a city department of commerce and development to spur the enticing of new industry. A decade later Mayor Dutch Morial created such a department, although it has since fallen into ineffectiveness, pending the election of a mayor who will use it aggressively. As the campaign wore on, each day was a tough, new battle.

As the days drew closer to the November 8 primary, I felt increasingly confident and encouraged. Fund-raising was going extremely well, and we were gaining the bulk of the political organization endorsements. The Metropolitan Democratic Organization, a very effective uptown group run by Frank Siccone, a Washington

Avenue tavern owner, endorsed me early in the campaign. The Crescent City Democratic Association, Chep Morrison's old organization, was strongly behind me. It was joined by the Regular Democratic Organization—its bitter rival, in which members braved telephoned death threats to endorse me. This was one of the last endorsements decided by the RDO in its historic Choctaw Club headquarters. I had the bulk of the other major endorsements in the city. The late attorney, Sewall S. Fine, helped put together an endorsement by the two-thousand-member Amalgamated Meat Cutters, Butchers and Allied Food Workers, which he represented. Many other labor groups got on board also.

Times were changing in New Orleans, however. The old political organizations and alliances did not command the universal power and respect of other campaigns. "New politics" began to emerge, such as the defeat of my council candidate Woody Koppel by the hip, young Eddie Sapir, now a judge. In fact, in some quarters, my support by all of the old-line political organizations cost me the backing of others. The Alliance for Good Government endorsed Guste in the first primary and would later switch to Landrieu in the runoff. The alliance was a respected, generally conservative, reform organization with which I had been friendly through the years. Its rationale for not endorsing me was that the candidates it selected were "uncontrolled" by other political organizations, thus presumably free to make wholesale changes once elected. The flaw to this reasoning was that the other candidates had sought the same endorsements from those groups and, failing to get them, now pretended that they were somehow "cleaner" by the absence of such support. It was a false issue, but it did hurt me in some quarters.

In the second primary, the *States-Item*, at that time independent from the *Times-Picayune*, backed Landrieu as a new, independent man of substance, and charged me with equivocation and empty rhetoric. The paper said, "As the candidate of City Hall, as the man who has the support of virtually every old-line political organization in town, how can Mr. Fitzmorris bring change? The answer is, he cannot. His hands are tied." It was a charge I bitterly resented. Throughout my political career I had been one of the few candidates to make thoughtful, substantive recommendations—really addressing the issues. Sometimes my candor had cost me the election, and now to be dismissed as a vague lightweight was unfair and inaccurate. The notion that I would be hamstrung as mayor because of my political support was particularly offensive. However, there was no margin in attacking the newspaper for its smear campaign. A wise man once said, "Never pick a fight with an organization that buys ink by the barrel."

The fact was, Moon Landrieu had been in the public eye during the three long years I had been out of office. He probably seemed like a bright, new face—just as I had earlier in my own career. It was another case of a candidate being in the right place at the right time, and that is just the way the cat combs its hair!

Seeking the Black Vote

In the second primary it was a race between Moon and me, and everyone agreed it looked close. The consensus was that I had overwhelming white, business, and moderate support and needed only about a quarter of the black vote for a convincing victory. Given my history of black support, I had not thought that would be a problem. The older black leadership in New Orleans was well aware of my record of sensitivity and support for equal opportunity, and I depended upon them to tell this story to the city's growing community of young, black activists. In fact, during the Fitzmorris-Schiro race, I had lost considerable white support from the public perception that I was overly concerned with the plight of our black citizens.

In this campaign, I made a conscious decision not to court the black voters, believing that there were sufficient black leaders who remembered my personal commitment to helping them gain their full share of the American dream. When television newsman Alec Gifford asked me pointedly, during a TV interview, if I would appoint more blacks to city positions, I replied that I would appoint the best qualified person to each position, regardless of color, religion, or political affiliation. Pressed on that point, I reiterated my position. That was not what Alec wanted so he continued to raise the question. At that time, my response was out of fashion. Today, its the "in" thing to say! It was the proper position, and it was the law, but it was not enough. The Landrieu campaign openly embraced the new, young black leadership and freely hinted that it would open the floodgates of city employment to black applicants. It was a studied assessment of the changing complexion of New Orleans political power. I had the same information and could have taken the same position. I chose not to do so, and blame no one for this campaign strategy for it was of my own choosing, in keeping with my own personality and beliefs.

I depended, instead, on the traditional black leadership like the Community Improvement Association. I combined that with endorsements from state senators Nat Kiefer and Ted Hickey and representatives Arthur Crais, Edward Boesch, Donald Fortier, Ben Bagert, William Gill, and Earl Schmidt and numerous other present and former elected officials including New Orleans district attorney Jim Garrison.

Raising a Negative Issue

Late in the campaign, it was clear that I was narrowly ahead. Then, against my own best judgment, I took an uncharacteristic approach: an open televised attack on my opponent. The Metropolitan Crime Commission had, for many years, criticized Landrieu for his representation of TAC Amusement, one of the nation's largest pinball and amusement companies. The MCC believed that illegal pinball gambling was widespread and that Landrieu's association with TAC was inappropriate for an elected official.

There was considerable factual basis for questioning Landrieu's allegiance to TAC. The TAC organization had set up many local barrooms in business and, when employees and customers of those bars had been charged with offenses ranging from gambling to prostitution, the establishment's licenses had been reviewed by the city council for possible revocation. On a long series of these votes, Landrieu had simply avoided voting against the interests of his friends at TAC.

I revealed some of these associations in my television attack, and the repercussions were immediate. Many of the little corner bars, located in every nook and cranny of the city, depended on their income from the pinball machines and jukeboxes to pay the rent and stay in business. The owners of these largely blue-collar bars saw my attack on Landrieu as a threat to their very survival. Many of the customers thought I intended to close down one of their principal avenues of entertainment. Overnight, my signs disappeared from these bars, and the talk turned viciously against me. Many of the owners had previously been against Landrieu because he supported the "open accommodations" law but, after my television attack, they switched energetically to Moon's side.

For my part, having once embarked on this negative campaign strategy, I failed to follow through. While I had bulging files of evidence, I liked Moon personally as well as his wife, Verna, and their attractive young family. Having opened the door by raising the charge, I did not present the evidence to support my claims. I was just not put together in a way that allowed me to "move in for the kill." I just never did have the political instinct to go for the jugular, in mean or personal attacks, and should never have raised the issue in such a tentative way without being willing to expose the bulky details which supported the initial charge.

Election Day Arrives

Election day saw a beehive of activity. As usual, Gloria and I were the first voters at the polls at 6:00 A.M. in the Twenty-Third Precinct of the Fourth Ward. I brought Lisa along for good luck. After casting our vote, we had a quick breakfast; then it was back on the campaign trail. I must have personally visited some 150 voting precincts. Norris and some other folks were busy working the streets; we really turned out a great army of Fitzmorris supporters working in every area of the city.

As the day wore on, I would sense a feeling that something was wrong. I was not getting the kind of positive response I had always enjoyed in previous elections. Some of my black friends told me that the word was out in their neighborhoods, "Don't vote for Fitzmorris." When the votes were counted, there was a heavy turnout from both the working-class neighborhoods along the river front and from the black precincts downtown, and I was faring badly. Landrieu was getting a third of the vote or better in the blue-collar neighborhoods, where I should have held him to no more than 10 percent. He was winning the black votes which had gone to other candidates like Guste and Gertler in the first primary, pulling 90 percent of the black vote, where I had expected at least a quarter. His endorsement of the council candidacy of Dutch Morial, whom I had not supported, and his vigorous support by the new black organizations, SOUL and COUP, contributed mightily to his victory.

The old-line political organizations and traditional black groups were unable to turn out the vote I needed. Only assessor Jim Comiskey's mid-city political organization held solid behind my candidacy; it was not enough. Landrieu won the runoff by 89,554 to 78,726. He went on to defeat Republican Ben Toledano, who drew votes mostly from the George Wallace precincts of the year before. I supported Landrieu against Toledano, but the outcome was painfully clear: I had lost an election I could and should have won, and there was a very real question as to whether Jimmy Fitzmorris had any political future at all. If I did have any future, it was obviously going to depend on some new combination of circumstances beyond the city limits of New Orleans for after a half-million-dollar race for mayor, this was to be my last campaign for a municipal position.

Chapter 6

The Lieutenant Governorship

The Lazarus Campaign: The 1971 Race

After I had lost back-to-back campaigns for mayor of New Orleans, many of my friends assumed that my political future was over, and there was certainly some merit to that argument. I believed, however, that there would be some future opportunity for me to serve and that it would eventually make itself obvious. In the meantime, I threw myself back into the daily whirl of railroad, civic, social, and religious activities of New Orleans.

Many observers believed that Mayor Schiro's election-eve promise of a domed stadium in New Orleans East had provided him the necessary thin margin for my 1965 defeat. Thus, I found it ironic that one of my first tasks as a private citizen, in 1970, was to put together the necessary land to make the Superdome a reality. When Schiro first proposed the stadium, he suggested that it be built on land in New Orleans East to be donated by Marvin Kratter, a political supporter. Even the most casual observers agreed that such a remote location made the project highly non-feasible. I dared not say so during the last hours of the campaign for it would have made me appear a grumpy obstructionist, but I agreed with the gloomy forecast of the chances a stadium would ever operate successfully in that location. Moreover, I had serious doubts that Kratter would live up to his commitment. I was convinced from the beginning that it was only a political ploy. Governor John McKeithen agreed with that assessment as well. He believed strongly that the domed stadium should be built in the center of the city, within the transportation hub and close to the major population area of New Orleans, within a short walking distance from the major downtown hotels.

There was only one problem: virtually the only tract large enough to accommodate the Superdome was on the other side of Poydras, opposite the civic center complex, and it was in several sections, each owned by interests which had no reason to part with this invaluable property. The largest portions of the tract were owned by two major railroads, the Kansas City Southern Lines, which I represented, and the Illinois Central Railroad, represented by its president, William Johnson. McKeithen knew me very well so he was not concerned that I might harbor some selfish motive for wanting the domed stadium project to fail. Instead, one morning about 6 A.M., Governor McKeithen called me and expressed a strong interest in trying to obtain the railroads' land and asked for my help and support. Additionally, he asked that I persuade Bill Johnson, then president of the Illinois Central, to join us at the governor's mansion to discuss the possibilities. Johnson reluctantly agreed, and we went together to Baton Rouge. All the way up, Bill told me all the reasons he was not going to sell. He knew full well that if the Illinois Central could keep its land, it would one day be priceless. McKeithen and I spoke fervently, at length, about the critical importance to the New Orleans economy of making this land available so the project could proceed.

We both knew that the KCS and IC would be making a significant sacrifice by parting with the land at that time. I knew that selling our portion would cause us to lose some customers to other railroads because we would no longer have sufficient warehousing for them in the downtown area of New Orleans. However, after discussing the matter with Bill Deramus III, president of the KCS, I assured him that the Kansas City Southern Railroad was willing to sustain that loss as an investment in the future of New Orleans and Louisiana. Johnson finally agreed and, after a number of telephone calls and meetings, the deal was done. On Tuesday, September 6, 1970, at a ceremony attended by Mayor Landrieu, stadium executive director Dave Dixon, and me, I presented the city with title to the vital 13.7-acre tract and received a check for $3,375,000, a fraction of what the property would be worth today, thus clearing the way for construction of the Louisiana Superdome. Curtis and Davis, Architects and Engineers, were eventually

The September 7, 1970, land sale from Kansas City Southern Lines to the city, 13.7 acres which made the Superdome construction possible, l-r: Mayor Maurice "Moon" Landieu, Superdome commission executive director Dave Dixon, and me, representing the railroad.

selected to design this great structure, and construction finally got under way August 11, 1971. Only two other small parcels on the fringes of the project remained, and they were acquired by the state without any major problem.

The Superdome, after a period in which its management was embroiled in politics—for the spoils system was still alive and well in Louisiana—became an international symbol of the city and one of the most important mainstays of our economy. It dominates the skyline of downtown New Orleans, covering some fifty-two acres, rounding out a remarkable square-mile area that includes the central business and shopping district, the French Quarter, the Aquarium of the Americas, a rejuvenated warehouse district, and riverfront developments. It did much to sustain and revitalize the downtown area of the city. It opened up Poydras Street to growth and development. For a time, it hosted up to twenty thousand fans at New Orleans Jazz professional basketball games and is home to 76,791 loyal and enthusiastic supporters of the New Orleans Saints professional football franchise as well as the WFL New Orleans Breakers, when that team existed, the USF&G Sugar Bowl, and a new arena football team, the New Orleans Night. It has also held some of the world's largest concerts and festivals, with room for 87,500 persons under the dome, and is home of the annual Doll and Toy Fund distribution of toys.

The Superdome has four ballrooms which can be subdivided into twenty meeting rooms. It also has Star Suites for visiting performers and VIPs, team locker rooms, a private Stadium Club, forty-four refreshment stands, eight bars, five cocktail lounges, a gift shop and sixty-four lavish, private suites on the loge level. Just recently, Saints owner Tom Benson added another sixty-eight boxes on the third level. The dome can accommodate five thousand cars and 250 buses. During the week it is heavily utilized by commuters working downtown in conjunction with the city's and private sector's "Park N Ride" program. Its official opening on August 3, 1975, made it one of the nation's premiere multipurpose sports and entertainment facilities. It was not built without considerable opposition for this was a very big step for a city which sometimes seemed accustomed to thinking small. One of the most common complaints was that "our children will be paying for it." That, of course, is true, just as they will pay for the bridges and highways that brought Louisiana into the twentieth century, improved our commerce and agriculture, and raised everyone's standard of living.

In a larger sense, the foresight and courage required to construct the Superdome was symptomatic of our belief in and commitment to the city's future. I like to compare contemporary cities to offshore oil platforms in the sense that, even though rooted in the earth, they are pounded by wind and wave, threatened by hurricanes above and corrosion below, part of the dynamic standoff between men who build and forces which destroy. When people ask whether a city can survive, any city, they are really asking whether that city has the determination and the vitality to survive. In New Orleans' case, the local sale of bonds to fund stadium construction marked the city's blow for independence from the money markets of the North and East. What did we get for the $129.5 million investment? We got more than the list of amenities and facilities I discussed earlier, more than just a structure in which a twenty-eight-story building could fit on second base. We really got a catalyst, a financial rocket with which to propel our city into the economic future. Much of that investment stayed in town through jobs, taxes, and purchases of goods and equipment.

We got a huge influx of tourist dollars which would otherwise have gone to other cities, not to mention revenue from the hotel-motel tax which, in turn, is invested in tourist and convention promotion to continue the cycle. I often remember what a press secretary to a vice president of the United States once said about New Orleans, after the Superdome became a reality. He was questioned about why the vice president seemed to come to New Orleans so often. "You don't understand," he said, "because you still believe all that stuff about the backward South. Out of all the invitations we get to speak at trade conventions, two out of three are for conventions held in New Orleans. That is where the action is, and you don't realize it." My point is that when you compare a project like the Superdome's cost with its benefits, you have to go beyond balancing ticket sales and direct revenue to the long-term indebtedness. You have to take into account the revenue pool we created for all kinds of people in New Orleans. So while it will take forty years for the domed stadium to pay itself off, in the meantime, it will provide a better living for thousands of people. That is why I believed so strongly in the Superdome and was pleased to have played a part in making it possible.

Life after City Politics

My years out of government were not all filled with business, for New Orleans is one of the legendary social communities of the world, and nowhere is that more colorfully evident than in our Mardi Gras season. It has been said that Gloria and I attend more Mardi Gras carnival balls than any other living people in New Orleans today, and that may be true. Our carnival season in New Orleans begins the night after Christmas and ends at midnight on "Fat Tuesday," Mardi Gras day. Carnival comes from two Latin words: "carni" (meat) and "vale" (removal), and thus means, by implication, "farewell to flesh," a reference to the beginning of Lent. Carnival in New Orleans is a series of almost-nightly, invitation-only masquerade balls put on by the various "mystic krewes," secret organizations whose membership is never revealed, which vie with each other in the beauty of their costumes and the splendor of their pageants. Gloria and I attended our first carnival ball in 1945, while I was still in the army and since that time continue to be a part of that entertaining experience. Over the years we have made many lifelong friends in the carnival community. Chep Morrison, Vic Schiro, and I were always on hand to escort queens, past queens, maids, and distinguished and honored guests to be presented to the various kings and queens at literally thousands of Mardi Gras balls at the Municipal Auditorium and other locations.

The Mardi Gras Tradition

Mardi Gras is a Fitzmorris family tradition: I narrate balls and parades. Daddy and Norris were members of Carrollton, one of the oldest and most prestigious of New Orleans' many carnival organizations. Norris writes and narrates balls, as does George Simno III. Many participants in these activities came to call me "Mr. Mardi Gras," and I always had tremendous political support from the captains and members of the carnival organizations. Participation in Mardi Gras cuts across all economic and social lines, ranging from the august krewes of Comus, Rex, Bacchus, Hermes, Endymion, Zeus, Venus, and Iris to the more ribald revelry of the black Zulu Social and Pleasure Club and Young Men Illinois. I do not believe that one can really understand New Orleans without first experiencing and understanding Mardi Gras,

The first Mardi Gras reviewing stand at the new city hall, 1958, l-r: my nieces Irene and Beth Ann Simno, me, unknown person, Chep Morrison's secretary Rosalie Grad, and Gloria. (Courtesy city of New Orleans, photo by J. R. St. Julien)

for this season takes place on a scale approached by no other city in America.

Continuing Commitment to Community Service

I remained dedicated to and intensely involved with a host of community and civic activities, as had been my practice throughout my public career as well.

My varied roles throughout the years included service on the State Board of Public Welfare, the board of governors of the Louisiana State Civil Service League, the Regional Planning Commission, the Total Community Action, the National Conference of Christians and Jews, a hospital, a recreation group, a bank, and a savings and loan. I had been president of the Mississippi Valley World Trade Council and advisory board member of the Small Business Administration. I had been presented the 1969 Award of Honor by Jesuit High School as the "finest public servant in the city of New Orleans" and held honorary life memberships and gold membership cards in the New Orleans Chamber of Commerce, the Young Men's Business Club, the World Trade Club, and the Knights of Columbus.

Pondering Another Campaign

Yet, with all those activities, I genuinely missed the action and the passion of public service in elective office. I believed that I had a unique combination of background, experience, and commitment to offer, and I determined to present myself as a candidate for statewide office.

I had really given some thought to running for governor, but I dared not discuss these plans with anyone. I believe they would have called "the man with the net." After some real soulsearching, I talked to my family and a very few close friends, including my dear friend Bill Helis, and finally decided to run for lieutenant governor, an office being vacated in the 1971 election as the incumbent, C. C. "Taddy" Aycock, had decided to seek the governorship. Many of Aycock's friends had spoken to me about managing his campaign, rather than seeking office on my own. Their belief was that I would add considerable strength to Aycock's campaign in the metropolitan New Orleans area, where he had traditionally run poorly. I gave some consideration to that idea. My main concern was deciding in what role I could best serve the interests of Louisiana in general and the New Orleans area in particular. After weeks of debating the pluses and minuses of all possibilities, I decided that I would be happiest and most effective as a candidate in my own right, rather than as a spokesman for someone else. On August 2, 1971, I announced my candidacy. The business and political community gave my candidacy little chance of success.

A One-Man Draft

A few years earlier, former presidential press secretary Pierre Salinger had described his candidacy for the U.S. Senate as "a groundswell consisting of the candidate himself," and my race for lieutenant governor was much the same. As always, I entered the race long on enthusiasm and ideas. There were, however, significant holes in the fabric of the Fitzmorris campaign plan. I had no money. I was a twice-defeated candidate for local office in New Orleans. I was virtually unknown outside the metropolitan area. I was a Roman Catholic facing the prospect of an election which might well be decided in the largely protestant, rural section of the state. Finally, another New Orleans figure, my friend state senator William J. Guste, Jr., was about to announce for attorney general against the embattled incumbent, Jack P. F. Gremillion, another good friend, and it was not at all certain that the people of rural Louisiana were ready to surrender two top elective positions to "big city" candidates. I felt a little as though I was swimming upstream as I viewed the other three major candidates in the primary: state senate president pro tempore, Jamar Adcock of Monroe; chairman of the joint legislative budget committee, state representative P. J. Mills of Shreveport; and public service commissioner, Ed Kennon of Minden.

Tough Competition

They all had name recognition and money. If the election had been held only for members of the state senate, Adcock would have won hands down. He was a floor leader for Governor McKeithen and extremely well connected politically in every nook and cranny of the state. He was well-heeled to boot, with affluent friends in addition to his own personal resources as a banker and real estate developer. If the race were to be decided by money and personal influence, I would be in big trouble. Mills, who later

My close friend and longtime campaign manager, the late William G. Helis, Jr.

went on to serve as administrator of the LOOP super port, a successful insurance executive and chief of staff to Gov. Buddy Roemer, was associated with Pioneer Bank in Shreveport and had his own circle of friends developed as a member of the state house of representatives. He was articulate, honest, hard-working, and aggressive. I, on the other hand, had a Ford station wagon, the use of Bill Helis's car and small plane, and an address book with a few names from my army days, the railroad, and the Knights of Columbus—pretty meager armament for a political war on this statewide scale.

I did have a few secret weapons: William G. Helis, Jr., agreed to be my state campaign manager. My brother Norris served as state coordinator, certified public accountant the late Anthony E. Armbruster was our campaign treasurer, Hughes Walmsley, chairman of our state finance committee. Harry McCall, Jr., was chairman of our state legal committee, and Carol Daigle took on her usual role as secretary and campaign coordinator. With that small team in place, we decided to get moving. We started to work, hitting every little community in the state. We literally wore the wheels off that old station wagon, occasionally supplemented by my friend Bill Helis's small but effective plane. The other candidates had campaign staffs of experienced professionals. I had the volunteer service of John Massa, a young, former Secret Service agent, and the late Steve Auerbach, whose principal asset as the campaign began was that he had free time to contribute and a sincere desire to help me. They both proved to be invaluable assets. Both were hard workers, met people easily, and never complained about the long hours or the seven-day-per-week campaign schedule. I had never met either of them but, with each passing day, they became more important to me, not only as campaign aids but as loyal, dedicated, faithful, personal friends.

We spent many wonderful days together—the three of us. Some weeks Steve would start out in the station wagon and make the major shopping centers. It was equipped with a sophisticated public address system which played our campaign song, "You've Got a Friend," and allowed us to speak as well. Along the way he would distribute and install the big "Fitzmorris for Lieutenant Governor" signs. John and I would start out by car or in Bill Helis's plane in another direction and arrange to meet Steve at a predetermined location, where we would continue our campaign tour in the station wagon. I've had many wonderful supporters along the way, and many lonely disappointments, but the three of us kept smiling and moving along. I also had the services of Bauerlein Advertising in New Orleans, under the capable leadership of Ken Gormin, the agency which had for many years handled the campaigns of U.S. senator Allen Ellender. They didn't have much media money to work with, but they at least knew the newspaper, radio, and television markets around the state and delivered more than anyone could have asked for the limited resources at their disposal; Ken and his staff could not have been more helpful.

The Back Roads Campaign Trail

For my part, I mostly worked small groups and individuals, speaking in shopping centers and office buildings, wherever anyone would listen. I quickly came to the conclusion that I could meet no voters on the interstate highways, so I traveled the back roads, some of them not even on the maps, where many of the people had never seen a statewide candidate in person. We never missed stopping at a gas station or small, mom-and-pop restaurant. Steve and John would always find some kind of excuse to buy candy bars or cookies because they knew we might not stop to eat lunch and maybe skip dinner, depending on our travel schedule. As "The Chief," a nickname I picked up early in the campaign, I always sat up front with the driver. Steve and John would split this chore; as one drove, the other would sit in the back seat and map out our schedule for the evening and the next day. We spent many lonely nights together. Sometimes our prearranged meetings with elected officials or civic leaders did not work out, and I would ask my favorite question, "Who arranged the schedule?" We had to blame it on somebody, so usually we blamed it on Carol Daigle.

We tried to arrange our schedule to return to New Orleans each Friday night and at exactly 7:00 A.M. Saturday morning Steve, John, and I would drive to 600 Iona Street, the residence of my campaign manager and dear friend Bill Helis, for an early morning breakfast and a blow-by-blow report to Bill about our week's activities. On many occasions Bill would know more about our schedule than we thought, asking why we failed to stop at one shopping center or another. We would try to find a reasonable answer, which most of the time was not accepted. Bill was great at keeping us on our toes, even when we indicated that we were exhausted. He would say, "I don't want to hear any of that. What time are you scheduled to leave tomorrow? And let me see your itinerary for the week." Under that kind of watchful eye we dared not miss another side road or shopping center. I'll always be grateful to John Massa and to the late Steve Auerbach for their company and encouragement in those long, hard, lonesome, and often disappointing days. Although they didn't realize it at the time, they were my strength.

Sometimes I really found it difficult to walk up to a complete stranger in a small community, put out my hand and say, "I'm Jimmy Fitzmorris, and I'm running for lieutenant governor. I hope you'll be able to give me your support." At times I just got a cold look, at other times a warm friendly smile, but all in all I felt well received. I will never forget early one Friday morning in Springhill, Louisiana, just five miles from the Arkansas border, we stopped at a very small shopping center. We had a disappointing meeting the night before, and I was really down (although I tried never to let the boys know that).

I approached a little old lady as she was selecting some fresh fruit, saying, "Pardon me, ma'm." To my surprise, she looked up and said, "You're Jimmy Fitzmorris. I saw you on TV last night, and I decided I am going to vote for you." I almost fainted. I said, "Yes, ma'm, I am Jimmy Fitzmorris, and I'm most grateful for your vote and support." Little did she know what she did for me that morning. I really got on a high. That sweet little old lady made my day, and I realized once again that the work of Ken Gormin and his capable staff, through the medium of television, had brought our campaign into the home of many Louisianians—and with that kind of support my confidence continued to grow.

Louisiana is a big state. You really don't realize how big it is until you hit the road, day in and day out. I must say, it was a wonderful experience. I saw some of the finest country, most beautiful homes, and most breathtaking scenery in the world, and drank some of the blackest coffee with some of the finest people in the world—the people of Louisiana. As time went on I really got to know the real Louisiana, and that's why I am so proud and honored to have served as lieutenant governor.

There was a lively and contentious crop of candidates for governor that year, including U.S. representative Edwin Edwards, state senator John Schwegmann, state senator J. Bennett Johnston, the late U.S. representative Gillis Long, heir to one of the great names in Louisiana politics, and former governor Jimmie Davis. Having so many challengers at the top of the ticket made fund-raising especially difficult. Total spending for all gubernatorial candidates exceeded $7 million. It is one of the great shames of politics that eight years later that amount would nearly triple. That election marked the first time the New Orleans Alliance for Good Government, a local reform group, backed Edwin Edwards. The next would be twenty years later in his successful fifth try for the governorship.

Issues and Endorsements

Each of the candidates for lieutenant governor ran independently, without linking up with one of the gubernatorial challengers. In the end, the runoff was between Edwards and Johnston, both of whom had seemed long shots at the beginning of the campaign. Some events called that independence into question: Former mayor Vic Schiro and others ran a full-page, four-color ad backing Jimmie Davis for governor and endorsing me for lieutenant governor. We responded, through Bill Helis, Jr., with our own full-page ad saying, "Jimmy Fitzmorris Is Independent." In late October, the Lake Providence Jaycees responded to Jamar Adcock's advertisements, which said, "Jamar Adcock Listens to People." The group pointed out that it had written him five times and telegraphed him twice on a community project and never received a reply. The Jaycees asked, "Do you call that listening?" New Orleans lawyer Darleen Jacobs created a group called "Association of Independent Democrats" which endorsed Adcock. Mayor Landrieu endorsed both me and Billy Guste. Both the *States-Item* and the *Times-Picayune* endorsed Mills.

In the runoff I was endorsed by Senator Schwegmann, who had been defeated for governor in the primary. He said, "James E. Fitzmorris, Jr., has a long record of public service that has proven him to be a friend of the people, and I endorse his candidacy wholeheartedly." I was also endorsed by P. J. Mills, who had finished fourth, just behind commissioner Kennon. Mills issued a very kind statement in which he said, " . . . I feel Mr. Fitzmorris' ideas and ideals most closely coincide with mine, particularly as to what public office should be and where Louisiana should go in the next four years. Also I have come to know Mr. Fitzmorris during the past six months of campaigning and find him to be a man of honor, integrity, and, most importantly, dedication. The fact that he has been in public life over twenty-five years and is not a wealthy man speaks loudly to me of the fact that he has devoted himself to public service and not personal service. . . ." The basis of my platform was that I would be a full-time lieutenant governor. Of course, the lieutenant governor had the statutory job of presiding over the state senate and serving as president of the board of pardons, but I wanted to expand the role.

Seeking an Expanded Role

I told anyone who would listen that the office of lieutenant governor was underutilized in Louisiana. I said that the office of lieutenant governor should be more than ornamental; it should be used for tourist promotion and industrial development, two subjects in which I had a considerable and proven expertise. It was inconceivable to me that a man would serve a heartbeat away from the governorship and not be given some specific duties and responsibilities. Senator Adcock concentrated on stressing his role as presiding officer of the senate, promising to make that body more independent of the governor and to appoint committee chairmen without concern for their seniority in the senate. His newfound independence struck some as a little incongruous, since he had long served as an acquiescent floor leader for Governor McKeithen without ever seeming to chafe under the governor's firm control of the senate process. When questions arose about his involvement with his banks and whether he would be able to be a full-time lieutenant governor, Adcock said that he would not sell his bank stock but would disclose his interests to the public. He was also questioned about several banking bills he had introduced in the previous session, in response to which he promised not to promote bank legislation if elected.

Both of us endorsed the notion of a constitutional convention to streamline and modernize state government. I defeated Senator Adcock, who returned to complete his term in the senate, by a vote of 689,007 to 395,055. He was later appointed chairman of the state tax commission. We maintained our friendship, and I had the opportunity to meet and visit with him on many occasions as time moved on. In the general election I easily defeated the Republican candidate, gathering 815,794 votes in the process.

Advent of the Open Primary

Edwin Edwards, having survived a financially destructive first primary, then a costly runoff against Johnston, faced an equally demanding financial challenge from David Treen, the Republican candidate. Treen, who was to win the governorship on his own eight years later, was in the enviable position of being able to save his campaign resources until the final election, while Edwards had already twice extracted and cajoled as much money as possible from his supporters in the process of just making it to the general election. Edwards won, but emerged about $120,000 in debt—a considerable sum in those days. Not long after he was inaugurated, he steered through the legislature a bill creating open primaries in which all candidates of any party ran at the same time and on the same ballot.

That strategy worked to the great advantage of the Republicans, who generally only ran one candidate for each major office, but Edwards believed it would level the financial playing field for future campaigns. So, after an exhausting and financially draining campaign, Edwin Edwards and I took office on a bright spring day, May 9, 1972. Some three thousand volunteers were assembled to serve the four hundred thousand who came to witness the swearing in and participate in the celebration. With Edwin Edwards taking his oath of office in both English and French, the day—in terms of both food and fervor—had a decidedly Cajun flavor. In addition to Gloria and Lisa, I shared the platform with my loving sister Florence, my wonderful brother-in-law George Simno, my devoted brother Norris, and his great helpmate, my sister-in-law Ann. I was particularly proud to have my father with me on the platform as I gave my inaugural address. I was honored to be sworn in by the president pro tempore of the U.S. Senate, my old friend, the late Allen Ellender, as my own congressman, the late F. Edward Hebert, one of the most powerful members of the U.S. House of Representatives, looked on.

As I took my oath of office, I had the powerful feeling that my dear mother, who had passed away a few years before, was standing by my side, as she had always been since my early childhood. I knew that Mother was also proud of her "big boy" at that moment, and I dedicated my service as lieutenant governor in her memory. She was indeed the "Queen Mother."

I looked forward to the challenges of being lieutenant governor

My first day as lieutenant governor and presiding officer of the state senate, May 9, 1972.

Inaugural day, May 9, 1972. My brother Norris, my sister Florence, and me.

Taking the oath of office from U.S. Senator Allen Ellender, l-r: Lt. Jim Borgstede, State Police; Congressman F. Edward Hebert; state representative Joe Delpit; and Donald Thibodaux, State Police superintendent.

with great enthusiasm and optimism, and to the crowd assembled that beautiful day I spoke of hope, coupled with sacrifice. I said that the election proved that the people of Louisiana wanted a new direction, new leadership, a new course of action. I told them that accomplishing the improvements we had promised in the way state government operated would require a new attitude about how it should be run, new initiatives that would require the involvement and the cooperation of all our citizens.

As I assumed the office of lieutenant governor, I could not help but think that, following my disastrous defeat in the 1969 New Orleans mayor's race, not many people gave me a chance to be elected to any political office—much less the second highest office in the state of Louisiana. All along, I believed it could be done, with my little army of loyal supporters and dedicated friends. I set out to prove myself right. Only in America, anything is possible!

Organizing the Senate

The principal role of the lieutenant governor, at that time, was serving as presiding officer of the state senate. In that role, it was my responsibility to appoint all of the committee chairmen, a very powerful duty. With my dear friends Sen. Mike O'Keefe, then president pro tempore of the senate, and Sen. Fritz C. Eagan, I spent considerable time trying to select the right man for the right job (there being no female members of the senate that session). As always, chairmanship of the senate finance committee was the most treasured post. I appointed the dean of the senate, B. B. "Sixty" Rayburn. He had a great knowledge of the state and was a good man to have on your side. There were some outstanding men who served with me in the senate, some of whom I had known previously, others I had not yet met. We developed a strong and lasting friendship, and I had nothing but the highest regard and respect for each of the thirty-nine senators.

It was also my responsibility to appoint the senate membership on all conference committees. These committees are formed when the senate and house have each passed similar legislation and cannot agree on one version acceptable to both bodies. Under that system, I appointed three senators to the conference committee, and the speaker of the house appointed three members from the other body. Bill Roberts, now a judge, was secretary of the senate. He was a very capable attorney who had a comprehensive understanding of all the procedural matters which came before the senate and knew its operation like the back of his hand. Bill had served a long time and had the respect of all who knew him. We developed a wonderful relationship and worked as an effective team during my years as presiding officer. I selected Larry Weidel to be my administrative assistant and as we worked through our first session I later asked Larry to serve as sergeant at arms.

The Constitutional Convention

Early in our administration came an event that significantly changed the way Louisiana state government worked. Both Edwin Edwards and J. Bennett Johnston, as candidates for governor, had endorsed the idea of holding a constitutional convention. I supported the convention concept as well. Unlike the Declaration of Independence, which we honor for the great beauty of its language and the force of its ideas, a state constitution is a "working document," designed to detail the thousands of small but important daily rules by which state government functions. In Louisiana, we try to keep this document current with our changing situation by the constitutional amendment process, but it is healthy, at least every century, for a broad section of our best and brightest citizens and everyday people from all walks of life to update the document. That opinion was not universally shared. As he exited public life, Gov. John McKeithen said, "I can't for the life of me see how a new constitution will bring better government to the state." Concerning reform, McKeithen said, "There isn't much left to be done—I did literally everything good government people asked us to do. There isn't much left to do."

I disagreed then, and I disagree now. Important progress is yet to be made in reform and modernization of state government, challenges which will likely outlive us all. The convention comprised some of the most outstanding people from all around Louisiana. Jefferson Parish assessor Lawrence A. Chehardy served, later becoming an appeals court judge. His son succeeded him as assessor and became a power in parish politics. He wove the "homestead exemption" into the constitution, and protected it. State senator Tom Casey, later executive counsel to Governor Roemer; Rep. Avery Alexander, a distinguished black leader from New Orleans; Rep. John J. Alario, later speaker of the house; my longtime friend from the Morrison years, the late Constable Clyde F. Bel, Sr.; Donald T. "Boysie" Bollinger, a prominent Republican; New Orleans councilmen Joseph Giarrusso, Sr. and Johnny Jackson, Jr.; Camille F. Gravel, Jr., longtime counsel for Edwin Edwards; state representative Woody Jenkins; Public Service commissioner Louis Lambert; New Orleans assessor Claude Mauberret, Jr.; Plaquemines Parish political leader Chalin Perez; state senator B. B. "Sixty" Rayburn, who participated in Louisiana political history from Huey Long through today; and many other distinguished public servants also served in the convention.

There were many new, young faces involved with the convention as well, many of whom have gone on to serve with distinction in other state positions. A skinny young man named Buddy Roemer was elected a delegate from Shreveport. At the time, no one would have imagined that this brash youngster would go on to become a United States congressman and serve one term as governor of Louisiana. A young Ferriday lawyer and senator, Jim Brown, served as a delegate. He later became secretary of state, candidate for governor, and commissioner of insurance. As speaker, the convention selected house speaker E. L. "Bubba" Henry of Jonesboro. Henry later became a gubernatorial candidate, successful lawyer, and lobbyist. Many other delegates went on to become legislators, lobbyists, and judges and served in other important roles after the convention. The convention was not the free-flowing, independent "citizens convention" it was sometimes thought to be; the Edwards forces were firmly in control most of the time.

Nor were the delegates unanimously in support of the final fourteen-article, forty-seven-page document which was presented for public vote and approval. Delegates Emmett Asseff, John Clyde Fontenot, and Shady R. Wall did not even sign the proposed constitution. There were strong feelings in the media and other interested groups as well, on both sides of the issue. By mid-March 1974, the Monroe *News-Star*, Shreveport *Times*, New Orleans *Times-Picayune*, *Shreveport Journal*, and New Orleans *States-Item* had all editorialized in favor of voting down the new constitution. The powerful Louisiana Association of Business and Industry also opposed it. A poll showed that most state legislators supported passage of the constitution. So did the Louisiana Education Association, Municipal Association, and clerks of court. I had endorsed the idea of holding the convention as early as May

Key Louisiana legislators in 1972. First row, l-r: Reps. John Johns and Risley "Pappy" Triche; Sens. Edgar "Sonny" Mouton and B. B. "Sixty" Rayburn; Gov. Edwin Edwards; me, lieutenant governor; Sens. C. R. Blair and Fritz Egan; Reps. Jimmy Long and Shady Wall. Second row, l-r: Reps. Matt Fowler, Joe Tieman, later a judge, and John Alario, later House Speaker; Sen. Adrian Duplantier, later a federal judge; Rep. Lance Womack; House Speaker E. L. "Bubba" Henry; Rep. Bill Strain; two unknown persons; Rep. Billy Tauzin, later congressman; and Sen. Billy Brown.

15, 1972, in a speech in Thibodaux. However, I took a "hands off" position on passage, saying that I thought every citizen had a responsibility to read the document and decide for himself which way to vote in the April 20, 1974, referendum on the proposed constitution. I voted for it, and so did a majority of Louisianians.

I later announced my support for holding a special legislative session to enact some portions of the document, although I agreed with the Metropolitan Crime Commission's opposition to the new constitution's section automatically restoring civil rights to criminal offenders immediately upon termination of their state and federal supervision. The system of having the lieutenant governor serve as presiding officer of the senate had come under increasing criticism from senators, frequently those, like Adrian Duplantier, who had backed some other candidate for lieutenant governor. They wanted to elect their own presiding officer and control their own committee appointments. The new constitution abolished the lieutenant governor's responsibility as presiding officer, and I was thus the last presiding officer of the senate chosen by the people of Louisiana; that choice is now entirely up to the members of the senate. I could understand the position of some senators for "home rule," however, I was disappointed that the convention delegates did not balance the removal of that responsibility by giving the lieutenant governor some other meaningful, statutory role to play. To this day, the lieutenant governor's job is mostly as large or as small as the governor wants and allows it to be.

The "Underemployment" Frustration

I chafed under this lack of real work and several times in my first term stated that I might not seek another unless I had some assurance that I would be a full partner in the business of state government. I finally reached such an accord with Governor Edwards and decided to run again, but my disillusionment and dismay were shared by other lieutenant governors throughout the South. It was a post I often called a "nostalgic link to the past." In Mississippi, for example, Lt. Gov. William Winter was paid eight thousand dollars and had a two-person staff. Arkansas's lieutenant governor Bob Riley received just twenty-five hundred dollars. The lieutenant governor of Alabama, after a dispute with Gov. George Wallace, found himself with no staff appropriation at all and was forced to go around soliciting contributions to keep his doors open. In the meantime, along with House Speaker Bubba Henry, we made big gains in improving the image of the legislature and the way it conducted business. There had been a time when the legislature, as well as most every other political position in the state, was accurately described as "government by gentlemen." Under Gov. Huey Long, the entire legislature was subservient to the wishes of the executive branch.

Long ruled by executive fiat, frequently storming into committee meetings and announcing the results of votes on bills under consideration before there had even been any discussion. Deliberations on the floor were conducted under the same sense of executive influence. Sitting in the speaker's chair at the podium, Long once rushed through a whole package of bills with an average debate of three minutes each. The result was a deplorable lowering of morale and deportment in both houses. By the time I became presiding officer, it was a joke and a disgrace. The floor of the senate resembled more a party or a picnic than a serious, deliberative body. Outsiders and lobbyists roamed the chamber at will, buttonholing senators and interrupting debate. Lobbyists frequently voted in the place of absent senators. Henry and I called a halt to the virtual anarchy on the floor and in the committee meetings. I got the box lunches and fried chicken out of the chamber and moved the coffee urns to the back of the room.

Getting the Legislature down to Business

I insisted that lobbyists remain behind the railing on the senate floor and allow senators to do their job. I made sure that citizens were welcomed in the gallery, but not allowed to interrupt or intimidate senators on the floor. I personally visited the committees after appointing members, to make sure that they were attending sessions and discharging their responsibilities. There was considerable resentment from some of the "old guard," particularly among some powerful lobbyists who never forgave me, over this sudden change in procedure, but members of the press who had covered previous sessions and visitors to the legislature who had been aghast at the previous disarray and confusion were generally complimentary about the new rules. Another of my statutory responsibilities was service as a member of the board of commerce and industry. I also played an active role on the state tourist commission. I joined with Sec. of State Wade O. Martin, Jr., in opposing naming Metairie public relations man Bob Cole to handle commission publicity, to replace the experienced, non-political Swigert Agency. The job was too important to allow it to become a political plum, and the incumbent agency had done an excellent job. Cole later became a well-paid advisor to Louis Lambert in his 1979 campaign against me for governor.

One of the most heated legislative debates was that over "no fault" insurance. I did not believe the proposed bill properly protected the right to recovery of individual citizens, and I broke a tie which ultimately killed the bill.

Reforming the Pardon Board

I was also, by law, chairman of the state pardon board. The other members were the attorney general and the sentencing judge. I did not think that was a proper role for an elected official, and said so. I immediately stopped the board from hearing pardon requests until the prosecuting district attorney had an opportunity to make a recommendation and until the state board of corrections had made a formal investigation and report of each case. In 1972, I declared that the board should be comprised of full-time professionals in that field. I deplored the practice of legislators who were also attorneys appearing on behalf of clients before the board. The constitutional convention took that responsibility away from the lieutenant governor, which was fine with me, but gave it to a board appointed by the governor. I did not believe that the requirements for service on the board were anywhere stringent enough to prevent politics from controlling the board's actions. It has since been improved to become manned by full-time professionals.

I supported renewal of the death penalty in 1974 and had earlier, as acting governor, refused a request to commute all existing death sentences. Edwin Edwards had been elected governor as a "reform" candidate. We now tend to forget that, in his first campaign, he was endorsed over David Treen by both the *Times-Picayune* and the Alliance for Good Government. The days in which he could bask in the warm glow of media approval were very few, however, and only seven months into his first term he told the Shreveport *Times* that he would not seek a second term but would, instead, return to the private practice of law. He blamed his decision on what he called "the mad dog press corps." Nonetheless, by the end of his first year, polls showed that Edwards had a two-thirds approval rating by registered voters. He and Pres. Richard Nixon had a nearly 100 percent recognition by the state's voters. I was second among state officials with 86 percent. More than half the voters said that they approved of my performance and only 4 percent disapproved. I thought that was an outstanding rating considering hardly anyone had any idea what the lieutenant governor actually did!

As the 1975 campaign approached, it was obvious that there would be some serious challenges mounted to incumbents. My old friend, Sec. of State Wade O. Martin, Jr., decided to give up his secure position to challenge Governor Edwards. It was to be as much a personal vendetta as a campaign, but Martin had a long record and friends in every nook and cranny of the state. He had to be taken seriously. Former mayor Vic Schiro, now six years out of office, decided to challenge insurance commissioner Sherman Bernard. P. J. Mills, whom I had defeated for lieutenant governor four years earlier, decided to run for the seat Martin was vacating. He ran ahead in the primary but lost the runoff to state senator Paul Hardy, who later served as Republican lieutenant governor. State senator John Schwegmann, a prominent grocer, was pitted against former New Orleans councilman Dan Kelly for a seat on the Public Service Commission. These were years of transition in Louisiana politics, sometimes sadly so.

I was given a giant testimonial dinner, chaired by Bill Helis, at the Fairmont Hotel in 1972 celebrating my election. Governor-elect Edwards attended, as did hundreds of my old friends from throughout New Orleans who had never lost faith in me through the dark days I spent in the political wilderness. It was a wonderful, touching experience.

After the dinner, J. Bennett Johnston virtually announced his candidacy for the U.S. Senate seat held by the venerable Allen Ellender. Johnston was fresh from his gubernatorial defeat. Ellender, who had polled 75 percent of the vote in his last election, was not worried. On May 30, 1972, the Grand Old Man of Louisiana politics said, "If the Lord spares me, and I know He will, for another six years, I will have served longer in the senate than any man in history." Many newspapers endorsed him based on his record and his seniority. Yet, Johnston had only recently come off the campaign trail on which he had recruited a whole

"Second lining" with Mayor Moon Landrieu at my 1972 testimonial dinner.

new generation of political supporters. Ellender was in for the fight of his political life for he had never faced such a stiff challenge since his first election to the Senate. Suddenly running behind in the polls, he turned to a number of old friends like me to help him get around Louisiana and meet the many new voters who had never seen him. I genuinely admired and respected the senator and spent countless days by his side in New Orleans and all over the state.

After long, hard work we were confident of victory. Then, suddenly, he was dead, just twenty-three days before the election. We had campaigned together at the Grand Isle Tarpon Rodeo the weekend before. Senator Ellender died at Bethesda Naval Hospital. It was on the day some will remember as the moment Democratic presidential nominee Sen. George McGovern told the press that he was "1,000 percent" behind his choice for vice president, Sen. Thomas Eagleton, whose treatment for depression had just become known. Senator Ellender had served with both men, but he was not supporting McGovern's bid for the presidency. I was not much impressed by McGovern either and had not determined any role I would play in the presidential campaign in Louisiana. State senator Charles G. Smither, a co-chairman of Moon Landrieu's campaign for mayor, went even further, resigning from the Democratic party in protest over McGovern's nomination. All the signs pointed toward another national Democratic disaster. Meanwhile, Louisiana Democrats were astir about the Ellender death and its impact on the senatorial election. There was talk about holding a special Democratic convention to re-open qualifying for the Senate position.

Much talk centered around Moon Landrieu or me as possible candidates. Landrieu did not seek the nomination, and I had absolutely no interest in going to Washington in any capacity. I had promised the people of Louisiana to be a full-time lieutenant governor and thought it important to keep that promise. In the end, Johnston won the nomination. Former governor McKeithen, running as an independent, made a very poor showing. The Republicans, in a brutal three-man contest, eventually nominated Ben Toledano, who had run for mayor against Landrieu. The then-weak Republican party was no match for Johnston, and he was easily elected to the seat where he continues to serve, most recently staving off a serious challenge from state representative

David Duke who was in grade school at the time this election was held.

Louisiana Loses Hale Boggs

There were other sad political changes as well. In October 1972, a small plane carrying U. S. House of Representatives majority leader Hale Boggs disappeared on a campaign flight in Alaska. He was never to be found. We dedicated the new federal building on Camp Street to his memory; I spoke at the ceremony. Hale was a complex personality, a big bear of a man who dared to back progressive legislation at a time when much of the South was not yet in step. He had great personal courage and integrity.

I recall the lines from Stephen Spender's *The Truly Great*, "The names of those who in their lives fought for life, who wore at their hearts the fire's centre. Born of the sun, they traveled a short while toward the sun and left the vivid air signed with their honor." Hale's widow, Lindy, daughter of a distinguished Louisiana family, and one of the most gracious women of our lifetime, went on to succeed her husband, serving with great honor and effectiveness until her retirement in 1991. She was succeeded by state senator William Jefferson of New Orleans—our first modern black representative in Congress. President Lyndon B. Johnson attended Boggs' memorial service. Their families had come to post-war Washington when both were young congressmen. A few months later, on January 22, 1973, LBJ died at his ranch near Johnson City, Texas. I praised his legislative leadership. Governor Edwards praised his use of power. Of course, though much in Louisiana was changing, much stayed the same. Both the Young Mens' Business Club and the New Orleans Athletic Club voted to retain their "whites only" membership policy. The YMBC later changed its name to Your Metropolitan Business Club, Inc., and expanded its membership to include women, while the NOAC ended its segregated policy.

The rigors of running a re-election campaign must be sandwiched in between the responsibilities of official duties. Some of those are important, some primarily ceremonial, but all take time.

On March 3, 1975, I testified in favor of building a nuclear power plant in Louisiana, before the Atomic Energy Commission's safety and licensing board. I believed that, properly constructed and constantly monitored, nuclear power plants were safe, efficient, and absolutely vital to our future. This belief was an easy target for scare tactics in the 1979 governor's campaign. Two days after President Johnson's death, I opposed the U.S. Supreme Court's ruling prohibiting states from interfering with a woman's right to obtain an abortion during the early months of pregnancy. The following week, with the help of Attorney General Billy Guste, as a member of the Louisiana Bond Commission, I forced the commission to stop its historic "rubber stamping" of a favored few bond attorneys, opening up the process. The commission had been morbidly ineffective; in one instance it was asked to approve a proposed bond issue the week before the bond election!

The Re-election Campaign: 1975

Edwards, the erstwhile "reform" candidate of 1971, was being challenged by a new reformer, state senator Bob Jones of Lake Charles. Jones won the enthusiastic endorsement of the *States-Item*, which had lost its affection for Edwards during his first term. It was about this time that rumors first began to circulate that Edwards' one-time alter ego and confidant, Clyde C. Vidrine, was writing an exposé of his former friend and boss. The book, *Just Takin' Orders*, appeared in 1975 amid much press attention, but it did not resurrect Vidrine's own troubled personal life or career. He was eventually shot to death by a jealous husband outside a rural Louisiana courthouse. Edwards was easily re-elected, and my own victory, rolling up 924,325 votes, was the largest number of votes ever received by any candidate in the history of Louisiana. I had based my re-election campaign on the premise that I had kept my 1971 promises to the people of Louisiana: I had promised to give up my railroad career and be a full-time lieutenant governor.

I had promised to work to develop the Port of New Orleans, to stimulate Latin American trade, and to promote our economic development and tourism. I was honored and gratified that the people of Louisiana believed that I had kept my promises and rewarded me with such a tremendous victory.

An Important New Assignment

Edwin Edwards kept his word too and, as part of the reorganization of state government, appointed me to head the department of commerce and industry, giving me a free hand to name members of the board and to run the operation. I selected fifteen capable, dedicated citizens from all around Louisiana to serve on the new board of commerce and industry. It was a tremendous opportunity and challenge, the first meaningful administrative work any lieutenant governor had been given. Edwards was very plain-spoken in giving me the assignment: "If you can make this work, you'll have statewide approval. If you can't make this department successful, you'll be a political failure."

There are no training schools for running a department of commerce and nationwide industrial development program; I just had to jump in with both feet and learn the job as I went along. That meant working seven days a week from 6 A.M. till nearly midnight. I was soon putting five thousand miles a month on my Cadillac and making as many as three hundred personal appearances a month in Louisiana before all kinds of audiences. America was taken by surprise by this sudden burst of activity on the part of formerly sleepy Louisiana. When I attended a meeting of the National Association of Lieutenant Governors it was the first time a lieutenant governor from Louisiana had ever shown up. I established regular meetings with the foreign consuls in New Orleans, discussing ways we could develop or expand trade. This was to be a continuing interest of mine throughout my years as lieutenant governor. We established trade offices in Paris and Brussels.

Opening Windows to the World

In 1972, I proposed to the legislature that we should open a trade and development office in Japan. I could see that in the coming years Japan would become a vital factor in the international trading equation, and I thought that Louisiana would benefit by being one of the very first states to establish a beachhead there. Unfortunately, at that time we were still concentrating on trade relations with Europe and just beginning to think about significantly expanding our effort in Latin America. As usual, Louisiana was substantially behind the curve in reaching out to these new markets. We did finally open a Japanese trade office, after the marketplace was already crowded with competitors from many other states and nations. The competition was so brutal, in fact, that Louisiana simply gave up and closed the office in 1991, deciding to concentrate on developing the Mexican market closer to home. No more than the Japanese office cost, I thought that the state should have retained it (and should have kept the offices we closed in Brussels and Paris as well), but the point is: Louisiana arrived in the Japanese market too late to capture the lion's share of expanded trade.

Much was made, early in 1991, about the diplomatic wisdom of Gov. Buddy Roemer's wearing blue jeans to receive the Japanese general consul. I think that's perhaps an overrated concern; Huey Long used to greet visiting dignitaries in purple silk pajamas! What really counts is the professionalism, the determination, and the commitment of the state's trade officials. If Louisiana can demonstrate to prospective foreign trading partners that we have the long-term commitment to developing a trade relationship and the professional skill and ability to carry out our agreements, the personal style of a specific governor becomes almost incidental to our "big picture," long-range effort. I paid special attention to promoting use of Louisiana businesses. I met personally on many occasions with purchasing agents for major Louisiana corporations, urging them to issue purchase orders, whenever possible, to Louisiana manufacturers, wholesalers, and suppliers. It is a lesson we still have not learned. When the state placed a monumental order for bricks for the Aquarium of the Americas, the order went first to a company in Kentucky. When its bricks proved unacceptable, we reordered from a company in Texas, incurring long delays and greater cost. All the while, there are brick factories here in Louisiana and people who need the work.

I tried to pay attention not just to new businesses coming to Louisiana but to the support and expansion of existing businesses in the state; they are often the forgotten heroes of our economy. As early as 1977, I was saying that Louisiana could become a major new center for motion picture productions. Reporters who covered my energetic campaign to attract movie producers to Louisiana generally believed that it was an interesting but far-fetched dream. I did not agree, and recent developments in which as many as three major motion pictures were being filmed in New Orleans at the same time, proved me to be correct. Back in 1977, I pointed out to a meeting of the state film industry commission that in the preceding fiscal year, eight major motion pictures had been produced here. The filmmakers spent $11.4 million, and $3.8 million of that stayed in Louisiana. Six major nationwide television commercials were produced in Louisiana that same year. Motion pictures allow every section of the state to get a piece of the action, spreading around the jobs and the purchases of the production companies. As usual, we took the motion picture business seriously much later than many of our competitors.

We have not yet centralized and effectively coordinated state and local contact points to expedite and cut the red tape connected with the needs of producers, and that is a shame. I believe that is a shortsighted, costly mistake.

One of the big flash points of debate surrounding our efforts at industrial development was Louisiana's industrial tax exemption to attract new industry to the state by waiving state taxes on plants and equipment for up to ten years. Many factions believed that amounted to a "give away" to industry, unfair to working people and to existing businesses ln the state. They thought it ought to be repealed entirely. Governor Buddy Roemer, in 1991, compelled his state board of commerce and industry to reduce the amount of tax exemption depending on a complex scale of how well each company met environmental protection laws. Environmental protection is an absolutely essential element of maintaining our quality of life here in Louisiana and a problem which we ignored for much of our state's history. In fact, there were very few significant environmental statutes on the books prior to 1980. I never thought that new industry was incompatible with environmental safety.

After all, the industries we seek to induce to relocate to our state would, in all likelihood, be transferring significant numbers of people from other plants to new locations in Louisiana. It always seemed obvious that we could not succeed in attracting new industry if our environment were so degraded and destroyed that none of those people would agree to move here. The same considerations would be taken into account by industry in the areas of education, taxation, and other areas. So I never believed that meaningful environmental laws and firm enforcement would hinder our ability to attract the kinds of responsible industry we want and need. On the other hand, I also thought it absolutely essential we not accidently present the image of a state which is antagonistic to new industry. If a new industry believes Louisiana to be corrupt, and the rules for doing business here too complex and costly, we are simply not going to be competitive in the area of industrial development, no matter how aggressively we try. There needs to be an even-handed approach which cannot be misinterpreted by industry on either side of the environmental ledger.

As Louisiana's chief "industry hunter," I assembled the best support team I could find, led by a capable department secretary, Gilbert Lagasse, and Andrew Flores, now economic development director of Tucson, Arizona, and applied the proven principles of successful salesmanship. I adopted a "rifle" rather than a "shotgun" approach. We did not attempt to churn industrial interest by a mass marketing approach, hoping someone would take notice and contact us. Rather, my system was to specifically identify a target company and approach them personally and directly. For example, I spent a great deal of time talking with companies which already had a presence here but which retained their headquarters in some other state. I urged them to consider relocating here because of our pro-business climate.

Our Slipping Sales Effort

Our state seems to have run out of steam in the whole area of economic development. We're just now getting around to a meaningful tax exemption on inventories. I began to concentrate on attracting industries which created more jobs, labor-intensive companies, rather than just industries which were tied to our natural resources and thus required huge investment but created few permanent jobs, capital-intensive companies.

In fact, we have continued to slide in the business of attracting companies which created manufacturing jobs for our people. In 1979, my last year as lieutenant governor and chairman of the Board of Commerce and Industry, we were first in the nation in industrial expansion and second in the area of new and expanded facilities. It seems to me we are currently moving in the wrong direction, eliminating our entire fourteen-person international development section, concentrating, instead, on just keeping those industries which are already here. We're thinking stop-gap instead of long-range, which will prove to be a mistake of historic proportions. That is in stark contrast to the 1978 session, my last as lieutenant governor, in which we passed nine bills to spur the economy and attract new jobs, laws dealing with revenue bonding, leasing of public lands and buildings, tax credits, commerce and development corporations. By the end of 1979, the results were apparent with record-setting levels: $3.1 billion of investment,

10,788 new permanent and 26,540 new construction jobs spread among 71 new plants and 492 plant expansions. Most of those were directly attributable to our tax deferral and revenue bond financing programs.

Our efforts attracted national attention as well. Peter Greene, the experienced and respected editor and publisher of *World Marketing*, said, "Many U.S. states are currently quite active in soliciting new investment among both domestic and overseas companies. . . . One state seems to have an unfair advantage in this activity. That's because the individual who is the number one spokesman for the state is an outstanding promoter. The state is Louisiana and the individual referred to is Lt. Gov. James E. Fitzmorris, Jr." Greene, whom I had only recently met at a business development meeting I held for some two hundred Northeastern business executives at the Waldorf-Astoria Hotel in New York City, said, "He gets his message across in an easy manner, laced with sincerity, making it easy for one to become a believer. Other state promoters better watch out or he's going to corner the market."

I appreciated his kind review, but the real secret to effective industrial development this year is the same as it was in the 1970s: an excellent staff, sincerity, skill, and a high degree of salesmanship.

The Offshore Oil Port

One of the most important international investments Louisiana made was the $1 billion Louisiana Offshore Oil Port. LOOP was designed to receive the bulk of America's oil imports. This deep-water port, built off the Louisiana coast, was America's first facility designed to accommodate "super tankers" bringing crude oil imports to the country. It was planned to attract scores of new refining and petrochemical plants. We predicted that it would result in $2 billion in offshore investments and sixteen thousand new jobs.

Five years in planning, the LOOP was built in recognition of our continuing national dependence on foreign oil. No existing port could accommodate the super tankers, which were, at that time, forced to line up at sea, where their product was offloaded into smaller ships which could then shuttle the oil ashore. That time-consuming process added between ten and fifty cents per barrel to the price of oil. It would also be environmentally safer than the old system of having dozens of antiquated small tankers unloading oil in the middle of busy ports.

The super port was built near Grand Isle, site of one of Louisiana's few sand beaches. It boasted a depth of one hundred feet, easily sufficient for any tanker in existence. The platform at which the tankers tied up to unload could handle tankers up to 750,000 tons—half again as large as any tanker in use today. P. J. Mills, later executive assistant to the governor, was one of the first administrators of LOOP and did an excellent job. The port has not yet realized its full potential, due primarily to the depressed state of the American oil industry, but it will eventually prove to be one of the most important facilities in the nation and a wonderful, if rare, example of an instance in which Louisiana was farsighted and first to react to an important opportunity.

The Superdome Controversy

One of the great controversies during my second term was the cost and operation of the domed stadium. The Louisiana Superdome, as it came to be known, was operated by the Superdome Commission, of which I was a member. On November 10, 1975, I called a meeting of the commission, at which the question of an investigation of Superdome Services, Inc. (SSI) was the main item on the agenda.

I did not participate in the discussion, but former councilman James Moreau demanded that the corporation, which was headed by well-connected black leaders Sherman Copelin, now a state legislator, and Don Hubbard, be investigated for possible abuses connected with their contract to clean and maintain the dome. He was joined in that motion by commission members state representative Kevin Reilly of Baton Rouge and Shreveport mayor Calhoun Allen. Among those opposed were Mayor Landrieu, senate president Michael O'Keefe, restaurant operator Owen Brennen, Dr. Rene Pigeon, and Peter Babin. The principals of SSI were founders of COUP, one of the most potent black political organizations in New Orleans. They were highly controversial figures. Copelin had previously admitted receiving fifty thousand dollars in payoffs from the Family Health Foundation, a local agency which received federal funds. The head of the agency went to prison, but Copelin was not charged. Attorney General Billy Guste found no wrongdoing connected with SSI's

Superdome role, and District Attorney Harry Connick refused to recuse himself from the matter, despite complaints that he was politically connected to the SSI leaders and personally involved, since his brother, Billy, held a key management position with the Superdome.

Guste did rule, however, that all legislators on the commission must resign when their terms expired because the commission, as established by law, was really part of the executive branch of government. The same ruling was extended years later when insurance commissioner Doug Green, before his conviction, challenged a suit brought by the state ethics board which also had legislator-members. The dome, already suspect because of substantial cost overruns, was losing money consistently. In January 1976, it reported a loss of $660,677, which brought the facility's losses to $2 million over the previous seven months. Within weeks, the dome's contracts with an advertising agency and parking service were also under fire. The commission ordered a study conducted by the reputable consulting firm of Arthur D. Little. The report was held by Edwards' commissioner of administration Charles E. Roemer, who said that he was only holding the report because he was waiting for additions to the recommendations section.

I personally led the fight to hire a professional security chief to oversee ADF, which held the security contract for the dome. On January 15, 1976, the *Times-Picayune* praised that action, but that controversy was only the tip of the iceberg. Reilly complained publicly that Landrieu was an ineffective commission chairman and demanded that he resign; Landrieu refused. I believed strongly in the concept of the Superdome and knew what it could do for our economy, but I thought the whole facility was in danger of being destroyed by the suspicion, controversy, and infighting. I asked all members of the commission to refrain from second-guessing the consultant and making public comment until the report was made public. The study recommended that the dome's contracts with sub-contractors be redrawn, that appointments of commissioners be redone, and that a new Superdome Authority be created to place management of the dome with a professional, private, management company.

In the midst of all this controversy, we were seriously attempting to lure professional baseball to the dome, offering free rent and picking up 40 percent of the game-day costs, up to $1,200,000. Whether because of uncertainty about the management or for other reasons, we found no takers. By April, a grand jury had found no evidence of mismanagement at the dome, although Baton Rouge district attorney Ossie Brown strenuously disagreed. That month, the dome was forced to turn out the lights and suspend clean-up in order to make it through the end of the fiscal year. Much of the controversy centered around dome director Ben Levy, a former chief administrative officer of the city, and Billy Connick, brother of the district attorney. When Edwards announced that he was placing commissioner of administration Roemer in charge of reorganizing the dome, the district attorney asked him not to pick on his brother in the process. The commission adopted a drastic $22.8 million standstill budget and shortly thereafter Levy resigned. There was even talk that the dome might be sold by the state, and at least one bid was received and rejected.

Edwards announced that he would undertake to adopt the consultant's recommendation that dome management be privatized, and he entered into discussions with Ogden Foods, which had considerable experience in that area. I named Billy Connick to help develop guidelines for new management, to which state senator Nat Kiefer objected. Ogden finally assumed management of the dome, later to be succeeded by the Hyatt Management Corporation, and the original commission was allowed to expire. Primarily, what we learned through this expensive and sometimes explosive experience was what I had believed all along: Political figures and their friends are not particularly well adapted to the management and operation of multi-million-dollar public projects such as this. Privatization is frequently the only way the public's interest can be protected. I had the same reaction, years later, when certain forces suggested that the city of New Orleans buy and operate New Orleans Public Service. I thought this was a highly inadvisable idea for there are very real limits as to what any spoils system is capable of operating.

The World's Fair Success and Failure

Shortly after we extricated ourselves from the dome controversy, Edwards appointed me to the steering committee to plan for a proposed World's Fair for New Orleans. We had not hosted such an international event since the disastrous Cotton Exposition near the turn of the century. The executive director of that event had absconded with most of the money and gone to South America. This time, we optimistically predicted that the fair would generate $400 million for the local economy and bring twenty million tourists to the city. Unfortunately, management of the fair was once again mired in politics and controversy, and the marketing effort was, in my opinion, mishandled from the beginning. By the time the fair stumbled to the end of its summer run, there was no money around for anyone to abscond with, many of the contractors were bankrupt, and most of the exhibitors highly disappointed. Nonetheless, the World's Fair did completely refurbish a previously rundown area near the riverfront. In its wake, the successful riverwalk commercial development and the renaissance of the adjacent warehouse district as a residential and entertainment center became a reality, so, in historical terms at least, the legacy of the fair is an undisputed success.

Would the Third Try Be the Charm?

Perhaps the most important personal and political decision of my final term as lieutenant governor came quite soon after my record-setting re-election. Mayor Landrieu was reaching the end of his second term and could not seek re-election. On the other hand, at the end of his current term, Governor Edwards would also be unable to seek another. The question, then, was: What road would Jimmy Fitzmorris choose? I had ample advice and plenty of support for either decision. Mayor Landrieu, who had defeated me in a painful 1969 campaign, urged me to come home and be mayor. He offered his help, and so did many other business, political, and civic leaders. It was a tempting choice. I had wanted to be mayor of New Orleans as long as I could remember. It was the closest job to the political frontlines. I had seen how much a really effective mayor could accomplish through my years on the council at the side of Mayor Chep Morrison. I had seen how a vacillating or ineffective city administration could set the city back by decades. I had not forgotten the important challenges I had enumerated for the city in my two races for mayor. Indeed, there was a sense in which this was the post which, twice denied me, was the prize I valued most highly.

Yet, I had just won more votes in a statewide campaign than any man in Louisiana history. The future looked promising for a race for governor of Louisiana. Certainly I saw challenges and opportunities to serve in that role as well. In the meantime, I had a moral responsibility to those people who had just re-elected me. I had made very specific promises to them about what I would do in the areas of economic development, international trade, and improvement in the job opportunities for people in every part of our state. Having made those promises, could I suddenly walk away, in mid-term, to return to New Orleans? The polls all showed that I could be elected. I had the necessary network of friends and supporters to finance an aggressive campaign. I dearly loved the city and continued to live there even after my election as lieutenant governor, spending as much time in my New Orleans office as in my capitol suite. I knew each of the prospective candidates for mayor. I was familiar with their individual strengths and weaknesses, their collective assets and responsibilities. I knew that several of them would not run if I chose to try for this position once again.

It was time to end the suspense, to allow them to get on with their lives as I had to do with my own. Thus it was, that on October 12, 1976, I addressed an overflow crowd at the Fairmont Hotel in downtown New Orleans. I was flattered by their attention, their advice, and their support, I told them. It was now time to decide. "The 1977 mayor's election is about twelve months away; potential candidates want to plan their campaigns, and concerned citizens are interested in knowing who the candidates will be," I said. "The people of this city have been very good to me; the people of this state have been extraordinarily good to me. I feel that to continue to play games, dodge the questions of the press, banter the idea with my friends, spar with hopeful men and women with aspirations to be mayor would not be fair." I explained that I had promised the people of Louisiana that I would serve four more years as their lieutenant governor. "I made that pledge in good faith, honesty, and with the sincerity of my convictions. I have never, ever in public service betrayed the confidence and trust of the people, and I will not do it now."

"I am here to tell you this morning, and to end all speculation, that I will not offer myself as a candidate for mayor of the city of New Orleans next fall. That is a firm and definite decision, and it will not change." I told them that I would, in time, announce for governor of Louisiana and ask their help once again. I concluded, "Again I thank you for coming this morning. I can never repay your loyalty, dedication, and friendship. I only hope that each of you knows that deep in my heart, I have a special, personal love for each of you, for without your friendship and the loyal friendship of thousands more like you, I would be nothing." With the cheers of hundreds of my dear friends from my earliest days as an unknown, untried, young contender for the city council—friends who had stayed with me through the darkness, sadness and uncertainty of two bitter defeats for mayor—and new friends who had joined our campaign and our celebration in two resounding victories for lieutenant governor, I closed forever the door to my private, personal dream of becoming mayor of New Orleans.

I wondered what my parents would have advised. I wondered what counsel my friend Chep Morrison would have had. But this decision was one I had ultimately to make alone, as every candidate finally must. I could not, would not, look back. From that day on, my sights were firmly set on the 1979 race for governor.

Chapter 7

Bitter Harvest
From Vote Fraud to Brilab

Sunday morning, October 28, 1979, the "bull dogs," early editions of Louisiana's major daily newspapers, were already off the presses as Gloria, Lisa, and I wound our way through the darkened streets from the Fairmont Hotel to our lakefront home on Emerald Street.

"**It's Unofficially Official**," the banner headlines read: "**Fitzmorris to Face Treen in Governor's Race**." Vote totals reported to the state's sixty-four clerks of court by election commissioners in Louisiana's 2,899 precincts showed that I was firmly in second place with 280,490 votes, compared to Louis Lambert's 279,014. In other words, I had won a spot in the runoff election, set for December 8, by 1,476 votes. I felt relieved, though thoroughly exhausted. There was broad, general agreement among most political observers that I would defeat the Republican candidate, Rep. David C. Treen, decisively in a two-man contest. I had a far more comprehensive personal organization and much higher name recognition. I also had a strong, intuitive feeling that I would receive the endorsement of at least three of the other major Democratic candidates in the primary during the course of the runoff election. I knew Senator Mouton, Representative Henry, and Secretary of State Hardy very well. I knew their personal philosophies and their political agendas. I had spoken to Mouton and Hardy in the hours immediately after the primary and had been encouraged by both conversations.

Endorsements by Mouton, Henry, and Hardy would bring me a whole new cadre of supporters and potential contributors. Their support, added to my already substantial vote from the primary, meant that I was well ahead in the runoff. As a sheer matter of cold, rational, political judgment, I could not see how Treen, even with a well-financed campaign, could make up the distance in the time remaining. In fact, I thought it very possible he might withdraw from the race in view of that combination of factors. We were friends and had genuine personal respect for each other's ability and integrity, so I thought it possible he might not want to spend millions more in a losing cause if it appeared I would likely win. I was not alone in that opinion.

Beginning the Next Campaign

My mission in the next few days would be simply to appear confident, in firm control and command of my campaign. Thus, I decided to waste no valuable time before consolidating my base of support and getting my runoff campaign on the road. There had been some talk about taking a few days off to rest, after the breakneck pace of the primary, but I did not want to waste even one day before getting my organization into action again.

Dr. Jess Lair, in his book, *I Ain't Much, Baby, But I'm All I've Got,* talks about personalities "addicted to adrenalin," and I suppose I am a classic example. In three decades in public life, I never found a way to campaign hesitantly or half-heartedly; I always went full speed ahead. Nonetheless, I was tired that Sunday morning, my staff was tired, and I was certain that the long campaign had taken its toll on the media as well. Despite our exhaustion, I decided that we should only treat ourselves to a few hours' rest before kicking off my runoff campaign with a full-scale press conference at my home. Throughout my career, my relations with the press had generally been excellent. I had a reputation for answering questions honestly and for being accessible. In addition, the fact that I was generally in one stage or another of a constant stream of new programs and developments made my office "good copy," and we were a frequent source of news articles and interviews through the years.

I was seasoned enough in the business of politics, however, to know that opinion was not unanimously held by the media. Some reporters questioned my depth and substance, and I knew why: A key element of my role as lieutenant governor and chairman of the department of commerce and industry was business development. When a new business opened or a significant industrial expansion occurred, I was frequently asked to officiate at the event, and I thought it part of my responsibility to assist when I could. Thus, to some reporters who covered only those occasional, ceremonial functions, it was tempting to dismiss Jimmy Fitzmorris as a superficial, shallow, "ribbon cutter." I believe the reporters who knew me best generally thought I was as well read, as thoroughly conversant with the whole spectrum of challenges confronting Louisiana as any man in public life. Indeed, I had spent eight long years studying every state agency and program in an effort to become the best prepared governor in our lifetime. Nonetheless, not every reporter got to see that side of me.

Consequently, during the campaign—in conjunction with thoughtful advice from Kirk Melancon and Jim Harris, who handled media relations on my staff and from others—I made a concerted effort to solidify and enhance my relations with members of the media I had not previously known well. I tried to look more "gubernatorial" in dress and appearance. I tried to slow down the daily pace of my campaign to give reporters an opportunity to see the more personal side of me, so they might better understand my motivations, my hopes and aspirations for our state. Partly for that reason I decided to begin this second stage of the election campaign by shuttling the jumble of television cameras, radio mikes, and print reporters to the relative serenity of my home. Gloria, Lisa, and I lived in a comfortable, although certainly not grandiose, home on a corner lot in the "East Lakefront" section of New Orleans. The Crescent City is a rich mixture of distinctive neighborhoods, and the lakefront is one of the more secluded, on the suburban fringe of the city. Here, I was usually able to relax, working in my yard or sitting by my pool on the few occasions when I could steal a few personal moments from my hectic political schedule.

A standing-room-only crowd of statewide reporters collected that Sunday morning, the first day of daylight savings time for that season. Because of the time change, half the crowd was on time, the other half, an hour late. They were greeted by my family, key staff personnel, and supporters and given an enthusiastic welcome by "Governor Fitzmorris," our family dachshund. "Guv" had been a gift, months earlier, his name jokingly chosen so that, no matter what happened that year, there would always be a "governor" at our address. The conference was friendly and relaxed. Most of the reporters had questions about my plans for the rest of the campaign and any early intentions I might wish to reveal for my administration. That afternoon trooper Billy Booth and I kept a longtime commitment, flying by helicopter to help our trusted friend and supporter, former Donaldsonville mayor Dr. D. C. Foti, dedicate a shrine to St. Jude which he had built across the street from his home. Uncharacteristically for me, I was so tired I dozed on the chopper during the trip.

Early Warnings of Trouble

By the next morning, telephone calls were already coming into our office with ominous frequency. My friends and supporters, particularly from rural parishes, were deeply and genuinely concerned about serious irregularities which had apparently occurred in the election that had taken place just thirty-six hours earlier. I stayed in my office in the State Office Building on Loyola Avenue in downtown New Orleans, fielding the calls with a growing sense of alarm. We decided not to alert the press at that point. It was still generally assumed that I would be the nominee against Treen, and I saw no advantage in unnecessarily confusing the issue. Rather, I decided that until the voting machines were opened and checked and the results made official, I would continue to keep my normal schedule. Accordingly, that night I kept another longstanding commitment, flying to Monroe to address the Traffic Club. I returned immediately to New Orleans to coordinate our workers stationed throughout the state for the opening of the voting machines the next morning.

I did not attend the machine openings in either New Orleans or Baton Rouge, choosing to remain by the telephone so I could check developments around the state. In looking back, I realize how naive I was, even after thirty years in public life. I did not then believe that an election which had just been honestly won in the daylight could erode under cover of darkness. My staff did not share my confidence in the integrity of the electoral process, and we did our best to be represented at all the major events of that day. Bill Allerton, Pat Gallwey, and George Simno III went to the machine openings in New Orleans. The results were threatening as the official vote totals began to soften and shift around the state. The machines were opened, and we watched with mounting horror as Saturday night's lead evaporated and our total fell steadily behind that of Louis Lambert. Carol Daigle's daughter,

Michele, stationed in Baton Rouge with my old friend, the late Stanley Gross, called to say that votes appeared to have been "rolled," with at least one hundred new votes appearing on seven machines for Lambert, votes which had not been reported Saturday night, adding 925 votes to his total in that parish.

Along with this disturbing news from the voting machine warehouses, we were hearing of apparent vote buying, intimidation, curious voting machine failures, and unexplained irregularities with absentee balloting throughout the state. It presented a pattern and practice of wrongdoing on a scale never before seen in Louisiana political history. By nightfall, our worst fears had been realized. My Saturday night margin of 1,476 had vanished. In its place was a Louis Lambert lead of 2,458.

Going to Court

We quickly decided that if the election could not be won fairly in the polling places, it would have to be won in court. Thus, we embarked on the perilous and uncharted waters of a statewide vote fraud challenge. Louisiana law treated that subject almost as an afterthought. The few statutes on the books were confusing and sometimes contradictory. State law required us to be in court, complete proof in hand, within five days of the official outcome. Meeting that deadline would have required legions of lawyers, an army of local investigators spread throughout the state, and unlimited financial resources.

To meet this challenge the Fitzmorris campaign had only a handful of dedicated volunteer lawyers, a depleted bank account already seriously in the red, and a clock that ticked mercilessly toward that judicial moment of truth set to come the following Tuesday. Nonetheless, with our choice reduced to struggle or surrender, we began to investigate and to fight. In retrospect, we had no real chance from the outset; the complex stumbling blocks established by Louisiana law were too overpowering. What we had was a small, brave, brilliant team of volunteer legal talent, the likes of which I have never seen before or since. In New Orleans, we had Larry Smith from Levy, Smith and Gennusa. He was president of the Young Lawyers Section of the American Trial Lawyers Association and a member of the board of governors of the Louisiana Trial Lawyers Association. Larry was a ferocious fighter and friend who devoted over fifty thousand dollars worth of time to our case. Charlie Cabibi, my devoted friend and chief counsel for the campaign, also played a crucial role in the case.

Charlie researched Louisiana's election laws, prepared pleadings, coordinated transportation of the volumes of documents from various officials around the state to Baton Rouge for the trial, attended the trial, and represented our interests at various court-ordered recounts in individual precincts. Charlie, who had already done so much on our behalf during the campaign, now devoted another fifty thousand dollars in time during these crucial days. He was tireless. One morning, he worked until 3:00 A.M. and, when he returned to the hotel to ask for a 5:00 A.M. wake-up call, the clerk asked why he even bothered to check in. Charlie replied that it was worth the price of the room just to get a good shower. Working with him were my brother Norris, George Simno III, Frank Courtenay, Chuck Zatarain, and a handful of young lawyers. In Baton Rouge, we had Charlie Grey, my executive assistant, the late former secretary of state Wade O. Martin, Jr., and the incomparable Rolfe McCollister, Sr. Rolfe had been my friend for thirty years, since we were first appointed to serve on the Board of Public Welfare, one of the "blue ribbon" boards established by Gov. Robert Kennon. Rolfe, and members of his firm, McCollister, McCleary, Fazio, Mixon and Holliday, had signed substantial bank notes to finance our campaign. We used their firm as a headquarters throughout the court challenge.

They contributed lawyers, investigators, and clerical personnel, and asked nothing in return. We became the firm's virtually sole and non-paying client for the duration of the trials. Through our subsequent fund-raising activities we were eventually able to repay the $10,500 in actual costs for the depositions, filing fees, and expenses the firm had advanced us, but Rolfe never sent us a bill for the hundred thousand dollars worth of time he and his associates devoted to attempting to salvage this election for us and the people of Louisiana. It is an act of friendship I will never forget and which I could never even begin to repay.

We began to investigate the leads which poured into our offices. We ran ads in newspapers throughout the state asking, "Did Your Vote for Governor Really Count?" and detailing the kinds of fraud and irregularities which might have occurred. We asked voters who might have been victimized to contact us so we could investigate further. The ads resulted in literally hundreds of complaints of varying validity, each of which we painstakingly investigated in detail.

What Did We Find?

We discovered the most pervasive, widespread pattern of abuse, fraud, and voting irregularities ever seen in Louisiana political life.

The picture of wrongdoing knew no parish boundaries; it extended into every sector of the state. We also learned that discovering widespread vote fraud and proving every instance of what we found were two distinctly different tasks.

Bill Allerton spent the entire weekend in the secretary of state's office examining voting registers from individual precincts and became convinced that a giant, wholesale election fraud had taken place. In some cases, the signatures on the register, where each voter signs in, were obviously in the same handwriting. In many cases, more votes were cast than the corresponding number of signatures on the register. In other cases, there were more signatures on the register than votes recorded. The glaring irregularities were too numerous and widespread simply to dismiss as "accidental." We came to believe that there was a one-word explanation for the shocking events surrounding this election: *fraud.* We began with the most widespread area of irregular activity, the absentee ballots. Because of the manner in which Louisiana absentee voting was then conducted, it had historically been one of the most attractive and pervasive sources of fraud.

In earlier times, absentee balloting had been tampered with through a "daisy chain" system in which a political organization furnished a prospective absentee voter with a premarked ballot. The voter took that ballot with him to the polling place, where he requested a fresh, absentee ballot. He then gave the premarked ballot to the officials, took the new, unmarked ballot to the political bosses, and collected his pay. The new ballot was then marked and the whole process began anew with the next absentee voter. Our 1979 investigations revealed variations on that theme, widespread irregular and incorrect activities in the way absentee ballots were cast, handled, and counted. The situation was so serious that we asked the court to have all absentee ballots in each of the state's sixty-four parishes recounted. In fact, some seven hundred absentee ballots were found to be so tainted that they were simply thrown out by the court. Some ballots were premarked by clerks of court, indicating to the absentee voter the clerk's preferred candidates in the election. In other cases, ballots cast for candidates the clerks opposed were simply defaced, erased, torn, or smudged so they would later be automatically discarded when the absentee ballots were opened and counted.

We had numerous reports of local clerks opening and reviewing absentee ballots before they were sealed into the voting machines. Absentee ballots from eight precincts in East Baton Rouge Parish simply disappeared altogether! Louisiana law provided that absentee ballots could only be cast at the clerk of court's office or, in Orleans Parish, at the civil sheriff's office. We found many instances in which absentee ballots were cast at private residences, nursing homes, and other locations. Some absentee ballots were opened and registered on the poll lists before the closing of the polls, contrary to law. Some people were allowed to vote by absentee ballot and then return on election day and vote again. It should be clearly noted that Commissioner Lambert consistently denied any personal involvement in the planning and direction of improper election activities on the part of persons who may have supported his candidacy or any personal knowledge of such activities. No such personal involvement or knowledge was ever proved, and I believe his assertion.

A Statewide Pattern of Abuse

In *Ascension Parish*, home of Louis Lambert, voter turnout was 78.7 percent, fifth highest in the state. That compared with a statewide average of only 70.5 percent. We received numerous complaints of vote buying and voter intimidation. The clerk of court allowed absentee ballots to be distributed, cast, and tabulated on election day.

In a subsequent investigation of voting machines in the warehouse, we found a device attached to one machine which mechanically advanced the vote counter. In Ward 7, Precinct 2, one driver took people to the polls and accompanied them into the voting booths. Lambert received his largest majority in this disputed parish, 73.7 percent. I was a distant second with 8 percent. In *Beauregard Parish*, we received numerous complaints of vote buying for Lambert including one instance in which a voter received a cash payment of fifty-seven dollars to pay his utility bill in return for casting his vote for Lambert. One of the most flagrant cases was that of *East Baton Rouge Parish.* That clerk of court has only recently been convicted in an unconnected criminal matter and removed from office. In 1979, we were told that he reopened and reviewed absentee ballots after they had first been counted. In seventy-eight precincts, more votes were cast than the number of voters who signed the poll registers. Lambert was the big winner in each of these disputed precincts, drawing 14,332 votes to my 6,409. The votes cast in excess of persons signing the registers totaled 1,670.

Conversely, in other precincts, 637 more persons signed the poll registers than the number of votes counted. Apologists for the system insisted that these were not Fitzmorris votes removed from the count but voters who signed the register, got tired of waiting for a machine, and went home without voting. I found this hard to believe because the wait at most precincts is *before* the voter gets to the table where he signs the register, a few feet from the machines. At that point, the wait is usually minimal. We found 4,436 votes cast in precincts where the public counter on the machines did not match the ending number on the same machines' protective counters. This was later explained as "harmless machine malfunction." In seven precincts, when the machines were opened, at least one hundred votes per machine were added to Lambert's vote more than the number the commissioners had reported seeing on election night. The clerk admitted that it was "very unusual," but denied wrongdoing on anyone's part. Lambert gained 925 votes more than the commissioners had reported seeing on election night, and wound up getting 30.2 percent of the vote, one of his largest wins in the entire state.

In *Richland Parish,* the tools to control, repair, and manipulate the equipment in the voting machines simply "disappeared" ten days before the election. In *East Feliciana Parish,* more votes were tabulated than persons who signed the poll registers. This was another big parish for Lambert; he won 51.9 percent of the vote in the six-man race. *Livingston Parish* was one of the most notorious examples of irregular activities. Plainclothes police chased poll watchers away from some polling places while parish law enforcement personnel spent the entire day electioneering and campaigning for Lambert in at least seven precincts. Could not the register of voters have complained to the sheriff? Probably not, since registrar Winona Graves' husband, Odom, was in a fierce battle for sheriff against the incumbent. Sheriff Watson was very busy in what would prove to be a desperate, losing battle for re-election. He sponsored a jambalaya party and "garage sale" inside one polling place, Ward 1, Precinct 2, and, when state police intervened after a complaint, simply refused to move. His activities were recorded by a Baton Rouge television station.

Voters from outside the parish were allowed to come into precincts, sign affidavits stating that they were properly registered but somehow omitted from the polling list, and cast votes. Poll watchers complained to the commissioners who decided, on a 3-2 vote, to ignore the complaints. One of those complaining, William King, was subsequently threatened and warned not to testify about what he saw on election day. And Louis Lambert received 62 percent of the vote.

Orleans Parish had more precincts than any other parish in the state and complaints were rife there as well. There were numerous reports of vote buying, with five-, ten-, and twenty- dollar bills taped to the back of Lambert ballots. This practice was particularly pronounced in the lower Ninth Ward, where one of the black political organizations used physical intimidation and threats to support its ticket, with Louis Lambert at the top of the ballot. Numerous election commissions intimidated voters, telling them, among other things, that there was a strict three-minute limit on completing the ballot, after which they entered the polling booth and forcibly "helped" the "dawdling citizen" cast his vote.

In Ward 9, Precinct 23, a commissioner forced his way into the booth, over the objections of the voter, and simply cast that person's vote for Lambert, even after being told he was not the voter's choice. Wards 3, 4, 10, 11, and 12 all reported a similar pattern of intimidation. Numerous voting machines simply failed to work; others were found jammed with match sticks so Fitzmorris votes would not register. Several voting machines in Ward 7 were found to already have one hundred votes for Lambert on the machines when they were opened to begin voting at the start of election day. We have no way to know how many similar incidents we failed to catch and correct as voting began. In fact, in Precinct 8 of this ward, almost 10 percent of the persons shown as having voted that day later swore that they did not go to the polls at all. The same was true in other precincts. We uncovered numerous Ninth Ward cases in which paid, "roving voters" went from precinct to precinct. At each stop they signed an affidavit stating that they lived in that precinct and had been accidentally left off the voters' register, whereupon they voted for Lambert and moved on to the next precinct to repeat the process.

In a number of precincts the poll registers were located well away from the voting machines, making it impossible for commissioners stationed at the machines to tell whether the persons in line had already signed the register or, in fact, whether they had already voted. Some thirty-three precinct polling places were suddenly moved without first gaining the permission of the federal court or the U.S. attorney general, as was required by the federal Voting Rights Act. Even Lambert subsequently agreed, in his own court petition, that such wholesale changes could have affected the outcome of the election.

In *St. Helena Parish*, forty-seven federal poll watchers supervised the precinct commissioners as they wrote down their vote totals at the end of election night. Yet, when the machines were later opened, three of the machines suddenly showed an additional one hundred votes each for Lambert. Two voting machines had no absentee votes shown at all and, in several instances, more votes were tabulated than persons who signed the poll registers. Two persons swore that they actually saw votes changes from 5 to 105 for Lambert by commissioners. In one instance, the commissioner simply took the keys to the machine home with him while the machine was unattended after voting ended, before it was opened for the official count.

In *St. Landry Parish*, several commissioners swore that seals were attached to the machines on election night as the law required. Yet, when the same machines were later checked at the warehouse, the seals were missing and three of the machines suddenly showed a difference in votes from that recorded election night. We found this to be a recurring complaint, with as many as one-third of the protective seals missing in some parishes when checked after the election. Without such seals, anyone with access to one of the many unaccounted-for keys and a simple tool could easily have changed votes on any of those machines.

Tangipahoa Parish reported similar problems with vote buying for Lambert. In Ward 6, Precincts 7 and 7A, commissioners tabulated seventeen Lambert votes election night. When the machines were opened there was an even one-hundred-vote increase for

Lambert.It was of interest to us that this sudden hundred-vote increase pushed the voter turnout in Precinct 7A to 84 percent. The average turnout in the parish was 73.2 percent. If these sudden, mysterious hundred votes were subtracted, the turnout for Precinct 7A went back down to 69.24 percent, more closely in line with the average for the rest of the parish.

In *Iberville Parish*, a woman named Edna Molden was said to have taken at least fifteen persons into the voting booth, contrary to law. We also found persons who had been paid for their votes, persons who had voted both absentee and in person, and numerous instances of intimidation and interference by commissioners. Another hundred post-election votes for Lambert appeared on a machine in *West Feliciana Parish*, while the public counter on one *West Carroll Parish* machine showed 94 votes while the machine certificate indicated that 187 votes had actually been counted. In *Lafayette*, Donald G. Bertrand signed an affidavit swearing that when he went to vote at Ward 5, Precinct 1, in the Scott school gymnasium, he tried to vote for number one on the machine for governor (Fitzmorris), but the lever failed to work so he selected an alternate choice. Based on his complaint, it is impossible to know how many votes I lost in that precinct. In the early days after the election, that is part of what we found, what we believed to be just the tip of the iceberg. And then we found Jerome Sauer.

Jerome Sauer had once been a key and trusted employee of the Fowler family which, through the late Doug Fowler and then his son Jerry, had controlled the Louisiana commissioner of elections position for decades. Sauer contacted Carol Daigle of my office when he heard a rumor that we were attempting to determine whether voting machines could be mechanically "rigged." He was plainly afraid for his personal safety when he spoke with us. He had insisted on a secretive, secluded meeting site. Sauer wanted no money or anything else from us. He just wanted someone to listen and take seriously what he knew, and what he knew was plenty: He showed us a small stick, similar to what you might find in a candied apple. With this thin, pointed device, he showed us how a person, after quickly and easily disarming the protective cover on the rear of a voting machine, could manipulate votes in favor of any candidate he wished. He had told this story before. When he first discovered that such machine tampering was possible, he contacted the manufacturer and arranged to demonstrate the device.

The manufacturer's representative, whether from fear that public knowledge of the machine's fallibility to tampering would harm his business or from some darker motive, secretly arranged to have Sauer arrested midway through the demonstration on charges that he was trying to extort payment for what he knew. Sauer was acquitted but he lost his job, and his reputation was ruined. The surrounding publicity made it virtually impossible for him to find suitable employment for years afterward. He showed us the device. Later he showed it to the court and a legislative joint committee.

So What Else Is New?

So we were now armed with the mechanism, the means by which machines could be rigged, as well as with scores of examples of vote fraud and irregularities. It was only then that we discovered one of the most disturbing, depressing, and discouraging facts of Louisiana political life: Few persons were surprised by our revelations, and hardly anyone was offended. I received a call Sunday, November 4, from one who understood my predicament—the president of the United States.

I had admired much of what Jimmy Carter had accomplished as governor of Georgia; his blend of fiscal restraint and social responsibility was much like the administration I hoped to create in Louisiana. I had been one of the first, few prominent Democrats to risk supporting his dark-horse candidacy for the presidency, and we had kept in touch after he was elected. His call to my office in the State Office Building that Sunday morning was taken by one of my security people, a black, ex-New Orleans Saint football player. His appearance as he announced the call made it plain that this was the first time he had ever answered a telephone to find the president of the United States at the other end of the line. Carter was sympathetic and understanding. He, too, had once gone to sleep thinking he had been elected governor and awakened to find his victory had evaporated during the night. Louisiana was not the only state in which such an event could occur. Consequently, he was not shocked to hear the news, but he understood better than almost anyone my sense of pain, and he shared my disappointment. His kind call did much to lift my spirits as we prepared that Sunday for the following week's trial.

Politics in Louisiana had been so corrupt for so long that the average voter and much of the press simply dismissed our findings as one more example of "Louisiana politics as usual." There was certainly an abundance of evidence to support that notion. During this election, before it and later, major and minor elections in every part of the state, including two prominent congressional races, were challenged.

In *St. Charles Parish*, a former police jury president who had resigned shortly before being convicted of extortion was released from prison, whereupon he ran for the police jury again. Legally, he should have been denied the right even to vote, let alone run for office, following his conviction. After an illegal candidacy which resulted in victory, the state simply applied the Louisiana solution: The governor hastily pardoned him so he could take his oath of office and return to a position of trust and power.

In *Vernon Parish*, police jury candidate Jack Singletary died between the first primary and the runoff. Nevertheless, he managed to defeat his opponent, Allie James, by more than two hundred votes. Cynics said that this proved that in Louisiana the dead could not only vote; they could be elected!

In *Calcasieu Parish*, District Attorney Bill Knapp obtained indictments against five employees of elections commissioner Douglas Fowler for perjury, theft, and illegal campaign activities on behalf of Fowler's son Jerry, who succeeded him in office. In the months following the election one conviction was reversed and the other indictments just faded from the headlines. In addition, allegations were made that thousands of dollars in state contracts were awarded by Fowler's office to friends, supporters, or even employees of that agency for the transportation and storing of voting machines. Several other district attorneys made headlines with criminal charges or pledges of grand jury investigations but, for the most part, they were soon forgotten after the interest in the election subsided. *Newsweek* magazine, reporting the election outcome, simply sighed and titled its piece, "Louisiana: How Votes Are Rigged."

Attorney General William Guste had been my friend since our days at Jesuit High School. He had later been a New Orleans state senator before winning his statewide position the same year I won the lieutenant governorship, where he remained until his retirement in 1992. He had endorsed my candidacy for governor. Guste was always sympathetic and considerate.

His staff revisited the results of our own investigation and referred eighteen incidents to local district attorneys, but little action took place on most of the 124 specific allegations we presented to his office. He was traveling in Israel during the weeks after the election but returned in time to tell the next legislature that the election fraud proved that his office needed more staff and money. The *Times-Picayune*'s Iris Kelso perhaps explained it most succinctly in a column entitled, "Votes for the Birds." She quoted a political expert who said that I lost because I didn't get enough "extra votes." "In Louisiana," he explained, "its like growing figs in your back yard. You have to grow enough for both you and the birds." In other words, the Fitzmorris campaign failed because I neglected to get enough extra votes to make up for those I should have known would be stolen from me! It was an attitude reminiscent of the late Gov. Earl K. Long when, in the 1950s, reformers unveiled voting machines to replace the notoriously corrupt paper ballot system. "Man made 'em," Uncle Earl snorted. "Man can cheat on 'em."

I had believed that we had grown beyond that. I surrounded myself, during thirty years in public life, with idealistic young people who shared that belief. In my campaign, I told the people of Louisiana that we had grown beyond that. The events of October 27 and the days which followed proved that we were wrong. By late in the week following the election, we all realized that the differences between the vote reported Saturday night and the results shown when the machines were reopened were historic and monumental. That Tuesday, Richard Hughes, elections divisions director for the secretary of state, told the press that mistakes are often found on the unofficial total but that such mistakes are usually off-setting, so the official and unofficial vote totals usually wind up only a couple of hundred votes apart. But this year, my candidacy had gone from a twenty-three-hundred vote lead to a twenty-four-hundred vote deficit in two days. Clearly, this shift was of massive proportions. In a statement to the people of Louisiana on Sunday, November 4, 1979, I said that we would be going to court in an attempt to have the genuine will of the people, as shown by Saturday night's totals, reinstated.

Facing the Insurmountable Obstacle

We knew that the task would be incredibly difficult, involving superhuman efforts to subpoena voting documents from individual precincts in every parish of the state, bringing the documents and the clerks of court and other election officials to Baton Rouge for depositions and the subsequent trial. Our task was made much more difficult because, despite a Wednesday order from Attorney General Guste that voting machines not be cleared until this challenge was decided, many clerks of court ignored the order and wiped out all the machine totals, thus destroying vital evidence we needed in the trial.

The Legal Team Needs a Leader

As the huge dimensions of the problem confronting us became increasingly apparent, we began to give serious consideration to naming a paid lawyer with extensive vote fraud experience to lead our legal team. I had the utmost confidence in the volunteer lawyers from throughout the state who had been investigating and preparing this case; they will have my gratitude forever.

The simple fact was: We were running out of time and we believed that retaining an attorney with a high-profile track record in handling such challenges might boost our effort. The Lambert camp took this challenge seriously as well, as you might expect. After all, between the two of us alone, we had already invested about $7 million, and the outcome of the primary was still in doubt. Lambert wasted no time in fielding his own top-flight legal team including the late state senator Nat Kiefer, the late Gibson Tucker, and Gerald and Gilbert Andry. Tucker and the Andry brothers had previously represented former New Orleans city councilman, the late James A. Moreau, in a suit two years earlier to invalidate the congressional election of Rep. Richard A. Tonry. The list of attorneys with experience in vote fraud is not lengthy. As we discussed possible lawyers, one name was on everybody's list: New Orleans lawyer John R. "Jack" Martzell. Jack Martzell is a Shreveport native, a graduate of Notre Dame University and Law School. He had been a law clerk for federal judges J. Skelly Wright and Frank B. Ellis. He had later been special counsel to Gov. John McKeithen. Although I had known him casually for many years, he had supported Sonny Mouton in the primary.

Throughout the years, I had been impressed by his personal characteristics of integrity, thoroughness, intelligence, and tenacity. Unlike the stereotypical defense lawyer, Martzell had no sharkskin suit, no cigar or theatrical manner. Only his trademark, "riverboat gambler" hat distinguished him from the most courtly, corporate lawyers in our community. After considerable deliberation, we decided to ask him to join us. We reached him in South Bend, Indiana, where he was attending a Notre Dame football game. Carol Daigle spoke with him and explained our predicament and our progress toward the trial, then just two days away. Jack Martzell agreed to abandon his own legal schedule and serve as point man for our legal team on short notice. As one of Louisiana's premiere attorneys, his fifty-thousand-dollar fee was a bargain, especially since he wound up contributing another two hundred thousand dollars worth of free service. Considering the investment we already had in this race, fifty thousand dollars was a negligible cost, although we had no idea where we would find the money. We sent a plane to South Bend to bring Martzell back to New Orleans, and our legal team was complete.

Our Day in Court

Our case, number 229,974, was assigned to Division L of the 19th Judicial District Court, Parish of East Baton Rouge, with Judge Douglas Gonzales presiding. Martzell believed strongly in what he called the "Oh, my God" theory of election fraud litigation. That is, his experience suggested that the only way to win such complicated cases, in the face of Louisiana's archaic and contradictory election code, was to show evidence so shocking and compelling that the judge would be shocked into saying, "Oh, my God." It was the electoral equivalent of the "smoking gun" in the impeachment case of Pres. Richard M. Nixon. Our entire case was based on two sparse sections of Louisiana law: Section 1431 had long held that, in a challenge between two candidates seeking a position on the runoff ballot, actual, specific proof of fraud and illegal activity must be shown on a case-by-case basis. A new section, 1432, had just been enacted in 1978 and never before applied in an election challenge. Indeed there had never been so broad a challenge as ours in a race for governor.

The new section stated that when a challenger sought to have the entire election voided, the court had to consider if "serious irregularities" made it impossible to determine the real outcome of the election. We believed that the new section about "serious irregularities" meant any breakdown in the election process, including mechanical failure and human error, not just actual vote fraud. That assumption was at the heart of our case. It would be decided, for the first time in Louisiana history, by Judge Gonzales, a slight, intense man with a well-established reputation for judicial independence. Throughout the trial, he showed exacting attention to every detail presented. He was not only thorough, he was unerringly fair and sympathetic. I felt then, and feel now, that he did his best to reach within the dry, precise language and letter of the law to find some spirit, some implied provision that would have allowed him to rule in our favor. The trial opened on Tuesday, November 6, 1979. The judge's first order was that all absentee ballots be recounted. In fact, he stayed up all night, personally supervising the examination and recount.

The next morning, November 7, he completed the recount of unchallenged absentee ballots and certified those results. He then ruled on some of the absentee ballots we had challenged. After that, he heard Louis Lambert's argument that the entire case should be dismissed because no cause of action existed under Louisiana law. Judge Gonzales stayed up all night a second time, researching the law on that point. Thursday, November 8, he overruled Lambert's exception, and we began to present our evidence as the most important part of the trial got under way. Our case was interrupted briefly at four forty-five that afternoon when the judge ordered Rep. David C. Treen included as a defendant in the case. That possibility had been foreseen, and Treen had been represented in the courtroom by New Orleans lawyer Martin Feldman, now a federal judge. After Gonzales' order, Feldman joined the growing assembly clustered around the counsels' tables. Neither Lambert nor Treen appeared during the trial, but I was there every day, along with Gloria, Lisa, key staff members, legal advisors, and supporters.

Early in the proceedings, Gloria fell in our house and suffered a severe fracture to her leg. She attended the remainder of the trial in a heavy cast, watching from a wheelchair and in considerable pain. Our old friend, Dr. D. C. Foti, had ordered special campaign buttons for the trial. Printed in our trademark gold and green campaign colors, they were boldly emblazoned, "I Believe in Miracles—Fitz #1." We wore them throughout the trial, and I have one in my office to this day to remind me of the wonderful faith and encouragement of my friends in those dark and troubled hours.

The courtroom was not nearly large enough to accommodate the numerous witnesses, media, the various candidates, and their supporters. It meant that we were co-mingled in the audience, friends and adversaries sometimes seated right next to each other. I was far too intent on the testimony taking place before the judge to pay attention to the strained seating arrangements, but Treen's lawyers noticed such details. A prominent Baton Rouge Republican lawyer was seated next to me during the first days of the trial.

Since he was a large man whose presence next to me was impossible to miss, Treen's people thought some observers might believe that there was some collusion between us so they asked him to move to the unused jury box, a safe distance away. As luck would have it, almost immediately thereafter, Judge Gonzales expressed concern for my personal comfort, sitting for long hours each day on the hard courtroom bench behind the railing. The judge moved me to the more comfortable seats of the jury box where I wound up, once again, sitting next to the same man, to the Treen camp's continuing discomfort!

Presentation of evidence continued through Friday, November 9. Judge Gonzales made it known that he intended to reach a verdict by that Saturday. He was not being abrupt in doing so, for Louisiana law, in fact, actually required that he reach a verdict within twenty-four hours after the case began. The obvious impossibility of meeting that requirement in such a complex case as this further illustrates how Louisiana law never contemplated such a massive, statewide election challenge and made no provision for the time and effort involved.

Because of the severe time restrictions, we limited our presentation primarily to the parishes of Orleans, East Baton Rouge, St. Landry, St. Helena, and Lafourche, presenting the examples of fraud and irregularity I have previously shown, challenging 12,002 total votes. We also presented the testimony of Jerry Sauer that the differences on a voting machine between the number registered on the protective counter and those of the public counter were important because the public counter could be easily tampered with. We then presented the curious testimony of Elmo Villar, voting machine specialist with the commissioner of elections' office. He swore that it was the custom of election officials to ignore differences of five to ten votes per machine between the protective and the public counters and to simply disregard such discrepancies as "machine malfunction." In Louisiana, with 3,860 voting machines of that type then in use, that policy meant that the vote count according to the public counters could be off by as much as 38,600 votes in a statewide election without anyone questioning it.

Arranging for all the witnesses to travel to Baton Rouge, where we paid for their stay at the Prince Murat Hotel, was a major undertaking. Many of them reported receiving threats at their homes. Such threats were reported to each local district attorney, but no actions were taken.

Moment of Decision

By late Saturday we had concluded, and the judge was prepared to rule. Judge Gonzales mounted the bench slowly and deliberately. Tension and anxiety hung ominously in the courtroom like the chilling fog that engulfs a Louisiana swamp before the dawn. No sound was audible, save the ragged breathing of the spectators, as he began to speak. In measured tones, the judge disallowed another 307 votes from the 2,296 difference between Lambert and me, lowering the distance between us to 1,989. Proving 307 specific, individual instances in which an improper vote had been counted had been a monumental task in the few hours we had been allowed for investigation. The question now: Would Judge Gonzales go the extra mile, to interpret the law to mean that an election riddled with hundreds of examples of unexplained "machine malfunctions and human error" could be voided?

He looked up from his notes and surveyed the courtroom, meeting my glance for a long moment. Then, in a tone of profound sadness and with tears in his eyes, he said that he could not find it in the law to give us what we prayed for and needed. He could not, he said, read the law to say specifically that he had the power to void the entire election based on our assumption that "serious irregularities" should include those contested votes we had not had time to prove. There would be no new election. He was later to say that it was impossible for me, or any plaintiff, to prove the number of fraudulent votes needed to change the outcome within the time allowed. Jack Martzell had prepared me for this possibility, but there was no way to plan for the awful pain, the sickening realization that our dream was dying before our very eyes. The judge's official ruling was signed and dated the following Tuesday, November 13. We immediately filed an appeal with the First Circuit Court, in which Lambert then lost his argument that the court lacked jurisdiction.

The appeals court took into consideration all of the evidence we had first presented, including the testimony of Jerry Sauer and other evidence the trial court had excluded. It discarded another seventy-five tainted votes plus a number of absentee ballots we had earlier challenged unsuccessfully in the lower court, but then it ruled that we still had not proved that enough specific votes were cast fraudulently. The court ruled that those we had not proven could be explained by "machine malfunction and human error," and that explanation was satisfactory for the court. The Court of Appeals ruling came on November 15, 1979, my birthday. It was a bitter birthday, a cruel conclusion to a brutal year. We immediately appealed to the Louisiana State Supreme Court, knowing that the odds against us were very long indeed, for trial and appellate courts are rarely overruled in our state. Nonetheless, we told the supreme court that the new section, 1432, should have been interpreted to mean that we did not have to prove fraud in order for an irregular vote to be discarded. On the contrary, we asserted, human error or machine malfunction which affects the outcome of the vote was specifically intended to qualify as "serious irregularity," sufficient by itself to void the election.

In addition, we argued that the stringent time provisions in the law were unconstitutional. The supreme court ruled on November 17 that there was no showing that the legislative intent was to allow an election to be voided unless specific vote-by-vote fraud had been shown. It found that the lower court had extended additional time to us by allowing us to amend our petition and by ignoring the law requiring a decision within twenty-four hours of the commencement of the trial. It then upheld the previous verdict and dismissed our appeal.

Facing Facts: Calling It Quits

Could we have appealed to the federal courts? Possibly, but only by hoping that the federal courts would overturn a state's sovereign election laws. Except for a glaring showing of unfairness such as in the "one-man, one-vote" trial, federal courts had been extremely reluctant to tamper with states' election procedures. In addition, we were exhausted and our financial resources completely depleted. There was the additional question of fair play. The other candidates' campaigns had been "on hold" for crucial days, awaiting the outcome of the trial and the appeals process. If I now mounted a federal appeal, the suspense and uncertainty would only continue.

If I were unsuccessful, I might only be seen as a sore loser, a "spoiler," and that was not the memory I wanted the people of Louisiana to carry of Jimmy Fitzmorris. I determined that it was time to put away our dream and get on with life. Three days later, November 20, I issued the final statement of the Fitzmorris campaign. I told my friends and supporters, " . . . having exhausted all legal recourse provided by state law, my challenge and candidacy for governor have ended." I said that I hoped my challenge to the overwhelming evidence of vote fraud and manipulation would change the course of Louisiana politics: "We are *entitled* to fair elections." I was proud of the way we had conducted the campaign and the election challenge and said so: "I entered the governor's race wanting, hoping, and expecting to win—but, at the same time, knowing I could lose. I tried to set the moral tone of the campaign. I ran on my own merits. I avoided the name-calling and mud-slinging, and have no need for it now. I, therefore, accept the courts' decisions with honor, dignity, and respect."

The Endorsement Quandary

Then I turned to the major piece of unfinished business confronting me. I had been the first choice of nearly 300,000 citizens of Louisiana to lead their state. In the days after the election and particularly after the courts' decisions, my office had been deluged by calls and letters from supporters and friends asking what role I intended to play in the runoff and what I recommended they do. It was a painful and difficult decision. I had been a working Democrat all my adult life. Yet, in the runoff, there was no question in my mind but that the Republican candidate, Rep. David C. Treen, was closer to my personal philosophy. He shared my commitment to honest, open, responsive state government. I had privately concluded that I would cast my personal vote for Dave Treen. But should I take a public stand in the race? The easiest option was to do nothing, to just "go fishing" as the politicians put it, until the race was over. By choosing that course, I might disappoint some Treen people but I would run little risk of alienating or offending the powerful forces within the state's Democratic party. Democrats might understand a lukewarm endorsement of Lambert and would probably be sympathetic if I took no stand at all.

I was subjected to immense pressure, telephone calls, telegrams, and personal visits from high officials in behalf of the Lambert candidacy. Nonetheless, I concluded that I could not, in good conscience, recommend Lambert to my friends and supporters. Thus, the safe course of doing nothing looked increasingly appealing in the harsh light of political reality. I knew that if I endorsed the Republican candidate for governor, I might be throwing away any chance I could hold elective office as a Democrat during the remainder of my lifetime. There was just one problem with the safety of silence: I knew that this would be a razor-thin election, perhaps the closest governor's race in Louisiana history. My supporters were most likely to drift toward Treen if I gave them any encouragement, and they were vital to his chances. If I did nothing, he would likely lose. In other words, my inactivity could make Louis Lambert governor. Neither Treen nor Lambert offered me any inducement for my support; each knew me too well to think that I would violate the state law in return for a promise of help paying off my campaign debt or for a key position in their administration.

In the end, I remembered the words of President John F. Kennedy: "Sometimes party loyalty asks too much," so I endorsed Dave Treen. I asked my supporters to work for his election. I promised my supporters that I would personally play an active role in the Treen campaign: "Mine is no empty endorsement, no hollow pledge—but rather it is a total commitment." I told them exactly where I stood with Treen: "In making this endorsement, I have asked Dave Treen for only one thing—and he has promised me only one thing: I want a firm, strong, honest, and highly moral government for this state for the next four years, and that he has pledged to do." Finally, I told my friends that I intended to remain active in Louisiana public life: "What about Jimmy Fitzmorris? You know I firmly believe that when the Lord closes one door on you, He opens another. You haven't heard the last of me. This is not the end; I won't just fade away. I'm not retiring, so don't close your files and mail your clippings back to me. Don't write any memorials for Jimmy Fitzmorris."

As I pronounced the termination of my race for governor, the other Democratic candidates faced a similar decision. Bubba Henry had earlier announced his own support for Treen. Sonny Mouton and Paul Hardy followed my lead within days. Like me, they had no promise of any role in a Treen administration. Like me, they concluded that Dave Treen best shared their personal aspirations for open, honest government. Like me, they knew that their actions entailed a costly political risk. In fact, none of us was ever elected to public office as a Democrat again. Only Paul Hardy ever won office again, as the Republican lieutenant governor. Each of us was officially censured by the state Democratic party leadership for daring to follow our conscience and support the candidate we believed best suited to the office, even though he happened to be a Republican. It was a possibility we had each foreseen and a risk we had decided we simply had to take. We crisscrossed the state in Treen's behalf. Since each of us represented a distinct, personal constituency, we rarely traveled together. Rather, we worked to contact our own organization of friends and supporters, asking them to join with us in the Treen crusade.

Because my own campaign was so deeply in debt, it was not possible for me to be very effective in raising campaign contributions for Treen. I did, however, provide my own staff organization, which worked diligently on Treen's behalf without any charge to him for salary, travel costs, or expenses. I paid particular attention to the matter of election security. I made a private, personal vow that what happened to me would not happen to Treen. We helped the Treen staff prepare a complex, ten-step procedure to provide security for the voting machines in the December 8 runoff election. There were security volunteers in each precinct, applying special security tape as the machines were sealed prior to the election, inspecting the tape prior to the commencement of voting, monitoring the election-day process, providing on-site review of the election results, and re-taping the machines that night.

A private security officer from Pendleton Guard and Security Services was stationed at each machine storage warehouse. Security for the machines was so tight the guards were instructed not even to leave for meals between the time the machines were stored until they were reopened for the official count; they brought food to the warehouses with them.

In addition, the Treen election benefitted from a cadre of federal poll watchers and from my own personnel, stationed throughout the state at individual precincts, determined to see that this one was a fair, open, and honest election. Our goal was to provide so much public attention and so many security personnel that the opportunity for abuse would be removed. Even then, on election night the Treen election seemed to be slipping away just as mine had, as Treen suddenly lost about ten thousand votes in the count. Alerted, we redoubled our security and scrutiny, and the slippage stopped as suddenly and mysteriously as it had begun. David C. Treen was elected, the first Republican governor since Reconstruction, by the narrowest margin in Louisiana history: 50.5 to 49.5 percent. In retrospect, there was no slack, no margin for error. Had any of us let down his guard or slacked his campaign efforts, even for a day, the outcome might well have been different.

Election Reform

The difference in attitude and emphasis brought by the new administration was marked and unmistakable. The "good government" agenda of David Treen placed a high priority on election reform. In addition, the unrelenting scrutiny of the Louisiana media made the need to combat campaign corruption impossible to ignore. Powerful voices like WWL Television's articulate, impassioned editorial writer Phil Johnson called for action. Thus was born the Special Legislative Committee on Election Reform, a unique joint panel from the state senate and the house of representatives. It was chaired by state representative Billy Tauzin and wound up providing him excellent statewide exposure prior to his upcoming campaign for the U.S. Congress as well.

The Fitzmorris Plan for Reform

I appeared before the committee on January 9, 1980. Knowing that the public attention span for reform in Louisiana has historically been very brief, I urged the panel to make immediate, substantive reforms to the way political campaigns were financed and conducted.

I also realized that many committee members were "old guard" political figures, not particularly known for their dedication to or interest in the "politics of reform," so I did my best to keep the light focused and the heat turned up on the subject in order to achieve as much improvement as possible within the narrow window of opportunity this committee offered. I told the committee that my purpose was not to cry and complain about my personal misfortune, not to play the martyred victim, but to affirm that serious election irregularities had occurred and to ensure that steps were taken henceforth to protect the integrity of the electoral process. I discussed the problem presented by the requests for funding which all candidates received from political endorsing organizations. I pointed out the obvious dangers in six candidates spending $15 million running for the office of governor, which only paid $50,000 per year. I called for a ceiling on campaign contributions and loans to a candidate from individuals, corporations, labor unions, political committees, and political parties. I urged a limit on campaign expenditures and on the duration of the expensive "media" portions of the campaigns.

I urged a combination of tax deductions for candidates' out-of-pocket expenses and tax credits for individual contributions to campaigns. I said that we should prohibit candidates and committees from paying political organizations or committees for campaign activities. I called for a "Fair Elections Commission," an independent, bi-partisan agency to supervise elections, enforce strengthened campaign laws, and investigate charges of campaign corruption. I called for a uniform system of voter registration in Louisiana and an end to the procedure of allowing persons whose names did not appear on the registration list to simply complete an unverified affidavit of eligibility and then vote anyway. I said that registration lists should be computerized, updated, and centralized. I told the committee that the existing procedure for absentee voting was wide open for fraud and abuse. I said that absentee ballots should be sealed and kept in the custody of the clerk of court and then opened there on election night, in the presence of candidates' representatives and the board of election supervisors, rather than simply being shipped to individual precincts.

I said that the law should be tightened so persons could no longer vote by absentee ballot and then show up on election day and vote again. I called for a thorough investigation of how voting machines could be rigged and how computerized machines could stop such abuse. I said that seals on the machines should be intact and the public and protective counter numbers should concur. I said that machines should never again be left unattended. I urged that machine results not be cleared until the election results were officially promulgated by the secretary of state. I urged that machines be opened on Monday after the election rather than on Wednesday, to prevent abuse. I asked that minimum criteria be established for establishing precinct polling places. I recommended lengthening the time allowed for mounting a legal challenge to a contested election. Finally, I assured the committee that I did not intend to call into question the integrity of the vast majority of the twenty thousand persons involved in the statewide election accounting system. Rather, it was my hope that election reform would result in a political system which would guarantee the integrity and respectability of the entire process and all who participated in it.

The committee's work went on for several years, its hearings consuming some thirty-eight tape recordings. Hundreds of witnesses and documents were involved. Individual testimony ranged from the sublime to the ridiculous. Newly elected secretary of state Jim Brown presented some innovative, substantive possibilities for change, ranging from mechanical changes all the way to holding elections on Sundays as do many European nations. On the other hand, the commissioner of elections had to be threatened with a contempt citation before he would even deliver requested documents. The attorney general's office asked that no new governing authority be established but that his own agency be enhanced and funded more generously.

Legislative Election Reforms: A Start

The committee eventually divided into two sections: one dealing with procedural questions about the actual conduct of elections, the other dealing with campaign finance and reporting. Governor Treen successfully sought creation of a new body, the "Elections Integrity Commission," which was to serve as a watchdog agency to investigate election complaints, intervene in contested election suits, and bring such suits on its own behalf.

To ensure that the commission was "non-political," the members were named from lists submitted by three private organizations and the presidents of the private colleges and universities in the state. In August 1980, Treen named the first members: Jean Reeves, Sam J. D'Amico, LeDoux Prevosty, Jr., Donald P. Weiss, Dr. Elton C. Harrison, Dr. Thomas Howell, Sidney H. Cates III, Dr. Robert S. Robins, and Dr. Peter E. Dawson. The members were informed and dedicated individuals, although the commission never received sufficient funding or legislative support to achieve major, substantive accomplishments. In 1981 it was replaced by the Ethics Commission for Public Employees and Elected Officials. To enforce the state's new campaign finance laws, the legislature named a committee comprised of both legislative appointees and executive branch members. The attorney general said that such a combination was unconstitutional, whereupon the responsibility was transferred to the Board of Ethics for Elected Officials, where it still rests. The results of this legislative attention were mixed, in my view. While substantial progress was made, not nearly so much was done as was needed.

Candidates were divided into "major," "district," and "other" offices, with varying expenditure limits, after which specific campaign costs had to be reported. The law now requires that all campaign contributions be reported and any "anonymous" contributions be transferred to the state. Reports by and registration of all political committees were instituted, ending last-minute committees which operated under the shield of secrecy. The time for which expenses and contributions must be recorded and disclosed was extended from the time a person becomes a candidate all the way through the time any contribution is still on hand or any debt owed. Reporting deadlines were changed, including itemized election-day costs and special reports covering large, last-minute contributions, loans, and expenditures. Individual contributions to political action committees were limited in a minor way, and some basic guidelines for the operation of PACs were enacted. All cash contributions above a hundred dollars were prohibited, and such gifts in any amount forbidden from corporations, labor unions, and trade, business, and professional groups. Using campaign money for personal purposes was prohibited, meaning that unused contributions must now be returned, donated to charity, spent on behalf of another candidate, or retained for some future race. The new rules also outlawed making contributions or loans through the name of another.

Election Day Improvements

Some substantive improvements were made to the election procedures themselves: Perhaps the most important was institution of absentee voting on "punch-card" ballots, which is now in place in all sixty-four parishes. This also eliminated the problem of an absentee voter returning to vote on election day, because the local precinct now has that voter's signature from his previous absentee balloting on hand during election day. Absentee ballots are now handled and retained by the parish registrar of voters, who is appointed, not elected, and the votes are counted election day by the registrar, clerk of court, political party chairmen, and an appointee of the governor. The results are not released until after the polls have closed. Unfortunately, it is not possible to determine the absentee vote results on a precinct-by-precinct basis since they are all grouped together in one "absentee ballot precinct" report. A statewide board of election supervisors is in place with a representative from each parish. The parish registrar of voters, clerk of court, and chairman of each recognized political party's executive committee (in Orleans Parish, the registrar of voters, civil sheriff, clerk of criminal district court, and political chairmen) serve as ex-officio members of the board.

Judicial System Changed

Time for challenging an election was increased to nine days following the date of the election. The trial must now begin four days after the suit was filed. In the case of a primary, the judge may postpone the runoff election for up to five weeks. If the trial is still going after 5:00 P.M., fourteen days after the primary, the judge may reset the runoff for a Saturday which is at least thirty days after the court's decision. The judge must now render a decision within twenty-four hours after the case is submitted to him, and appeals must be filed within twenty-four hours after the judgment is announced. The appeal must be heard no more than forty-eight hours after the appeals court receives the record of the first trial, and a decision must be made within twenty-four hours after the case is argued. The appeal to the state supreme court must be made within forty-eight hours after the appeals court rules. In addition to subtracting illegal or fraudulent votes, a judge may void an election if he finds that it is impossible to determine the outcome of an election or if unqualified voters were allowed to vote or qualified voters denied the right to vote in such a number that the election outcome could have been changed. The judge may also order a re-vote in precincts where a machine malfunction could have changed the result.

Commissioner Qualifications, Rules Changed

Some improvements were made to the qualifications for becoming an election commissioner. There is now a written test administered, and commissioners-in-charge must successfully answer additional questions. All commissioners-in-charge now bring election results to the local clerk of court, so there is a central location from which reliable results may be obtained. Unfortunately, no meaningful requirements for location or selection of precinct polling places were ever enacted. Commissioners-in-charge receive $125 for their service on election day, certified commissioners get $75, and non-certified "ad hoc" commissioners, $35. The person providing the polling place receives $100, and the "custodian" another $50. The idea of returning the machines to the warehouses Sunday, immediately after the election, didn't work. Machines are still transported to the warehouses on Monday and Tuesday and opened Wednesday. The job of transporting and storing the machines is now awarded through public bid, eliminating the major controversy surrounding operation of the commissioner of elections office.

The protective seals placed on the voting machines were improved; the front doors of the machines are now sealed and resealed and so are the binders containing the names of voters. The ballots themselves, however, are still printed by one firm in Baton Rouge. The idea that this lucrative business should be shared or spread among the parishes went nowhere. Presumably, additional changes or improvements could still be made, since the work of the joint committee continues in the form of sub-committees to the house and senate governmental affairs committees.

The Day the Sky Fell

Almost one month to the day after my appearance before the joint committee, arguing for "good government" and "political campaign reform," a shocking series of events unfolded which called into question my very commitment to such ideals. It was called the "Brilab Investigation" and it marked the first time in thirty years in public life that anyone had even suggested that Jimmy Fitzmorris had used any public office for personal gain. The story broke on what should have been one of the happiest days of my life, Friday, February 8, 1980. My daughter, Lisa, was scheduled to reign as Queen of the Krewe of Carrollton during Mardi Gras.

Queens are traditionally selected not on the basis of talent, good works, beauty, or ambition. Rather, their selection is part of the deeply rooted carnival tradition. If you are a member of such a krewe, you register your daughter for this honor when she is a baby. Then you participate in the krewe's activities through the years, waiting for the day when she is old enough to be a member of the krewe's royal court or even the queen during its Mardi Gras parade. Riding that float as a member of the "royal family," past the cheering throngs of thousands of visitors from home and throughout the world, is a thrilling experience those young girls will carry with them the rest of their lives. In Lisa's case, I had hoped that the thrill of being a Mardi Gras carnival queen might, in some way, compensate for the terrible heartbreak and disappointment of the election defeat. Then, the Friday before the parade, the *Los Angeles Times* broke a story which suggested that I was part of a statewide scandal reaching into the highest echelons of state government—that I had peddled my influence.

Was I now not only to be denied the governorship, but also to have my most prized possession, my previously unquestioned reputation for honesty, ripped from me as well? The subpoena for my campaign finance records had seemed innocent enough when it arrived some days earlier. Since I had no indication of the scope of this investigation, I was completely prepared to deliver what amounted to a small warehouse full of campaign contribution records and to appear voluntarily before the grand jury. Our campaign had established very strict guidelines about those from whom we would accept contributions. I knew we had abided by those guidelines and had not knowingly taken any action which was contrary to law. I was absolutely certain that we had never promised a job or any other consideration in return for a contribution. Therefore, I felt confident that we had nothing to fear. Through my years in state government, and particularly in connection with the recent election fraud investigation, I had developed an excellent working relationship with many agents of the Federal Bureau of Investigation. I did not, however, recognize the names of any of the agents who called on me relative to those campaign records.

Because I was curious about that situation, I called Jack Martzell to mention the incident and asked if he had any thoughts before I provided the records. He spoke with his own contacts in the bureau and learned that this was not a routine campaign finance review. Rather, this was a full-scale criminal probe, being conducted at the highest levels of the bureau's public integrity section, which dealt with public corruption.

The FBI "Sting"

The *Times* story made it clear what the FBI believed it had unearthed. Apparently, Joseph Hauser, a longtime confidence man, had been convicted of racketeering, bribery, and conversion of funds in an Arizona insurance scam. To reduce his own sentence, Hauser offered or agreed to become a federal informant. Essentially, his assignment was to work for the FBI's Organized Crime Strike Force, trolling for trouble in neighboring states. Our state's political reputation being what it was, I suppose it should have been no surprise that they selected Louisiana as a prime target.

Hauser, with the aid of undercover officers, simply invented a new insurance company operation and began to approach state officials seeking state insurance business in return for bribes and campaign contributions. To facilitate these contacts, he enlisted the aid of reputed New Orleans Mafia kingpin Carlos Marcello. In the trial which began that summer, it was revealed that twenty-five thousand dollars had been given to the gubernatorial campaign of Sen. Sonny Mouton. The contribution was routed through Charles E. Roemer II, Governor Edwards' commissioner of administration, who was then running Mouton's campaign. Roemer is the father of former governor Buddy Roemer. An undercover agent also bought ten thousand dollars worth of tickets to a Louis Lambert fund-raising dinner after the event had already taken place. Neither contribution was disclosed on either campaign's initial report; both were later revealed in amended reports filed after the investigation was reported in the press.

Martzell and the Fifth Amendment Decision

Jack Martzell agreed to represent me in the intricate hearings before the grand jury. He immediately gave me one piece of advice which I first heatedly refused to accept:

He said that I must invoke my Fifth Amendment protection against self-incrimination and refuse to answer questions before the grand jury. Because I knew I had done nothing wrong, I believed that taking this approach would surely make it look as though I had something to hide. I argued bitterly against his position. Martzell explained, patiently but firmly, that most persons convicted after a grand jury appearance are not charged with illegal activities but with perjury. Their legal problems come about because they fail to remember some minor incident precisely and correctly. Martzell believed that, in a lengthy, massive campaign such as ours, I was in danger of being trapped or tricked into "guessing" at the details of some incident I could not precisely remember. Reluctantly, I took his advice. In retrospect, his counsel, while still distasteful to me, was correct, and I was fortunate to have the benefit of his experience and expertise in this area. No amount of money could ever have repaid him for the time he devoted to our cause, his wise and patient counsel, and the tremendous research done by his legal assistant, Carol Godbold, and other staff members.

The Case against Jimmy Fitzmorris

The basic allegation against me was that I had met with one of the undercover agents and another intermediary they were trying to gain evidence against, the late New Orleans lawyer Vince Marinello. The story was that I had discussed using my influence in their behalf and, in return, had been given ten thousand dollars by Marinello later the same day as the conversation. Marinello was an old and trusted friend I had known since my 1965 campaign for mayor. He had worked as a volunteer in every subsequent campaign I ran. I would probably have scheduled a courtesy meeting with any business contact of his, had he told me that such a session would help his law practice. I agreed to just such a meeting at his request in this instance. The meeting took place at 7:45 A.M. on Thursday, September 27, 1979—one of the busiest days of my campaign. It was not held in any secret or obscure location. We met, in broad daylight, in my lieutenant governor's office in downtown New Orleans. Marinello was accompanied by a man I later learned to be undercover agent Wacks.

He introduced himself as Michael Sachs, president of Fidelity Financial Consultants, representing Prudential Insurance Company of Beverly Hills, California. As we spoke, I jotted on the back of his card where he said he was staying, "Royal Orleans, Room 636," because he suggested that I call him there to arrange a subsequent meeting. I never did make that call, but I did keep the card for my files, an old habit of mine. Later that day, Marinello phoned Hauser and Marcello to say that he had just delivered "the papers" to me in a separate meeting between just the two of us. Little did they know that their conversation, along with some thirty thousand others, had been taped by the FBI as part of the Brilab Investigation.

Proving It Never Happened

There was just one minor problem with the story as they told it: It could never have happened. At the exact time the second meeting was supposed to have taken place, I was aboard a private plane, returning from campaign appearances in Thibodaux, at the other end of the state. Also, by a remarkable, fortunate coincidence no one could have anticipated, I just happened to be wearing a body mike for a news documentary WDSU Television was preparing; the entire day's activities had been recorded. The mike was removed only later that night, just before my endorsement by New Orleans mayor Dutch Morial.

Eventually we had an opportunity to present to federal authorities that tape, along with a minute-by-minute campaign schedule for that day which had been kept by Carol Daigle. The two pieces of evidence proved conclusively that such a meeting could never have happened. When indictments were eventually handed down, my name was nowhere mentioned. Marcello and Roemer were convicted, although their convictions were overturned on a technicality after they had already served their sentences.

Washington lobbyist I. Irving Davidson and veteran state employee Aubrey Young, also charged in the case, were both acquitted. Marinello was acquitted and later moved to St. Tammany Parish where he practiced law until his mysterious murder in 1991, a crime which has never been solved. The brutal realities are these: When the government believes it can connect you to a crime, it is on the front page of every paper in the state. When the decision is later made that you are innocent of any crime, no government prosecutor appears on the steps of the federal building to announce that decision.

Your name just does not appear on the list of persons indicted, and there is a sense in which you can never be fully exonerated because some people will always remember that you were somehow connected to charges of corruption. The point is: No matter how honestly you have conducted your public career, you are at all times vulnerable. Your reputation as a public official can be ruined at any moment, by any person acting to advance his own interest or career. That is simply a fact of life and should give serious pause to any idealistic young person contemplating a career in public service. Fortunately, the confidence that governor-elect David Treen had in me, based on our years of friendship and my established record of integrity, was not shaken by this crisis. He went on to offer me one of the greatest challenges of my career: service for four years as his executive assistant for economic development and international affairs and the position of chairman of the Louisiana Board of Commerce and Industry.

Chapter 8

Life after the Election

The weeks immediately following an election defeat are dark and difficult days, filled with uncertainty and indecision as you try to figure out what happened and what to do with the rest of your life. In some ways, the experience is almost like a death in the family as you come to the realization that the specific dreams and aspirations connected with the office you sought will never be realized.

Of course, many people apply for a job and don't get it, and in politics you know that is always a possibility. On the other hand, I had really prepared myself to be governor. Few people spend every single day, seven days a week, 365 days a year for eight long years seeking a specific job they don't get. Most people don't have to give up their present job to seek the new one; they don't conduct their job search in full public view with intrusive press coverage of their failure, and they usually don't wind up a million dollars or more in debt after the experience either. As any person would, I read the various media accounts of why I lost and what the future might hold. WWL Television's Phil Johnson repeated an editorial he had broadcast after my earlier defeat for mayor, praising my class, dignity, and lack of bitterness in defeat and calling me, "a man who has given the greatest part of his life to this city," saying "sing no sad songs for Jimmy Fitz. He'll come back. He always does." It was not clear to me, in those weeks of interlude and introspection, just how I would come back or as what. Political writer Allan Katz, for whom I have great respect, added an interesting piece in which he said that the problem with my political career was that I wasn't "mean enough," that I lacked the instinct for jugular attacks and for revenge.

I always thought that it was not so much that I didn't know how to fight mean and dirty; I had learned from the best political infighters in the business. My avoidance of gutter politics was a conscious decision, partly because I wasn't very comfortable campaigning that way (and consequently not very effective at it) and partly because of my own personal and religious beliefs. I had, quite early in my political career, deliberately chosen the way I wanted to be remembered, a decision influenced by family upbringing and my religious training, and I was unwilling to change, even if that was the only way to win. But none of those columns, nor the good wishes and sympathy of my friends and supporters around the state, paid the piper. The harsh reality was: I had given up the lieutenant governorship and lost the governorship. Now I faced the twin challenges of retiring my substantial campaign debt on the one hand, supporting my family on the other, and carrying on my life. I was eventually able to retire the campaign debt through a combination of forgiveness of loans, sales of cookbooks and other items, and a post-election testimonial dinner I have already discussed. The question of how best to serve still remained.

Shortly after the election, I met with governor-elect David Treen in his pre-inaugural office in the Southern Savings Building in Metairie on several occasions. He expressed genuine admiration for my track record in government service generally and economic development and international affairs specifically, and asked if I would be interested in taking on a similar task in his administration. I had many other offers from the private sector, inside and outside of Louisiana. Treen, to his credit, had never asked me to campaign for him against Louis Lambert as a condition of possible future employment. In fact, he laid down no conditions at all. To his credit, Treen also stuck by me throughout the Brilab controversy, expressing his belief in my innocence based on our many years of familiarity and friendship. I thought it made great common sense to utilize the skills and talents of the various contenders for governor in the Treen administration, and I thought he made wise choices in naming Senator Mouton his executive counsel, Secretary of State Hardy as head of the Department of Transportation and Development, and Speaker Henry as commissioner of administration.

The Appointment Controversy

The statewide press had a field day with the appointments. Some questioned whether there had been a pre-election "deal," essentially trading jobs for endorsements. I can say without fear of contradiction that nothing could have been further from the truth, and none of the former Democratic challengers had spoken to one another about our decision to endorse Treen. Others in the media saw the appointments as mere "window dressing," and various informal pools emerged, betting on which appointee would leave first. As it happened, each of us stayed to the very end of the Treen administration, serving enthusiastically in the posts to which we had been appointed.

The Democratic Party Position

Our appointments did not sit well with the Louisiana Democratic party. I had expected some resentment, obviously from the Lambert wing of the party, but I underestimated the depth of the bitterness, how long it would last, and how far-reaching it would be. I had not been particularly worried about such feelings. After all, many Democratic Louisiana governors and elected officials had either openly opposed or ignored their party's choice for president, and they had never been formally called to task by the party.

In the 1991 campaign for governor, U.S. representative Clyde Holloway was the officially endorsed Republican candidate. Nonetheless, many prominent Republican officials, including Pres. George Bush, publicly supported the candidacy of Gov. Buddy Roemer, who had only recently joined the Republican party. Nobody seriously suggested that the president should be censured for his failure to abide by the party's position. Similarly, when Roemer and Holloway were both defeated in the primary, and the runoff was between state representative David Duke, a maverick Republican, and former governor Edwin Edwards, a Democrat, literally scores of Republican officials, including former governor Treen, rushed to endorse Edwards. No Republican said that they should be censured for doing so, and no Democrat suggested that it was in any way wrong for Edwards to accept these Republican endorsements.

Politics has changed considerably since the acrimonious days of 1979. I like to believe that my having the courage to take a stand on principle and endorse a candidate of the other party—and the strength to sustain the resulting fire storm of Democratic party criticism—perhaps paved the way. Many of us remember former governor John McKeithen, then openly courting Republican selection for vice president of the United States, showing up in London, in striped pants and morning coat to call upon the queen.

Even had I realized earlier the lasting bitterness my endorsement of Treen would cause, I would not have been swayed for I had always put the man ahead of the party and, even in the light of my experience, I continue to do so as in the 1988 election when I served as state chairman of the Democrats for Bush. Following the 1979 election, however, the group which controlled the Louisiana Democratic Party struck back with a vengeance. A meeting of the state Democratic Central Committee formally censured each of us who had endorsed Treen. It was a curious action. None of us was ever informed that such a censure was pending. None of us was asked to defend our actions or to speak to the committee. None of us was informed that such a vote had taken place; we read about it in the newspapers like everyone else. I told the press that I was not upset by the party's action, saying, "I have never done what was politically expedient at the expense of what was morally right," and I pointed out that some 300,000 other Louisiana Democrats apparently agreed with me when they cast their ballots for the Republican candidate, Dave Treen.

Should I Fight or Switch?

None of us ever served in elective office as Democrats again, and both Hardy and Henry switched parties, becoming registered Republicans. Treen never asked me to do so, although many close supporters of his suggested that action to me. I vividly remember one such conversation with my friend, Rep. Bob Livingston. I told him that I feared such a sudden, convenient conversion on my part might be viewed by rank-and-file Republicans as opportunism. I believe that perception, among many other factors, seriously wounded Gov. Buddy Roemer, when he changed parties on the eve of the 1991 gubernatorial campaign, in which he was subsequently defeated. I declined, as a Democrat by both birth and by choice; I remain a registered Democrat to this day—although still placing the man above the party.

The World's Fair

Quite early in the Treen administration there opened the position of commissioner general of the 1984 World's Fair in New Orleans, a selection which was to be made by the Reagan administration. I expressed my interest and my willingness to serve.

Unfortunately, that selection came during the early days of the Brilab investigation, and I always thought that my connection with that incident doomed my chances for the commissioner general's job. Although I was completely exonerated, by that time the position had been filled by New Orleans lawyer Jack Weimann, who served well and later served the Bush administration as ambassador to Finland and later chief of protocol. I worked closely to assist Jack, particularly through my connections with the consular corps, and believed sincerely and enthusiastically in the concept of the World's Fair. Had I been commissioner general, I would have early on completely changed much of the organizational structure of the fair and almost all of the marketing effort, which I thought was misplaced and ineffective. I still believe that the World's Fair, handled differently, could have turned a profit. Nonetheless, and in spite of everything, it was a wonderful fair; everybody who attended expressed praise. I attended many times and took guests from throughout the nation and the world and thought it was an excellent event. Further, the development of the fair site, after the exhibition ended, did much to enhance New Orleans' commercial and tourism industries.

Considering Another Mayor's Race

At the same time the commissioner general's position was becoming available, 1981, I was under considerable pressure to run again for mayor of New Orleans. Many of my friends in the business community were deeply opposed to the re-election of Mayor Dutch Morial, and a substantial amount of contributions and support was offered if I would return home and enter the race. In fact, there appeared a "Draft Fitzmorris for Mayor" movement, headed by prominent business and civic leader Bill Baldwin. Dutch Morial and I were very different in style and temperament; I thought his confrontational style was often counterproductive.

Nonetheless, Dutch had stuck his neck out for me in the governor's race, against tremendous pressure and at considerable political risk, and I felt I owed him some allegiance. In fact, at Dutch's 1979 press conference endorsing me, Louis Lambert was positioned at the fringe of the crowd, hoping Morial would make a dramatic last-minute switch and endorse him instead. In addition, the changing racial demographics of New Orleans made it necessary that any white candidate for mayor get at least 75 percent of the white vote in a race against a black candidate, and I thought that was a tall order.

I did not think that the disclosure of a tape recording of a private conservation in which I had mimicked a question, during the governor's race, by a young black woman, would work to my advantage in the mayor's race either. But in the end, none of these considerations was as important as my basic feeling that, out of my many years of friendship and respect for Dutch, I should not run against him. I met with Dutch in his city hall office before my December 11, 1981, announcement at the Fairmont Hotel that I would not be a candidate for mayor, and told Dutch my decision. His principal opponent turned out to be former state representative Ron Faucheux, whose advertising firm had handled Treen's campaign. I knew he was close to Treen personally, and I knew that Treen intended to stay out of municipal elections in general and the New Orleans election in particular. I believed that as long as I was part of the Treen administration, that should be my position as well, so I did not publicly endorse Morial in the election. I think Dutch believed that I owed him more than just staying out of the race; I think he believed that I should have returned his 1979 endorsement of me by publicly backing him for reelection, despite Treen's strong feelings against such an endorsement.

Dutch personalized everything, and I don't think he really ever forgave me for not coming to his aid. In fact, when I ran again for lieutenant governor in 1983, he was a determined and vociferous backer of my opponent, Lt. Gov. Bobby Freeman. I felt bad about not being able to join Morial's campaign, although I voted for him myself, but sometimes politics creates that kind of uncomfortable choices, and I saw no other alternative at the time. When Dutch and I were both in the private sector, he asked me to serve as one of his personal advisors as he decided whether or not to run once again for mayor. A decade later, after Dutch's death, I was pleased to be able to endorse and assist the campaigns of his son Marc, who ran for Congress and has since been elected a state senator, where I am confident he will do an outstanding job. I had before, and continue to have, a warm and wonderful friendship with Dutch's widow, Sybil Morial. When Treen assigned me most of the same responsibilities for economic development and international affairs that I had previously had as lieutenant governor, it left the new lieutenant governor, Democrat Bobby Freeman, who had defeated Treen's running mate Jim Donelon, with virtually nothing to do. In fact, I retained my old lieutenant governor's office in the State Office Building in New Orleans.

Treen never sought my advice about what role Freeman might be asked to play. Had he asked, I would have reiterated my belief that either the lieutenant governor should be given specific, statutory responsibilities or the office should be abolished. The experience of the Treen-Freeman years, in which both men had great difficulty working with each other, proves my point. Treen eventually slashed Freeman's budget, forcing him to plead with the legislature for enough money to operate. In fact, Freeman eventually had nearly a half-million dollars per year and had a considerably larger staff than I did when I held that position. In addition, he had his capitol office, was offered additional space in the State Office Building in New Orleans, and opened field offices in Shreveport and Monroe as well—all that with geometrically less work to do. In fact, in his four years as lieutenant governor, he doggedly refused to attend even one board meeting as a member of the Board of Commerce and Industry, one of his few remaining functions, because Treen had appointed me chairman!

The Treen Management Style

In the meantime, I had developed an excellent working relationship with Treen. He operated much like the Reagan administration, with clear lines of command and generous delegation of authority. He believed in setting out the basic goals he wanted to achieve and then allowing his appointees great latitude in getting the job done. His door was always open to me, and I tried always to keep him informed, generally working through his executive assistant Billy Nungesser. If his administration had a major failing it was that Treen was so consumed with careful study of the major decisions facing him that he sometimes seemed unable to seize the initiative in routine, daily activities. He was not effective in dealings with legislators, whose ego and parochial concerns require careful, diplomatic, and constant attention. He had a special "hot line" installed between my office and his, but in four years I cannot remember his ever using it to call me. He was so concerned that his administration be a total contrast in ethics and approach from Edwards' that he sometimes achieved a kind of executive gridlock.

That should by no means obscure Treen's considerable accomplishments in restoring public confidence in state government, bringing a more businesslike atmosphere to state administration, protecting the wetlands, and many other achievements. I simply seized the opportunities and challenges my office provided and charged ahead, doing tasks which were familiar territory to me after my service in the same role for eight years. I said that we ought to try to attract the Japanese government's commercial trade mission to relocate to Louisiana from Houston, stressing that the Japanese were the largest foreign clients of the Port of New Orleans. I was unable to attract much support for that notion, and the trade office remains in Houston to this day. I suggested a high-level trade mission to Japan, to listen and to learn. That kind of mission really requires the active endorsement and the personal presence of the governor, not his designee, because only with that high-level presence will the Japanese, or any foreign government, take the mission seriously. I was never able to achieve that goal either, and, in recent months, Louisiana has closed its trade office in Japan entirely—a serious mistake, in my judgment.

I also supported the Regional Planning Commission's proposal to create a state fund to generate low-interest loans to small businesses. I thought that this was an unusual opportunity because large corporations generally have the ability to "self-fund" their own expansions, while small businesses usually lack the cash flow to undertake such projects. That proposal was never adequately pursued either. There was a substantial change between my economic development activities as lieutenant governor under Edwards and as executive assistant under Treen. Under Edwards, I had actually run the Department of Commerce. Under Treen, that responsibility fell to a black attorney, Don Bernard, and I served the governor directly without my former staff support and control. Bernard was one of the first high-level black appointees in the South. He and I enjoyed an excellent relationship, but I believe that the effectiveness of the department suffered because of the split in responsibility and authority. The limited nature of my staff resources necessitated my continuing the "rifle" rather than "shotgun" approach to economic development, which I thought was the more productive method anyway. I continued to identify specific companies within a particular industry which I believed could be convinced to relocate to Louisiana or to expand their Louisiana activities.

I worked to develop both company-based incentives, which worked well for small companies to whom the actual cost of doing business was the determining factor in their location choice, and investor-based incentives, which worked well for larger corporations to whom other factors played an important part in their selection of where to locate. We were able to achieve significant success on a number of economic fronts during the Treen years, although the state's economic conditions had considerably worsened as our petrochemical base was experiencing serious financial downturns.

The Last Hurrah: Running Again for Lieutenant Governor

At the end of Treen's first term, I was confronted by the need to decide what I wanted to do the next four years. Treen had been generous and supportive of my activities, but I genuinely believed that I would function more effectively as the elected head of my own operation than as an executive assistant to the governor. Thus, I decided to seek another term as lieutenant governor. This meant challenging the incumbent lieutenant governor, Bobby Freeman, whom I liked personally but with whom I had never had a close working relationship.

I made the decision without taking an early poll. Had I taken such a survey, I might have realized what serious damage the earlier Democratic "censure" had done to my standing with local, "courthouse Democrats" and labor leaders around the state. I seriously underestimated the amount of residual bitterness among local party workers who believed, rightly or wrongly, that my endorsement of Treen had been the key factor in his defeat of the Democratic candidate for governor. I spoke with both Edwin Edwards—attempting his own political comeback—and David

Treen about my intentions. Treen was encouraging, and Edwards promised to take a "hands off" position on the race. I suppose Edwards technically kept his word, for he made no formal endorsement. However, his wife at the time, Elaine, his brother, Marion, his son, Stephen, and key members of his staff soon surfaced as enthusiastic backers of Freeman. Former governor John McKeithen, for whom I had sent a private plane so he could join me at my announcement and add his endorsement of my candidacy, suddenly and mysteriously announced—without speaking to me first—that he had changed his mind and was now opposed to my candidacy.

Organized labor strongly backed Freeman, as did most local Democratic organizations. I had the support of the generally conservative Louisiana Association of Business and Industry, although I ran as a lifelong Democrat. I also ran as the one man who had proved he could work effectively with both Edwards and Treen, a record demonstrated by my previous close cooperation with each of them as governor. However, when Edwards achieved a smashing first-primary victory over Governor Treen—freeing personnel and resources to concentrate on defeating me in the runoff against Freeman—the handwriting was on the wall. I stayed in the campaign because I had never quit a race in my political life, but my close, immediate association with the now-discredited Treen administration made the outcome a certainty. The campaign against me was personal, it was bitter, and it was brutally effective.

Opponents suggested that I was benefiting from a generous state retirement, although I was drawing no retirement at all and had, in fact, taken a leave of absence from my state position in order to run. Democrats were repeatedly reminded of the previous censure which followed my endorsement of Treen. Black radio stations were saturated with commercials suggesting that I was a racist, based upon the secret tape recording of a private conservation in which I had humorously repeated a question, posed four years earlier, by a young black woman. I had meant nothing demeaning by the conversation; people quoting statements by Irishmen, Italians, Jews, and Eskimos all use the native dialect for purposes of humor, and no man in Louisiana public life had a stronger record of support for human dignity and equal opportunity than I. Nevertheless, within the state's black community the commercials were devastatingly effective. I had the endorsements of the *Times-Picayune, Gambit,* Shreveport *Times,* and others but it was not enough. The momentum of Edwards' $12.6 million first primary victory had been effectively transferred to Freeman, and it was impossible to overcome.

After the shattering defeat, I returned to the Treen administration and continued work on the projects I had begun, completing the term. Then, suddenly, the Treen administration was over, the Edwards administration, along with Lieutenant Governor Freeman, was in power, and Jimmy Fitzmorris was out of public life, probably forever. Given my previous state experience, and my own excellent working relationship with Governor Edwards, I was confident that he would ask that I continue to serve in my present position or a similar one. I waited until literally the final hours before his inauguration for his call, but no call from Edwards ever came.

Fitzmorris and Associates Is Formed

In retrospect, it was probably a blessing in disguise for it forced me to do what I should unquestionably have done years earlier: assess my personal goals and ambitions and, late in life, develop an enterprise that resulted in a productive, profitable, personal business career. I knew that I was interested in—and now had four decades of invaluable experience in—real estate development, government relations, sales and marketing and management, as well as a clear understanding of international trade.

In fact, I was equally interested in all those areas, and it was difficult to choose which to pursue. I also knew that, after a lifetime of working for private industry and for the people of Louisiana, I wanted a chance to work for myself. Thus was born Fitzmorris and Associates, a consulting firm in which I could utilize my experience, pursue all those areas that interested me, and control my own destiny as well. It was a decidedly modest beginning, although I had many wonderful offers from friends to take space in their offices or buildings. Three days before leaving state government, I toured the International Trade Mart, now the World Trade Center, and found a small, "model" office that contained exactly the "executive look" I was after. I convinced the building management, under the leadership of my good friend Eugene Schreiber, to let me have the "show room sample" office, exactly as it was, and we moved in overnight. With the assistance of my friend from South Central Bell, Carl Bailey, we set about to find a telephone number that could be easily remembered by my friends. The closest he could come was 581-FITS, and I have that number to this day.

It was a harried, last-minute beginning, but I had enough confidence in myself to believe that I could develop a very active and successful corporation. My first client was JIMCO, Inc., a major heavy-duty concrete supplier, under the leadership of two of my very dear friends, Jim Schwartz and his son Johnny. After a flurry of telephone calls and letters to companies I had known for many years, I emerged with several dozen corporate clients circling the globe. My office space doubled, and then doubled again, and my days became as busy as they had ever been during my years in public life. I found, after four decades in government, fulfillment, contentment, and constant challenge, and am relieved to report that there is "life after politics."

Chapter 9

Public Faces, Private Places

One of the remarkable fringe benefits of a career in public life has been the opportunity to meet, and often to develop a personal friendship with, many of the major figures in the political, athletic, and entertainment worlds. I am frequently asked to tell the stories of my meetings with some of the personalities who strode the front pages of history during the last half-century or more, and I am happy to recount some of these experiences again. There can be no doubt that my life has been enriched, perhaps even changed, by my personal experiences with these outstanding individuals.

Certainly, for a young boy of modest means, the chance to actually meet and visit with them was a wonderful and exciting experience. I always tell my audiences that some of the persons who most deeply affected my life, in lasting, personal ways, were not the rich, the famous, or the powerful, but those who had dedicated their lives to other callings, and I have included some of their stories as well.

Presidential Profiles

I have already mentioned my first encounter with Dwight D. Eisenhower, then a colonel in the U.S. Army, years before anyone seriously thought he would become president of the United States. After his election, Ike came to New Orleans to participate in the re-enactment of the signing of the Louisiana Purchase. Denis Barry, now a judge, was then president of the Young Mens' Business Club, in which I was also very active. He and I were honored to serve as civilian aides to the president on this occasion.

It required the first of many Secret Service security clearances I was to have during my career. Mayor deLesseps Morrison threw an elaborate Mardi Gras parade to honor and escort President Eisenhower to Jackson Square, site of the re-enactment.

I remember industrialist Henry Kaiser, one of the most powerful business leaders in the nation, sitting on the curb in front of Jackson Square, awaiting the president's arrival. Judge Barry and I were on hand to escort the president to a temporary structure that had been constructed in the square, in which he could wash and freshen up before his speech. My line, to the leader of the Free World as he stepped out of the temporary structure that day, was: "Mr. President, your towel," words I can't forget! Ike was warm, friendly, cordial, and very much at ease. He had a kind of grandfatherly appearance which was very engaging. His visit was an important and exciting moment for everyone in attendance, but especially for those of us who had served in World War II and who had such devotion to and respect for him. He wore the mantle of the presidency with great dignity, but was by no means stuffy. He was not accompanied by Mamie on that trip, in fact he flew in on Air Force One and left immediately after the ceremony. In his remarks, he was able to draw on his considerable military knowledge about New Orleans in discussing our critical role in trade, commerce, and the military history of the nation.

My first meeting with Pres. Harry Truman was under much less formal circumstances. The late Bill Deramus, Sr., then chairman and CEO of the Kansas City Southern Railroad, where I worked for many years, called and asked me to come to Kansas City for a special assignment. When I arrived, he told me that President Truman was to take the railroad's Presidential Car, "Kay-Cee," from Kansas City to New Orleans, and that I would travel with the presidential party, serving as KCS president Deramus's personal representative. Truman had just left the presidency and he and his wife, Bess, were going to Pass Christian, Mississippi, to visit an elderly black woman, who had been a nanny for their daughter, Margaret. The woman was now in ill health, and the Trumans wanted to pay her a visit. Upon arriving in New Orleans, I accompanied the Trumans to the Roosevelt, now Fairmont, Hotel, where they stayed overnight. Although Truman was one of the most colorful storytellers I have even known, his tales were not always unchallenged. On many occasions Bess would interrupt him to say, "Harry, that's not the way it happened. Let me tell you

President Harry Truman came to New Orleans aboard the Kansas City Southern Line's presidential car, "Kay Cee."

how it really took place," and she would provide her own version of the event! They had that casual, unaffected relationship that old couples, who have been together many years, sometimes develop.

Truman was cordial and familiar; it was like hosting a member of my own family. He was much smaller than Eisenhower, with none of that awesome sense of "command" that surrounded Ike. Yet, I could not help but be struck by the notion that, in this nation, a man who seemed very average in many respects, could have risen to become president. Unlike Eisenhower, Truman's casual conversation was punctuated by occasional swearing. Yet, his conversation revealed a tremendous depth of knowledge about every aspect of government. He might have been an "accidental president," but he was impressive in his grasp of national affairs and particularly in his historical knowledge, for he was a great student of history. I did not accompany him and Mrs. Truman on their private visit to Mississippi, but rejoined them when they returned to New Orleans to reboard the "Kay Cee." The railroad's private car is still in service. Each time I am on board I remember how much Harry and Bess Truman enjoyed their journey in it. Travel on this car is the epitome of personal service. Private meals for four or six—never more than ten—are carefully arranged by the railroad's chef, well in advance of the trip. Because of the limited size of the galley, it is difficult to prepare elaborate gourmet banquets, but that was not Truman's style anyway.

He dined on steak, baked potato, soufflé, and ice cream with fruit. Always an early riser, he especially enjoyed the big breakfast of bacon, eggs, grits, and sausage, which he consumed after his early morning walk. Truman had a genuine fondness for rail travel; his 1948 campaign for the presidency had been marked by a nationwide "whistle-stop tour." Truman was of the generation which believed that one could see so little from the air that rail was the preferable manner of travel. He called his wife Bess "The Boss," and she was clearly in charge of the daily life of their family. She, on the other hand, told me that every night her husband would discuss with her the events of that day, so she always felt a part of his public life as well. She was a delightful conversationalist and a good listener. Truman corresponded with me several times after that trip.

I had worked very hard for the election of John F. Kennedy and was delighted when he agreed to come to New Orleans to dedicate the Nashville Street Wharf and to speak at city hall. Former mayor Chep Morrison, then JFK's ambassador to the Organization of American States, accompanied him on that trip. We staged the traditional motorcade to and from the airport.

Someone once said that the late Leonard Bernstein "exuded sex appeal like a leaky eel," and that description applied amply to Kennedy as well. When I was a young boy, women were depicted as "swooning" in the presence of a particularly dashing male. That's pretty much what happened to the rather large contingent of women who crowded around the motorcade and collected at each of his speeches, just hoping to get a glimpse of Kennedy or maybe to touch him as he went by. This was a brief, one-day trip on Air Force One, which he made without Jacqueline or any staff people. Chep returned to Washington with him. During his trip I had the opportunity to visit with him at some length. We shared a great interest in Latin American developments, and he was very knowledgeable on that subject. His image was that of a bright, fresh, vigorous departure from the old-time politics we had known. He had a fascinating ability to bring you into the conversation, peppering you with questions in that Boston-Irish accent. He was not pompous or overly intellectual, just a vigorous, young man on the move, brimming over with new, long-range goals. I saw JFK only one other time, during a trip to Washington, where I had an opportunity to visit with him again. The impact of his life and his presidency will prove to be very deep, but his stay among us was very brief.

I first met Lyndon Baines Johnson when he was running against Kennedy for the Democratic presidential nomination in 1960. Johnson, accompanied by Lady Bird and a bevy of campaign workers called "Johnson Girls," came by train and spoke at the Union Passenger Terminal. You could see the calculation in his eyes, sweeping the room, making note of every opportunity. He knew exactly how to talk to political people for he was a skilled and seasoned operative, though this was an ability that did not always translate into conversations with persons who had no deep interest in politics. The next time I saw him, Johnson had become president and he was in New Orleans for a small, fifty-person reception, prior to a large banquet at the old Jung Hotel on Canal

Street. The reception was mostly populated by the city's business leaders, many of whom were not Democrats and most of whom were not supporting Lyndon Johnson.

He was not accompanied by Lady Bird this time, but he had all of the fabled "Lyndon Johnson magic," as he gave every person in the receiving line the "Johnson treatment," looking them deeply in the eye, clasping their hand in his, and holding their elbow firmly by his other hand, pulling them close and telling them how their personal presence had been important to him. Before entering the main dining room, he clapped his hands together and told the assembled crowd, "My friends, your president wants you to know how much you have honored him by coming here this evening. I know how difficult it is for many of you to be for me, but your presence honors me." Minds and hearts were changed by the Johnson treatment that night. Stronger personalities than ours had been bent by Johnson's will—this was, after all, the man who could singlehandedly talk Arthur Goldberg, who hated daily political life, into resigning a lifetime seat on the U.S. Supreme Court to make a hopeless race for governor of New York. Johnson was immense, personally, in his Texas gait as he strode into the banquet room and in his gestures during his speech. He was not a particularly good speaker, but his personality filled the room.

I saw Johnson several times during visits to Washington, and Chep Morrison, who had resigned to run once more for governor of Louisiana, got a personal note from Johnson thanking him for his leadership. When Chep died, Majority Leader Hale Boggs, at my request, got the president to order a special military plane to bring the remains of all those killed in the air crash which took Chep's life to Alvin Callendar Field, rather than to the nearest air base, which would have been in Florida.

The Johnson approach was very different from that of Sen. Hubert H. Humphrey, who went on to become Johnson's vice president and who very nearly won the presidency for himself. Humphrey, a one-time college debating partner of Sen. Russell Long, and I appeared on a number of programs together, including one meeting of the state AFL-CIO at the old Heidelberg Hotel in Baton Rouge. Humphrey could speak, eloquently and fervently, on any subject for almost any amount of time. He had great respect for the Louisiana congressional delegation, for in those days Louisiana controlled many key chairmanships with Eddie Hebert, Hale Boggs, Allen Ellender, and Long. Those were the days when, if New Orleans had a problem with the federal government, the mayor could get Boggs, Hebert, Ellender, or Long to call the president directly.

I first met Richard Nixon when he was vice president. He came to New Orleans to speak to a packed hall at the Roosevelt Hotel. Nixon struck me right away by how trim and compact, conservatively dressed, and articulate he was. I visited with him at some length in an anteroom prior to his address. After he became president, he and Mrs. Nixon came to Houma for the funeral of Sen. Allen Ellender. He and I sat at opposite ends of the front row during the service. There was a large congressional delegation for the funeral, including Vice President and Mrs. Spiro Agnew, Majority Leader Mike Mansfield of Montana, and Sen. Edward M. Kennedy. Ellender had, through one of the longest senatorial tenures in our history, earned tremendous respect in Washington. The last time I saw Richard Nixon was at a White House function to which I had been invited by the late Rep. Eddie Hebert. He and Nixon had served together on the House Un-American Activities Committee at the beginning of Nixon's career, and they remained close friends through the years. Hebert offered Nixon some personal advice that night, saying, "You are being insulated by your staff from what is taking place in your administration. One day, you will get into trouble because of the actions of your staff."

Mrs. Nixon, quiet but gracious, was on hand that night as well. Nixon seemed serious and reserved; he never seemed to unwind throughout the evening. His speech was very precise, and he seemed very solemn. It was evident that Nixon was under tremendous stress and, of course, the reasons became evident in the months to come. I never thought that Nixon would resign. I thought that I sensed in Nixon a kind of resolve never to surrender, to fight against all odds.

Vice President Gerald Ford and I were at Children's Hospital for an event when Ford got a call from the White House. He returned to tell me, "I have to leave immediately to return to Washington. I cannot tell you why, but the reason will become apparent to you soon." Ford went back to Washington, and within hours Nixon had resigned and Ford was the next president of the United States.

One of the closest associates of both Nixon and Ford was Dr. Henry Kissinger, one of the outstanding diplomats of our time. He accompanied Nixon to New Orleans for an address to the

A whirlwind, 1974 New Orleans visit by my friend, Pres. Gerald Ford.
(Courtesy New Orleans *Times-Picayune*, photo by James Guillot)

Veterans of Foreign Wars national convention at the Rivergate. Dr. Kissinger and I were standing at the back of the Convention Center when Nixon grabbed press secretary Ron Zigler by the shoulders and shook him, reprimanding him for some error in scheduling. It was a jarring sight, a subordinate being shaken by the president of the United States. In January 1979, Gov. George Brisbee of Georgia invited me and a small group to a private meeting at the governor's mansion in Atlanta where Kissinger gave a fascinating briefing on international affairs. His thick accent belied a brilliant mind and a wonderful sense of humor as well.

With the possible exception of Jimmy Carter, I think Gerald R. Ford was the warmest, most relaxed president I have known. He has a genuine concern about people on an individual basis. I met him on several occasions when he was vice president and, as presiding officer, introduced him to a joint session of the Louisiana legislature. One day, we were on our way together to dedicate the France Street Wharf. President Ford asked, "What do you think about including some discussion of my commitment to equal rights in this speech?"

I suggested, as diplomatically as I could, that New Orleans would probably be the wrong place for that particular speech and that this dedication would almost certainly be regarded as the wrong setting. President Ford deleted that reference from his speech, and I was always impressed that he took time to ask some local advice before approaching such a delicate subject. I have enjoyed a long and friendly relationship with him since then. On one occasion, I mentioned to him that I was going to be in California; he was already there, preparing for a televised campaign debate with Jimmy Carter, the Democratic nominee. When I arrived at the hotel, there was a message for me from the Secret Service. President Ford was inviting me to attend a small, private gathering following the debate at a friend's home in San Francisco. I was pleased and honored to attend. When I arrived at the beautiful home, on a hill overlooking the city, my security man, Richie Hart, had to remain outside with presidential security agents. I was greeted at the door by Senate Majority Leader Howard Baker. It was soon evident that I was the only Democrat in the small gathering, but everyone made me feel welcome and at home because I was a special guest of the president.

Before we sat down to watch the debate on television, I thought it would be a good opportunity to call my home in New Orleans, as I always did when I traveled. I picked up the first available phone. Before I could dial, a voice on the other end responded, "White House." Realizing that I was holding the White House hot line, I replaced the receiver as quickly as possible and tried to move away without being noticed. I did not particularly want it known that it was I who was using the president's private line to make a call to New Orleans! Later, when President Ford arrived, he walked across the room to greet me, saying, "I'm glad you could come. Let me call Betty," whereupon he picked up the same phone. I didn't mention that I had already spoken to the White House and everyone had seemed fine.

This was the debate when President Ford created the major foreign policy faux pas of the campaign by saying that there were no eastern European nations under communist control. I never knew what he intended to say; of course he knew better, but there was an audible gasp from the group gathered around the television set, and we all knew he was in serious trouble. I met him another half-dozen times or more, and he always struck me as very decent, very knowledgeable, and very capable.

People made fun of Ford for what they saw as his lack of depth, even for his problems with physical agility. Chevy Chase's "presidential pratfalls" on "Saturday Night Live" became a national joke. I thought Ford was treated unfairly and inaccurately. Perhaps because of my personal experience, I thought it unfair to belittle a candidate's abilities without real knowledge of his true personality. In fact, President Ford had an almost encyclopedic knowledge of the national government, based on his many years service in the House of Representatives. He was a great friend of Eddie Hebert, Hale Boggs, and Dave Treen, who had served with him in Congress. Ford was very careful about watching his weight and his general appearance. In his conservative, vested suits, he looked like a professional football player who had gone on to become a corporate executive.

The man Ford replaced as vice president, Spiro Agnew, had a special affinity for New Orleans. He visited the city some dozen times, sometimes just for relaxation, probably the first vice president ever to develop such a fondness for the city. I think it may have been because New Orleans reminded him, in some ways, of Baltimore, but with a more relaxing atmosphere.

Agnew always stayed at the Royal Orleans and usually ate either lunch or dinner at Brennan's, nearby on Royal Street. He became such a "regular" they named one of his favorite dishes after him, "Shrimp Agnew," and it is still on the menu. Agnew was a burly man, but always impeccably dressed and well-spoken. My dear friend and campaign chairman, the late Bill Helis, Agnew, and I met for lunch or dinner at Brennan's on many occasions when he was in town. I must say he certainly never gave any indication of the improprieties which were to drive him from office, but his reputation for tough talk was as evident in private conversations as in public speeches. He had a deep-rooted distrust and dislike of most of the national press, and often said so. They, of course, delighted in making the most of his subsequent problems, so perhaps he brought some of that on himself. I think he understood the risks involved in attacking an enterprise which buys printer's ink by the barrel but he was, and remains, a very strong-willed personality.

I met former governor Jimmy Carter at the very outset of his presidential campaign, several years before the election. He had a disappointing turnout for a breakfast at the Delta Towers Hotel. I was one of a handful of persons in attendance. He later wanted to speak to a joint session of the legislature, which I arranged. He had a very cool relationship with Gov. Edwin Edwards so I coordinated most of his visit, although Edwards did appear at the session long enough to introduce him. At this point, he could have walked Canal Street unnoticed; no one thought he was a serious contender for the presidency. After his surprise victory he made several visits to Louisiana, and I also visited him in the Oval Office.

Once, he wanted to come to Louisiana and tour the oil rigs. Rep. Lindy Boggs, energy secretary James Schlesinger, Sens. J. Bennett Johnston and Russell Long, Edwards and I accompanied him on the presidential helicopter, Marine One. He wanted to look for oil spills. He had never been on an oil rig before and was intrigued by how the workers actually lived out there. Edwards dispatched me to see him off when he flew back to Washington the same afternoon aboard Air Force One. As we approached the massive plane, receiving the salutes from the military personnel positioned near it, Carter said, "Well, Jimmy, this is a lot different than the time you and I went to the Delta Towers."

I was more intrigued by his last statement before boarding the plane. Looking at his watch, he said, "By the time I get back to

Governor Edwin Edwards, Pres. Jimmy Carter, and me.

Washington it will be 5:00 P.M. I can visit with Amy because I have nothing on my schedule." Since I still had a full list of appearances on my own schedule for the rest of that day and evening, I was surprised that the president of the United States planned to just go home and relax with his daughter. His wife, Rosalyn, came to New Orleans for a subsequent dedication of developer Lester Kabacoff's international river terminal, and I escorted her on that occasion. Theirs was a remarkable political partnership. Probably not since Eleanor Roosevelt had a First Lady been so intimately involved in the inner workings of government. Although some resented her position, I sensed that President Carter relied on her greatly. Since leaving the White House, they have written books together and separately, and he has achieved the kind of respect and acclaim abroad that eluded him at home, working for human rights and exerting a positive presence at trouble spots all around the globe, not to mention his own work domestically with the Habitat for Humanity movement.

I first met his successor, Ronald Reagan, when he was governor of California. He came to speak at Tulane University, when I was a member of the city council. Because he was a Republican, no local elected official was anxious to meet him at the airport, so I went to greet him and escort him to the campus. I met him again in Indianapolis at a meeting at the TEKE headquarters. TEKE is a fraternity which had honored me in 1967 by giving me an honorary membership and inviting me to the next national board meeting. Reagan was serving as a member of the board. Unlike some political figures who accept such positions in a kind of ceremonial, disengaged way, Reagan was very interested, active, and informed on TEKE operation. He was always comfortable in pubic appearances because of his great showmanship and his training as an actor and broadcaster. Because of our similar early training in elocution, we shared some mutual experiences and interests and developed a personal friendship. I was with him once at the White House and on several other occasions with Dave Treen. He came to New Orleans several times and appeared at a meeting at the New Orleans Hilton on behalf of senatorial candidate Henson Moore.

He managed each of those affairs with the style of a board chairman, clearly expecting those to whom he had delegated responsibility to perform without a great deal of involvement on his own part. Both Treen and Rep. Bob Livingston had helped brief

I had great respect for Pres. Ronald Reagan, a fellow "TEKE."

him before the Henson Moore speech; he had strong personal relationships with both of them, and he already knew a good bit about Louisiana. His careful attention to his own physical health gave him the appearance of a much younger, vital, and energetic man.

I first met George Bush when he came to kick off a boat race between Michael Reagan and Pat Taylor. Governor Treen could not attend the luncheon for that event so I represented him and appeared on the platform with Bush. He was easy to get along with and had a delightful personality, but he was very intense. I met him only once after he was elected, in a campaign in which I had served as state chairman of the Democrats for Bush. He was very personable and sincere. In person, Bush seems even taller and thinner than he appears on television. He has a passionate interest in physical fitness, playing tennis and jogging, and believes it is very important to his ability to perform. Certainly he is, at his age, among the most active presidents of this century.

Presidential Contenders

Perhaps the best speaker I have ever known was the late Adlai Stevenson, former governor of Illinois, twice the Democratic nominee for president, and later U.S. ambassador to the United Nations. I rode in a parade with Stevenson and Chep Morrison that culminated in a speech at Gallier Hall. Stevenson was not a particularly handsome man, but he had riveting eye contact and a kind of luminescent aura surrounding him. He was a brilliant, eloquent orator—although I feared he spoke far above the average person's ability to comprehend.

At the other end of that spectrum was the late vice president and senator Alben W. Barkley of Kentucky. In our lifetime, only he and Hubert Humphrey have returned to the Senate after service as vice president. I was introduced to Barkley by the late assessor Jim Comiskey. The Kentuckian had no eloquent phrases; he spoke the plain language of the common man. He also had the most comprehensive repertoire of jokes of any figure in public life, many of which he recounted in a wonderful autobiography, *That Reminds Me*. He was denied the Democratic nomination for president in 1952, largely on account of age, in favor of Stevenson, a distant cousin. When he died, a friend, trying to comfort

Barkley's widow, said, "Well, he's surely at the right hand of the Lord now."

"Oh no," she said, "I'm sure he's not finished telling St. Peter all his stories yet."

I suppose I was theologically closest to Sen. Eugene McCarthy, a deeply committed Roman Catholic, with whom I appeared on a program at Loyola University. McCarthy was introspective and withdrawn in person but a very effective and witty speaker. I could never relate to his political philosophy nor did I participate in his quest for the presidential nomination.

I met Vice President Fritz Mondale when we were in New York where he was dedicating a building for homeless artists. I was invited to the program by a former New Orleanian who was one of his Secret Service agents. He made a good appearance and was a fashionable dresser, but I never developed any belief that he could win the presidency.

I had the same impression of Gov. Michael Dukakis, whom I met when he came, all by himself, to address a meeting of the Democratic State Central Committee. We sat beside each other at the shoeshine stand in the Baton Rouge Hilton. I introduced myself, and we visited before his speech. He was impeccable and polite but cool and distant; I could not believe that he would ever be able to relate well enough to the American people to become president.

An earlier presidential candidate of my acquaintance was the late Tennessee Senator Estes Kefauver. He had already gained considerable national publicity conducting one of the first televised hearings. Tall and intense, he was not particularly friendly despite his folksy "coon-skin cap" appearances. I went with him to visit Louis Rousell, Sr., at his office in the Whitney Bank Building. Kefauver's speech to the YMBC was covered by a capable young reporter, Ken Gormin, who later became head of Bauerlein Advertising in New Orleans and a close friend.

I rejected requests to assist in the campaign of Sen. George McGovern. I had met McGovern twice while he was visiting New Orleans, and we had discussed national affairs sufficiently for me to conclude that we had nothing in common. He was decent, intelligent, and polite, but somehow our life experiences had led us to diametrically opposed conclusions, and I never thought it would be possible to develop any personal relationship with McGovern—a feeling I have had only rarely among the hundreds of political figures from both parties I have met through the years.

I met Senator Lloyd Bentsen when he came to Gallier Hall for a 1976 political appearance. He was seeking the Democratic presidential nomination and knew of my friendship with Sen. Russell Long. He was, because of his personal makeup, not a particularly great mixer or backslapper but very knowledgeable on the issues.

Governor Nelson Rockefeller, on the other hand, was a tremendously outgoing person. I met him when he spoke to the lieutenant governors' conference in Mobile, accompanied by his new wife, Happy. The striking factor about Rockefeller was how small he appeared, compared to his magazine photographs which made him look much larger and more athletic. I greatly enjoyed our meeting, and we followed that occasion with several letters.

One of Rockefeller's presidential opponents, former Gov. George Romney, was a delightful personality whom I met several times. The most recent was only months ago when he came to New Orleans in the wake of the Desert Storm operation to make some awards in connection with his service on the Thousand Points of Light Commission. He hadn't changed much, retaining a wonderful touch with people and memory for names and places.

I was also very impressed with Republican senator Barry Goldwater, now retired, who was the Republican presidential nominee in 1964. Goldwater had great sympathy and support in the South in his very difficult race against Lyndon Johnson, particularly because of the Arizona senator's impressive military credentials and knowledge.

I also served as host of Alabama governor George C. Wallace when he visited Baton Rouge and, as lieutenant governor, introduced him to a joint legislative session. I found him to be much more cordial and reasonable in person than his public image might have led one to suspect.

The Lieutenant Governors' Conference

One of my most challenging and interesting experiences as lieutenant governor was hosting the Seventeenth National Conference of Lieutenant Governors held in New Orleans in August of 1978. As I discussed earlier, until I was elected, the lieutenant governor of Louisiana did not even participate in this national association, so this was our state's first experience in the national

Alabama governor George C. Wallace and me. (Courtesy Alabama Governor's Office)

spotlight as host of this conference, and we were determined to make the most of it. The role of lieutenant governor in the other forty-nine states is not markedly different from that in Louisiana: it serves as a training ground and possible springboard for future state and national officials. At the time of this conference, ten lieutenant governors had recently been elevated to the office of governor in their respective states.

Our conference was honored by a similarly outstanding roster of lieutenant governors who would, in future years, distinguish themselves in business and government. Most of the nation's lieutenant governors were in New Orleans for the conference including: my good friend, Alaska's Lowell Thomas, Jr., son of the famous broadcaster and now a successful business executive in his home state; Arkansas's Joe Purcell, now practicing law; California's Mervin M. Dymally, my close friend and now a congressman; Colorado's George L. Brown, now a New York businessman; Georgia's Zell Miller, now governor; Indiana's Robert Orr, who went on to become governor and U.S. ambassador to Singapore; Maryland's Blair Lee, later governor and now a lawyer; Massachusetts' Thomas P. O'Neill III, whose father was then Speaker of the U.S. House of Representatives; Mississippi's Evelyn Gandy, who later ran for governor; Missouri's William C. Phelps, who also ran for governor and is now practicing law in Houston, Texas; Ohio's Richard Celeste, who recently retired as governor; Oklahoma's George Nigh, who later served as governor; Wisconsin's Martin J. Schreiber, who became governor; Texas' longtime lieutenant governor William P. Hobby, who held that office until recently and was one of the most powerful lieutenant governors in the nation.

Also attending was Virginia's Charles Robb, son-in-law of the late former president Lyndon B. Johnson, who became both governor and U.S. senator from his state. We spotlighted Louisiana's offshore oil development, taking many of the lieutenant governors and conference attendees on a tour of an offshore oil platform, the first such experience for many of them. This was accomplished by a 135-mile helicopter trip to Consolidated Natural Gas Company's "Ship Shoal" rig in the Gulf of Mexico. The group also toured the Mississippi River and Port of New Orleans, the Superdome, and other areas of the city. The conference adopted a number of resolutions, putting themselves on record favoring adoption of the Equal Rights Amendment and of carefully controlled but expanded offshore drilling. The conference also spoke out on issues of aging, agriculture, the economy, and economic development. We sponsored a State Department briefing on the pending Strategic Arms Limitation Talks, Soviet relations, human rights, the Middle East, trade issues, and the situation in South Africa. It is interesting to note how many of those issues are of continuing concern after more than a decade has passed.

Since this was our first opportunity to host these nationwide dignitaries, we wanted Louisiana to shine and for the Conference's States Dinner we pulled out all the stops, staging one of the most festive, elaborate formal dinners the Fairmont Hotel has ever seen. As each lieutenant governor entered the hall and was formally presented, in order of the state's admission to the union, the National Guard band played that state's official song. Finally, conference chairman-elect O'Neill, chairman Orr and his wife, and Gloria and I were introduced and took our places at the head table. Following the presentation of colors, British singer Tessie O'Shea, then performing at the Fairmont's Blue Room, entertained the group. The Louisiana National Guard Band played during dinner, which was concluded by waiters presenting Baked Alaska, accompanied into the hall by the incomparable Olympia Brass Band. We then introduced our special guest, CBS Television personality Don Stewart, followed by entertainment by the nationally recognized Southern University Stage Band.

The conference guests had dined on Avocat Muscovite, featuring Louisiana shrimp, Lake Pontchartrain crabmeat with imported caviar; Mousse de Poisson en Croute, a hot redfish mousse; Sorbet au Poire; Beef Wellington; the traditional New Orleans Baked Alaska; and coffee. Each guest was presented the recipe for these famed Louisiana dishes, which subsequently were featured at formal affairs throughout the country. In my travels around America, I still run into former lieutenant governors and guests from that conference. They tell me that this impressive, five-day program did more to showcase our state's talents and assets than any program of its kind in their experience. I believe this kind of spotlight salesmanship can only help to boost Louisiana and its national image.

Foreign Leaders

Throughout my career I took a similar keen interest in increasing our exposure to international figures and potential trading partners. Particularly in my years as lieutenant governor and as executive assistant to Gov. Dave Treen, I coordinated the activities of key international visitors through my offices in Baton Rouge or New Orleans, working particularly closely with the Consular Corps.

These guests were frequently heads of states or ambassadors, but often they were also leaders of student groups, businessmen, or government officials in this country as our guests to be briefed on state and national economic matters. Through my relationship with the Consular Corps, I expedited official government requests as well as attending to the personal needs of foreign guests and dignitaries. Some of these experiences stand out keenly in my memory:

The late Gen. Charles de Gaulle, president of France, visited Louisiana on several occasions. Tall and distinguished, he had a stern, commanding manner of speech. The general spoke excellent conversational English, reverting to French only when he wished to be very precise. It is a trait that I found many Japanese dignitaries exhibit, but an ability few American emissaries—including me—are able to match. One of the most memorable de Gaulle visits involved New Orleans mayor Chep Morrison, his host for the visit, and Gov. Earl K. Long, who harbored both personal animosity and political competitiveness where Chep was concerned. Governor Long had to be forcefully persuaded to attend the banquet Chep was staging to honor de Gaulle at the Fairmont Hotel. Finally, Long arrived at the formal banquet, decked out in a seersucker suit and large Panama hat!

I asked the governor to join the general, the mayor, and other dignitaries in an anteroom just off the banquet hall so we could all enter together and be introduced. He refused and strode to the head table alone, before the introductions, where he quickly ate his dinner, still wearing the Panama hat, and then got up and left the room before the evening's program even began, walking straight through the crowd on his way out. When de Gaulle rose to recognize the dignitaries in his remarks, he included, "Your Excellency, the governor of Louisiana, who is no longer with us." It sounded like a line from a eulogy; the crowd roared at Long's expense, to the considerable consternation of the general.

The late Gen. Anastasio Somoza of Nicaragua was an entirely different kind of public personality. He was reviled by his critics as a ruthless dictator, and there seems considerable evidence to support such a contention. Yet he and I had a warm and cordial relationship that lasted several decades both here in the United States and on my own state visits to his country. I was his host and companion on a three-day state visit to Louisiana just before he was overthrown. I had previously been his guest at his palatial villa on the ocean. His residence boasted every luxury imaginable, but it was within a few miles of some of the worst human misery and squalor I had ever seen. I believe his years of public display of such wealth and privilege in the face of such tremendous misery and poverty eventually led to his downfall.

General Somoza was very interested in developing expanded trade between his nation and Louisiana. In fact, during Gov. John McKeithen's term there was some preliminary discussion about Louisiana interests being involved in oil exploration and production there, but that project never came to pass. Somoza made a trade trip to Louisiana in July 1975, during which he met with me and then-governor Edwin Edwards. In my last visit to his country, Somoza was under extremely tight security. He met with us for only fifteen minutes, attended by a whole phalanx of machine-gun toting security guards, then left abruptly. The physical strain was evident in his appearance, and he no longer even attempted the long, cordial discussion we had shared in earlier years. The attitude of the Nicaraguan people was evident in the streets throughout our visit, and was emphasized in several visits we had with dissident factions in the country.

They believed that their nation had been looted by Somoza; they thought that American foreign policy had been propping up the Somoza regime, and they deeply resented it. I was perplexed and troubled by this rising spirit of anti-Americanism, particularly in light of our longstanding efforts to help improve conditions in that country. As strongly as the Nicaraguan people disliked our continuing support for the Somoza regime, they equally deplored President Carter's widely publicized human rights program, bringing pressure to bear against just such totalitarian dictatorships as Somoza's. As much as they wanted a change, and as firmly committed as they were to ousting Somoza, they felt equally intensely that the United States had no business meddling in the internal affairs of her neighbors. It was a very tense time for any American to visit.

Jordan's King Hussein was honored at an International House reception ln New Orleans. During that trip I spent one evening

Governor Edwin Edwards, the late Nicaraguan president, Gen. Anastasio Somoza, and me at a 1975 state visit at the Governor's Mansion.

and the following day showing him around the city. He was very interested in our port. At that time he had just taken power. A very short, immaculately groomed man, Hussein was an extremely business-oriented leader who established a good working relationship with Mayor Chep Morrison.

I met Cuban dictator Fidel Castro before he came to power. It was in 1959, and I was on a trade mission to Cuba. This was the period just before Castro overthrew the Cuban dictator, the late Gen. Fulgencio Batista. Much of the American press was lionizing Castro in those days, celebrating him as the "savior of Havana." I was accompanied by a group of Louisiana businessmen, some with interests in the Havana casinos, attempting to expand the tourist trade between our port and Havana. Castro was invited to one of our sessions and appeared suddenly, one night, clad in the military outfit of the Cuban guerrillas, a much smaller man than he appears in photographs, his ever-present Cuban cigar clenched firmly between his teeth. This was one of the last such trade missions to Cuba, for just one year later he seized power, closed the casinos, nationalized the sugar companies, and adopted a stridently anti-American position. He was polite and conciliatory in his discussions with us, but I thought there was something untrustworthy about his approach. Many of us did not take Castro entirely seriously until well after we returned to the United States and found that he had a real chance of overthrowing the well-entrenched Batista administration.

The Fitzmorris Mission

In 1979, as lieutenant governor, I headed what was probably the largest trade mission ever conducted to Central America, visiting Guatemala, Honduras, El Salvador, Costa Rica, and Nicaragua. We had an audience with the president of each nation and, with the cooperation of the U.S. State Department, also met extensively with each country's trade minister. This thirty-two-person mission included representatives of the Dock Board, the International House, the International Trade Mart, Tulane University, and several business groups. These were dangerous days for the "Fitzmorris Mission," as the international business press called the group, for conditions of riot and revolution were fomenting everywhere we went. In fact, when we arrived in El Salvador, the

State Department formally advised us not to deplane but to leave the country immediately for our own safety. We declined, but we accepted the twelve-man motorcycle escort, armed with machine guns, which accompanied us everywhere we went. I attended early mass one morning and could see the armed military patrol outside the church throughout the service.

Our secret weapon throughout that trip was the late Poche Waguespack, Jr., then president of the New Orleans Chamber of Commerce. It turned out that he had a flawless command of Spanish and was an invaluable addition to our mission. Except for peaceful Costa Rica, we needed the constant protection of our armed escort in every nation we visited. We could not help but be struck by the stark contrast between the opulent presidential palaces in each country and the homes of the tattered crowds of the poor who were literally starving to death in the very shadows of the great mansions. This great chasm between the very rich and the very poor was the precise recipe for civil unrest and uprising, and none of us found surprising the revolutions which were evident everywhere.

Belize is a small, developing country with an economy based primarily on agriculture and tourism. After the independence of Belize, I established an excellent working relationship with Prime Minister George Price. He was that nation's first freely elected prime minister, then was defeated and later returned to office. One of his principal ministers, Said Mousa, has family in Gretna. The Minister of Tourism and the Interior once taught at Xavier University in New Orleans and was well acquainted with the late mayor Dutch Morial during the 1980s.

Belize is best known for its wonderful scuba diving, but it also has a gorgeous interior with many jungle animals. Belize is a very small nation, you can easily cover it in one day. For an English-speaking country, it is also remarkably disadvantaged. Just two years ago the country was still trying, largely unsuccessfully, to put into place a rural electrification system like the one the New Deal brought to the American countryside in the 1930s. Ralph Fonseca, minister of finance, and Prime Minister Price asked me to return as a private citizen, along with my friend Weeland Hyde, to review their efforts to develop greater trade between Louisiana and Belize. One persistent problem is the lack of shipping service between our port and Belize, a thorny, circular problem caused by the lack of sufficient trade to justify shipping. We are still working to overcome this significant obstacle to the economic development of Belize.

Stars and Good Sports

Those weighty problems of state aside, one of the great thrills of being in public life has been the opportunity to rub shoulders with many of America's outstanding sports and entertainment figures. I enjoyed working with Eddie Fisher when he opened the Lions' Telethon several years ago. Pat Boone was also a familiar figure in town as he worked on several occasions with the Easter Seal Campaign. Johnny Carson starred in a relief benefit program for the victims of Hurricane Betsy. Loretta Young was featured in a fund-raising event for the Sisters of the Holy Family. Bette Davis, in town to promote a film, also spoke to the YMBC. I had the great pleasure of escorting Ginger Rogers to several carnival balls while she was in the city on a film promotion tour. I also worked with singer Patti Page in several Muscular Dystrophy Telethons in the late 1960s. Robert Stack visited New Orleans when he starred in the TV drama, "The Untouchables." Younger viewers may know him chiefly as the host of television's "Unsolved Mysteries" series. Joan Crawford's visit to New Orleans was all business. She was married to the president of Pepsi-Cola, and I met her when they were in New Orleans for a major national sales meeting. Ed Sullivan was one of the most entertaining speakers I ever netted when I was program chairman of the YMBC.

One of my favorite actors, Pat O'Brien, chose to take the Kansas City *Southern Belle* when he came to New Orleans for a benefit performance, and it was my pleasure to greet him at the KCS Terminal. At that time the train arrived at 6:30 A.M., but passengers were allowed to remain on board the Pullman cars until eight. I was on hand when the train backed into the station and climbed on board, fully expecting to find O'Brien still asleep, but he was awake, dressed, and ready to start the day. We had a delightful breakfast in the dining car after which I took him to the Sheraton Charles Hotel for his appearance. The Sheraton Charles was the successor to the historic St. Charles Hotel, where so much of the political intrigue of New Orleans had taken place. When the Sheraton chain bought the old St. Charles, it bowed to heavy community pressure and retained part of the old name.

Meeting Mr. and Mrs. Robert Stack at the Lakefront Airport. (Courtesy Roosevelt Hotel, photo by Ray Cresson)

The legendary Bob Hope and me.

Unfortunately, the Sheraton Charles is gone, replaced by the Place St. Charles office complex at the corner of Common and St. Charles in downtown New Orleans.

Probably no single encounter was so memorable as meeting Bing Crosby. Always the showman, a fascinating storyteller, Crosby was here to appear at Archbishop Philip Hannan's annual benefit for the Archdiocese Community Development Program. I was part of a small group selected to meet him at the airport and accompany him to the Hyatt Hotel. That night, the archbishop hosted an intimate dinner for ten persons at his private residence. After dinner, Bing Crosby kindly agreed to sing a few bars of "White Christmas." Many of the guests from that evening are gone now, including Crosby himself, the archbishop has retired, and there will never again be such a unique opportunity to sit across from the man who made "White Christmas" famous across this country as he sang the lyrics almost every American knows by heart. The next day I took Crosby on a tour of the Superdome. He said, "It's a great building, but I bet Ray Guy (then the punter for Crosby's favorite LA Raiders) could hit the TV screen." That night he sang to a packed house in the Grand Ballroom of the Hyatt—as always, leaving the audience screaming for more.

As chairman of the dedication committee for the opening of the Louisiana Superdome, I had the pleasure of contacting Bob Hope and asking him to accept our invitation to perform in one of the most magnificent buildings in the world, the Louisiana Superdome. Bob immediately accepted our invitation and put together a star-studded show headlined by himself, along with Telly Savalas, Dianne Carroll, New Orleans' very own Pete Fountain and Al Hirt, and other luminaries. I met Bob on several other occasions when he came to New Orleans for various charitable events. He is, without doubt, "Mr. Entertainment."

While I was serving as a member of the New Orleans City Council, the "Kraft Music Hall" came to New Orleans to tape a show, and I had the wonderful assignment of hosting Perry Como during the two days he was in town. He was an easygoing, delightful man who could sing a song like nobody else could and seemed to enjoy every moment of it. In later years, Perry filmed one of his television "specials" in New Orleans, and I visited with him again.

Controversial, yet a man of tremendous accomplishment for the cause of Muscular Dystrophy, is my friend, Jerry Lewis. I first met

Gloria and I were thrilled to meet Perry Como, one of our favorite entertainers.

For many years I have worked with Jerry Lewis in the Muscular Dystrophy telethon.

Jerry Lewis at the Royal Orleans at a gathering of Muscular Dystrophy volunteers.

Because of my personal involvement, I was asked to serve as corporate vice president, a position I still hold. One of my most vivid recollections of my association with Jerry is after I presented a $250,000 contribution on behalf of the Helis Foundation. Jerry made a special trip to New Orleans to visit with Bill Helis and me. Regrettably, Bill Helis was then hospitalized and Jerry could speak to him only by telephone. Later, on one of his national telethons, Jerry said, "I'm directing this to the people of New Orleans: Please ask my friend Jimmy Fitzmorris to call me at this number." I immediately began receiving calls from friends around the city. When I called, Jerry asked if I could get him ten tickets to the World Heavyweight Championship Fight, which was to be held in the Louisiana Superdome—which I was able to do. Jerry later came to New Orleans at the invitation of Archbishop Philip Hannan to perform at the archbishop's annual community appeal banquet.

In July of 1962, the late Michael Landon, "Little Joe" of the "Bonanza" series, came to New Orleans as part of a nationwide tour, and I had the pleasure of presenting a key to the city and a certificate to him. He requested a seafood dinner, and I was pleased to entertain him that night at Fitzgerald's Restaurant on the lakefront. It was an exciting evening, for everybody at the restaurant immediately recognized him and came over for autographs and conversation. When we finally left Fitzgerald's, I took him by the house I had recently purchased at 700 Emerald Street. Little did I know that he would go on to become one of the major stars of motion pictures and television. He was a very warm, compassionate, and genuine individual, whose friendship I shall always cherish.

Some of the more colorful stars I fondly recall meeting were: the original Lone Ranger (before having removed his mask) along with his "faithful Indian companion, Tonto"; Winnie the Pooh, at the grand opening of Sears and Roebuck's store in Hammond; Mickey Mouse, on his national tour commemorating the Tenth Anniversary of Disney World; and Leonard Nimoy, Dr. Spock of "Star Trek."

Many of my favorite sports figures had a New Orleans connection as well. I met commentator Howard Cosell when he came to speak to one of the many report meetings of the United Way. I was seated next to him at the luncheon. When you chat with Cosell, the experience consists mostly of you listening and Cosell doing all the chatting, but he was a fascinating man to meet.

Dan Marino, then the handsome, impressive young quarterback for the Miami Dolphins, came to New Orleans to accept an award from the Italian-American Society. He was tremendously proud of his Italian heritage and told colorful stories of his NFL career. On an economic development trip to Pittsburgh I was pleased to be able to meet coach Chuck Noll at the stadium. I knew his impressive reputation, but I was especially struck by the tremendous respect his players had for him. I also had the great opportunity to meet and develop a friendship with the late Art Rooney, one of the original owners in the NFL. Mr. Rooney had a great interest in Louisiana because of his friendship with the late Charlie Degan, one of our distinguished New Orleans assessors. The two of them enjoyed watching the ponies run at the New Orleans Fair Grounds.

Baseball great Don Larson visited New Orleans after one of his many outstanding seasons. After a French Quarter tour, Mayor Chep Morrison loaned Larson and his guests the mayor's limousine for the remainder of the night. Early the next morning I was at my desk at city hall when the telephone rang. My friend, the late Eddie Gaudet, general manager of the Sheraton Charles, said, "I don't know how this came about but the mayor's limousine is parked up on the sidewalk in front of the hotel. You ought to have somebody move it before all the business people start arriving downtown for work." I immediately had the mayor's limousine quietly returned to city hall.

There was a constant procession of athletes through New Orleans functions such as the Sugar Bowl, then sponsored by USF&G, including Archie Manning, basketball player and businessman Bob Petit, Pete Marovich, Bart Starr, Bert Jones, Terry Bradshaw, Roger Staubach, Leon Spinks, Chuck Muncie, Alabama coach Bear Bryant, and others. One of the great benefits of living in a city like New Orleans is that so many of the athletes you've read about on the sports pages or seen on television are frequently visible on the streets and at public events. In years past, many of them came in conjunction with the New Orleans Pelicans, our remarkable minor league baseball team. Much of the credit for the Pelicans goes to the Gilbert family, Larry and his sons, Larry Jr., Tookie, and Charlie—all star athletes at Jesuit High. The Gilberts lived out on West End Boulevard and were tremendously respected by the baseball fraternity. I was active as president of the "Grandstand Managers' Club," a business support group for the Pelicans, and it gave me the wonderful opportunity to work with the Gilberts, team president Joe L. Brown, son of actor Joe E. Brown, Danny Murtaugh, the late Branch Rickey, and the many others who were part of the Pelicans legend. One of my fondest hopes is that baseball will return to New Orleans in my lifetime.

One of my great friendships in professional sports was Rocky Marciano, the late heavyweight champion of the world. Rocky was blessed with a wonderful sense of humor. Our mutual friend Harry Spiro, Jr., a major housing developer, brought him to meet me when I was a member of the city council. We all had lunch at the Roosevelt Hotel and then toured some of the Third Ward neighborhood bars, part of my councilmanic district. I could have brought the president of the United States on that tour, and it would not have caused the same sensation as a visit from Rocky Marciano. Through him I made many lasting friends in the boxing world.

Perhaps my most memorable sports experience was a long lunch at Antoine's King's Room with professional football coach Vince Lombardi. We were the guests of the late Rep. Eddie Hebert, and the three of us spent hours talking. Lombardi had strong facial features, accentuated by his favorite cigar, and a unique, decisive way of speaking. It was a remarkable experience and a rare insight into the personality of Coach Lombardi I will never forget.

God's Servants

One of the early thespians of the religious movement on television was the late Bishop J. Fulton Sheen, a dynamic orator with a persuasive personality. Bishop Sheen came to speak at Loyola University, and I had the opportunity to spend time with him in the holding room prior to his stage appearance. His piercing eyes, his religious fervor, his deep sense of interest and concern gave me the powerful impression that he was looking into my very soul.

Another great highlight was my brief meeting with His Holiness, Pope John Paul II. He visited New Orleans as part of his United States tour, and I, along with some other folks, had accepted Archbishop Hannan's invitation to greet His Holiness upon his arrival at New Orleans International Airport. The security was tight that evening as the plane landed and the red carpet was rolled out; the security people were trying to guide His Holiness away from the crowd, but, hearing the chant of "Papa! Papa!," he immediately broke ranks. To the delight and excitement of those of us behind the barricade at the airport, he shook each of our hands and extended a personal greeting.

Finally, a small remembrance and tribute on a very personal note: My life has been touched, enriched, and challenged by a lifetime of exposure to the religious community. In fact, my dear parents aside, I believe that my personal and private life—who I am and the way I have chosen to live—has been mostly shaped by my Jesuit training. I remember many of the priests and nuns fondly and the following five vividly:

Rev. Harry Tompson, S.J., served both as president and principal of Jesuit High. He is now director of the Manresa Retreat. He is a dynamic, effective speaker with a wonderful personality, but I remember Father Harry best for the deep currents of compassion which flow within him. In one of the darkest hours of my life, when the state supreme court had effectively ended my legal effort to gain the nomination for governor and the race was lost, he and Rev. Paul Schott—of the New Orleans packing company family—came to my home on Sunday morning, just hours after the court's ruling against me, and spent considerable time visiting with me.

Rev. Schott, who had also served as president of Jesuit, is in Dallas now. Together, he and Father Harry helped me put myself in touch with my inner religious resources at a time when I needed to remember that God has a plan and a purpose for each of our lives, that His plan is not always the same as our own personal agenda, and that we must not lose faith and the sensitivity to feel Him working, often in mysterious ways, in our lives.

Rev. Dan Partridge, now in his fiftieth year in the priesthood, was my old classmate at Jesuit High. We still maintain a close friendship which has survived and been strengthen by the half-century which has elapsed. My Jesuit years have become increasingly

Archbishop Philip M. Hannan and I worked on many projects together; I have tremendous respect and admiration for him. (Courtesy Roy Trahan)

important to me as I have grown older, my experiences there more indelibly etched into my memory. Next to my wedding band I still wear my original class ring from Jesuit—now worn and weakened by time—but I cannot bring myself to retire it in favor of a handsome new facsimile I received a few years ago.

I first met Archbishop Philip M. Hannan, J.C.D., S.T.B., S.T.L., in 1965, soon after he arrived in New Orleans to succeed Archbishop Cody, who had been transferred to Chicago.

While new to the local Catholic community, Archbishop Hannan was already familiar to many of us by reputation. A World War II chaplain and paratrooper, he had become a friend and confidant of the Kennedy family and a respected figure in Washington, D.C.

Once in New Orleans, he managed immediately to make an indelible impression on the civic and religious communities. He had a refreshing personal style, being both highly visible and easily accessible. He became what I would call a "pastoral archbishop," not merely an unseen administrator of the church's significant local interests.

He also became my valued, trusted friend and colleague in a myriad of local projects, both spiritual and temporal, for he was actively interested and involved in every aspect of our community. He was wise and brave and an awesome promoter and fund-raiser for religious projects in which he believed. I was lieutenant governor at the time of the Nicaraguan earthquakes in December 1972, and he used my capitol offices to help arrange logistics for sending medical supplies and relief to the refugees in that devastated area of the world. It was typical of the archbishop that he personally accompanied one of the first shipments to the area, so he could see firsthand what else needed to be done to help.

His retirement in 1989 was a difficult time for many, and for me in particular. However, in a wonderful way, Archbishop Hannan turned his retirement years into a whole, new career. Unfettered from his former administrative duties, he became a respected television commentator, co-hosting his own program on New Orleans station WLAE, in which he reported from religious events and trouble spots around the globe. He also became a believer in and expert on the miraculous events at Medjugorje, Yugoslavia.

I still see him regularly, and he continues to inspire and challenge everyone whose life he touches.

"Amazing Grace"

One of the genuinely extraordinary human beings of my lifetime was the late Sister Mary Grace Danos, O. Carm., who served a quarter-century as principal of Mount Carmel Academy in New Orleans.

Baptized Mary Cecilia Danos, she was born May 2, 1915, on Milly Plantation, near Plaquemine, Louisiana, the eighth of twelve children born to Dr. and Mrs. Joseph Louis Danos. She was different from the start: quiet, deeply religious, persistent, and sometimes impatient. From her earliest childhood, she felt the calling to a religious vocation, and by the age of fifteen she was ready to answer. She wanted first to be a nun and a nurse and could have achieved that ambition through the Sisters of Charity in New Orleans, had she but been willing to postpone her vocation until her eighteenth birthday. She felt strongly that her calling was to enter the Lord's service then, not three years later, so she came instead to the Order of Mount Carmel and a career in religious education which was to consume and crown the remainder of her life. Those who believe profoundly in the will of the Lord think it no accident that she was called to the Carmelite Order, which has as its centerpiece daily devotion to Mary, mother of Christ. In religious education and administration, Sister Mary Grace had found her life's work. She became the second principal in Mount Carmel Academy's history, and stayed for a quarter-century.

Working through sheer persistence and force of personality, she transformed the institution which became her home, graduating thirty-five hundred young women, increasing scholarships some 800 percent, always building and improving. Her "senior trips" for the girls being graduated from Mt. Carmel became legend: Once she led the class on a camel-riding expedition, with herself firmly atop the lead camel and very much in command. On another trip, she eagerly mastered the sport of para-sailing.

I first came to know her when she called to ask if I could stop by her office to help with a special problem. The night was filled with political activities and meetings so it was nearly midnight when I arrived at her office where she was hard at work. I later learned that this was no remarkable occurrence in the daily life of a nun whose workdays frequently lasted until two or three each morning. She had only a "small request." She needed fifty thousand dollars to continue the school's operation, and she needed it by

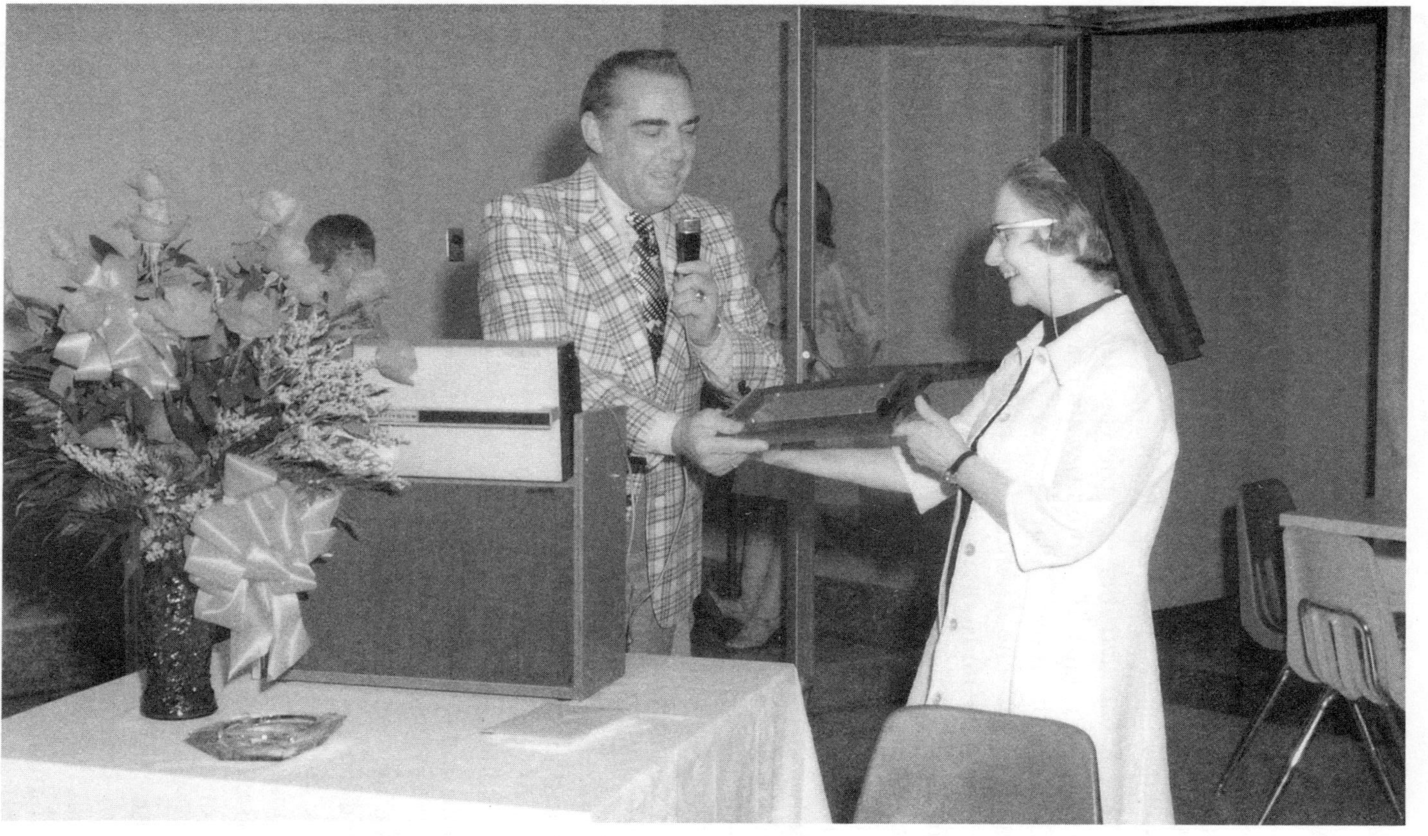

The late Sister Mary Grace Danos, one of the truly great ladies of our time, touched thousands of lives, including mine.

week's end. She was slight of build, a gentle woman; she spoke in a still, small voice which belied the torrents of faith, assurance, and ambition that raged within her. She assuaged the alarm which must have been evident in my voice as I warned her what a perilous quest it would be, this rescue mission to somehow find fifty thousand dollars against a deadline only hours away.

"When the Lord is on your side and the cause is right, it will all work out," she said with quiet assurance. She had no doubt that the Lord had led her, in this momentary crisis, to Jimmy Fitzmorris and that, if I would pay attention, I would find my way to the fifty thousand dollars scattered around our city that was meant for her school. And I did.

Later, in the midst of a political campaign, she asked me to head a "modest" $1.5 million effort she called the "Design for Excellence Campaign," with which she intended to build a full-scale performing arts center on the Mt. Carmel campus. Together, we went to seek the approval of Archbishop Hannan. I had previously called him, explained the nature of the project, and given him my assurance that we would be able to achieve our goal. After a brief discussion, he graciously added his support to our effort.

Undeterred by the fact that we had just gotten what we came for, she continued, unrolling a small mountain of detailed floor plans and architect's renderings. It was her hope that the archbishop would be as interested in the minute details of the project as she. Gently but firmly he reiterated his support and eased us from his office, telling us that the task now was to begin the solicitation of contributions. And so we began. Her approach was simple and devastatingly effective: The Lord had sent her to me as the best and probably last hope to accomplish His mission. She was only the intermediary, the messenger, in this transaction between the Lord and me; the decision was out of her hands and up to me and my own conscience and religious commitment! It was a proposition which always proved impossible to refute and, of course, the performing arts center stands today exactly where she had envisioned it.

She searched everywhere for a daily message from Mary, with whose spirit she was in daily communication. It was her greatest joy to be among the first Americans to discover Medjugorje, where the Virgin Mary spoke to Yugoslavian children and—through them—to a troubled universe. "I've been taking pilgrims to Lourdes and Fatima for years, to where Mary was. Now we can go to where Mary is, where she can be seen and her message heard now, today." She made a dozen trips herself, to Medjugorje, this slight figure weaving her way through the masses of humanity streaming to the rural mountainside to await Mary's appearances to the children. It was so typical of Sister Mary Grace that she not only went herself; she sent others, thousands of pilgrims from throughout the nation to see and experience for themselves.

Some, particularly the young, could not easily afford such a pilgrimage, so she helped them raise their own funds through the Youth for Mary movement. She had felt the powerful presence of Mary at Medjugorje in a very personal way. It was the Thanksgiving season of 1986 and she was descending the steep, treacherous mountainside at Medjugorje. By all reasonable accounts she should never have made the trip. Before leaving Louisiana she had suffered a terrible fall and sustained a badly broken left arm. Four pins held together the hundred bone fragments that had been pieced together to reconstruct her elbow. One of the pins had worked its way loose and protruded painfully from her limp, useless left arm. She was being helped down the incline by a guide when she slipped. Someone grabbed her left arm to steady her. "Tell him not to touch you," the guide shouted in alarm. "Tell him your arm cannot be touched." "It doesn't hurt," she said, swinging her arm in a wide circle. "I am free." And so she was. Even the protruding pin mysteriously returned to where it had been implanted, where it remained the rest of her life, and she had the complete use of her arm once again.

It was an event which could not be medically explained but served to ever deepen her already considerable personal faith. No such miracle was to appear for the cancer which was slowly, surely ravaging her body. The cancer had been discovered just after Christmas in 1985. It was to move from her colon to her liver and finally to her lungs, where, on one beautiful June day in 1989, it would finally claim her life. The disease which ravaged her body could not weaken her will or shake her religious faith. It served only to remind her of the preciousness of life and the growing scarcity of time. Earlier she had spent two days with Mother Theresa, learning to sustain herself on only a cup of water each day. That faith sustained her as, in terrible pain, she wrote a beautiful "Magnificat of Waiting," as a testament to her beliefs and an acceptance of God's will in her life. It reads, "You have changed my life; I was so confident in my unknowing. You have deflected my fervent thrust toward iron-clad goals, and spread before me your vision of fragile simplicity.

"My longing to be a healing and reconciling person to your people is affirmed within the daily comings and goings of my life: my illusions of my own wholeness are mercifully revealed. You are here now in this seeming emptiness of waiting, remembering your intent, . . . according to the promise made through the work of my life that your fullness may be known now, in our time. Amen."

Sister Mary Grace worked harder than ever before, her already superhuman days almost lapping each other as she attempted to complete as much of her mission as possible. "I am," she liked to say, "just the servant of Jesus and Mary, traveling when they call, to give their message of love, sacrifice, and prayer, to bring about world peace." She had always kept in close touch with those of us who shared her work; a little cake inevitably appeared for each of our birthdays, a small gift each Christmas, the Papal Blessing for our wedding anniversary. Now, she gathered us even closer, reminding me, in her wondrous, peaceful faith, of the words of Aeschylus, "In our sleep, pain which cannot forget falls drop by drop until, in our own despair, against our own will, comes wisdom through the awful grace of God."

She was less given to quoting Greek philosophy than the New Testament, as in a passage from Philippians she included in a letter to me—during one of the darkest periods of my own life: "I thank my God for you every time I think of you and every time I pray for you I pray with joy."

The flag at Mt. Carmel Academy was at half-mast June 14, 1989, as twelve hundred of her friends, a mere droplet in the vast sea of lives she had touched and changed in so many scattered parts of the world, gathered at St. Dominic's Church on Harrison Avenue to pay our last respects at the Mass of the Resurrection. Her old friend, Archbishop Philip Hannan, spoke with great feeling and emotion of her enormous faith and vision, how she drew from everyone she met and each of her experiences to apply her daily life to Christ's own vision for the world. "The day she died was the day of her birthday in heaven. We can pray for her and to her," he concluded. I can and I do, for I believe that she has a very special relationship with the Blessed Mother, and it is one of the miracles of our faith that you can too—and, in that wonderful way, Sister Mary Grace is still, and will continue to be, with us.

I recently completed my thirty-seventh consecutive year installing the student council at Mt. Carmel, and it was one of the highest honors of my life to have been given the first Sister Mary Grace Danos, O. Carm. Award in 1990. Presented by her successor, Sister Camille Ann Campbell, who had proven to be a tower of strength and inspiration following in the footsteps of her former teacher and mentor, the simple silver plaque is inscribed, "For Her Monument Look Around You."

Epilogue

This story has taken us through parts of eight decades of Louisiana life. The time has come for some final reflections on the past and a few thoughts about our future. My childhood was greatly influenced by the priests and nuns who provided most of my early education. At that time, the late 1920s and 1930s, they were inspired by the growing, international movement of Catholic social activism which had, as its roots, the teachings of St. Thomas Aquinas that God's people were called to balance individual rights with social responsibilities.

I came to accept that proposition almost as an article of faith, particularly as I saw how important personal involvement was from my own experience and perspective in business. I became involved in public life because much needed to be done by the representatives of the business side of government. I had a deep interest in people, and I believed I could make a difference. I was never particularly interested in amassing a great fortune, in climbing social ladders, or in promoting myself into some national role in Washington, D.C. From my point of view, all the interesting action was here, if a young man would just roll up his sleeves and get involved. This was not an altogether popular decision among my family, friends, and associates, but I put aside their negative comments and proceeded to devote myself to a career in public life. Did I make a difference, can I see any accomplishments from forty years' daily involvement with business and politics? I think so; I believe I proved that a person could be honest and in government at the same time. I think I showed that one man can make a difference, not just in his own life but in the lives of those he inspires to follow him. I brought two generations of young people into public service to work with me, and most of them are still there.

Not all of them rose to prominence, for that is not really the purpose of dedicating one's life to public service. Rather, they came to represent the honest, capable core of government at local, state, and national levels, and I am proud of each of them. I tried to speak out for my beliefs, which sometimes meant taking the unpopular side of an issue. I tried to encourage people to think beyond their immediate wants and needs, to consider what actions we could take today that would be important to our city and state's future success. Many of my proposals were well ahead of their time, heatedly criticized or simply ignored at the time I first brought them to light. I proposed regional cooperation with the parishes surrounding Orleans. From the standpoint of economy and efficiency, the duplication of efforts among governing bodies just makes no sense. Our effectiveness in the state legislature is greatly lessened because the metropolitan parishes have been unwilling or unable to speak with one, powerful voice. Decades ago, I said that if we did not clean up Lake Pontchartrain it would die—and nobody took that claim seriously. I urged all parishes surrounding the lake to cooperate to protect the lake, to consistently and carefully plan for its development.

That still has not been accomplished. Twenty years before either became a reality, I proposed a New Orleans Convention Center and the establishment of a Trade Free Zone, both of which I thought would have immense economic benefits for the city. I supported development of an international airport in New Orleans East because I always believed that the Moisant site was too small for the long run and, more importantly, because I thought it made no sense for the city to attempt to operate an airport in another parish. I tried to get people interested in a business/government/educational partnership to create a research facility at the University of New Orleans in the 1960s, an idea which is just now beginning to catch hold. I tried to run each of my campaigns on the leading edge of new thought and technology. Above all, I always tried to encourage business people to take an active role in government, beginning in the years well before the advent of the Louisiana Association of Business and Industry, the New Orleans Business Council, and Metro-Vision. I tried to tell business people that it was not enough just to speak out on the issues; they had to get personally involved in the political process itself, as workers and as individual contributors.

I believed then, and believe today, that is the only way they can have any meaningful impact or influence. Business is finally making a start in that direction, largely through LABI and the Business Council, but not nearly enough has been done. The business community does now provide some meaningful campaign contributions at the local and state level, but there is still a terrible lack of personal involvement. Organized labor, to its credit, on the other hand, provides not just campaign money but campaign workers, and that often makes the difference in a close election. There have been epic, monumental changes in how the public process works since my first campaign in 1954: The incredible growth in the communications and information industry is one. So is the tremendous number of special interest groups on all levels, now working on causes from the environment to women's issues. The result is that the old political organizations and the newspaper endorsements play a much less important role today. There is a growing gridlock of confusion and contention as public officials confront this whole spectrum of political organizations, each with its own agenda.

Yet, there is a growing sense of frustration and disillusionment on the part of the voters here and across America. It is very clear to me that if each citizen had to vote on the issue, senators and congressmen would never get a raise. Despite all these new organizations, voter participation is much less than it was when I first ran. Not since the eve of the Civil War, when Abraham Lincoln faced the succession of one-third of the states from the union, has there been such a lack of respect for the political process, such a refusal to participate. When half of our people fail to register to vote and only half of those registered actually go to the polls, we have public officials elected by 25 percent of the electorate. The result is that when people say they believe that no one considers their views or speaks for them, they often have only themselves to blame. When I ran for governor, I used to tell people, "If you owned one share of General Motors, you would follow your stock with great interest. You would be concerned about the expenditures of your corporation and the quality of the people who ran it." I told them that they each owned one share in America, that government was a much larger business with much greater impact on their daily lives. Therefore, I suggested, they owed themselves and their children at least as much attention and involvement in the political process as they would have given to that share in GM.

I spend a considerable amount of time now, when I speak to business, professional, and student groups throughout the state each week, trying to encourage them to identify and shape the emerging issues of the next century. Locally, we need to be working on an effective transportation system. Our present highway infrastructure, in addition to being increasingly antiquated and unsafe, is effectively gridlocked, and everybody who tries to travel the interstate at peak rush-hour knows it. Whether the answer is light rail transportation or otherwise, this is an issue that cannot continue to be avoided. We must find a way to restore public confidence in government and to encourage greater individual involvement. We must move toward regional government cooperation, finding a better way to utilize the manpower of government in an age of diminishing resources. We must find a way to give local governments broader powers to generate revenue and run their daily lives. At present, almost every major project a city might wish to undertake requires approval of all the voters of the state.

It is clear that federal funds will continue to decrease and state government will also have less to give to the cities. City government, with the active involvement of the business community, must prove to the voters that it is capable, competent, and worthy of their support of such programs. We must move to support and revitalize the Port of New Orleans so it can assume its rightful role as the major American port for Latin American trade. The market is clearly there, if only we will seize the opportunity to develop it. Similarly, we must aggressively encourage Caribbean nations to view New Orleans, once again, as the Gateway to America.

Finally, a closing word to young people: As I travel across Louisiana I am often asked if I would recommend that they make politics a career. After all, I first ran as a very young man and made politics my life. Should they do the same at their age? I think not. One of the few regrets of my life is that I was so deeply involved in daily politics I did not return to get my law degree. If I were guiding the life of a young person today, I would recommend that he or she stay involved in the political process, voting and supporting good people seeking public office. But I would recommend that they postpone seeking public office until they have first established their own careers and provided themselves some security. The costs of campaigning and the immense pressures of daily political life can so easily sink them if they have not first established some resources and security for themselves and their families. Would I have taken my own advice if someone had given it to me at the beginning of my own political career? Probably not, for once the political bug bites you, it is often an incurable infliction. Whatever our young people decide, I hope they will learn what Frank Mankiewicz said that we could learn from the life of Robert Kennedy: that life in politics can be both joyous and honorable.

Appendix

Special Acknowledgement and Appreciation

I especially wanted to take this opportunity, which may be my only such chance, to thank specifically some of the members of my personal staff as well as others who were particularly helpful during my campaign and in my years as lieutenant governor.

I do so knowing that it is not possible to list everyone whose name should rightfully appear; the list of campaign supporters and personal friends numbers in the thousands and is the size of a telephone directory. It is my hope and prayer that those whose names do not appear will understand and know that it is not because I do not deeply appreciate their efforts in my behalf. Indeed, every person who pulls the lever for a particular candidate believes that act establishes a special, personal bond between them. During each of my campaigns I always understood that special relationship and felt that connection between me and those who placed their trust in me.

I did, however, wish to conclude this book by offering a brief, personal word of appreciation and acknowledgement to some wonderful friends and associates:

The members of my personal staff during my twelve years of government service for the state of Louisiana were loyal, devoted, dedicated employees—who work far beyond the call of duty—and to whom I wish to extend a very special word of thanks and appreciation:

Bill Allerton
Mrs. Sue McCormick Bonacorso
Mrs. Kathy Ashby Bradford
Ms Cheryl Brown
Gregory S. Buisson
Ms Yvonne Comeaux
Mrs. Janet Simno Courtenay
Mrs. Carol A. Daigle
The Honorable Mike Early
Patrick J. Gallwey
Charles E. Grey, Jr.
Dennis M. Hammond
Jim Harris
Ron Luman
Kirk Melancon
Anthony R. Messina
Mrs. Hilda Nolan
Ms Michele DeMesme Ray
Mrs. Staci Warren Rehkopf
The Honorable C. W. Roberts
Ms Roycelyn Roberts
Mrs. Stephanie Walker Schaff
Mrs. Elouise Seay
Mrs. Frances Shay
Ms Beth Ann Simno
Mrs. Gay Duhe Smith
Ms Karen Waguespack
Mrs. Teresa Wann
Larry D. Weidel
Joseph F. Willis, Sr.
Charles C. "Chuck" Zatarain III

Executive Security

Lawrence "Larry" Antoine
Steve Auerbach
Billy Booth
Jim Borgstede
Joel I. Brazzell, Jr.
Donald J. Brisolara
Stephen F. Campbell
Kenneth E. Delcambre
Eric J. Durel
Louis Frost
Charles L. "Ronnie" Gill
Richard P. "Richie" Hart
A. J. Kahoe
Timothy Lawes
Stephen Dan Martin
John Massa
Anthony M. Monteleone, Jr.
Richard E. Nelson
Allen "Pete" Peters
Charles "Salty" Saltaformaggio
Michael J. Sunseri
Keith M. Wilkins

"The Fitzmorris Air Force"

Bill Bailey
James R. Baker, Sr.
James R. "Rusty" Baker, Jr.
Francis J. "Pat" Benezech
Danny Blanchard
Allen Campbell
Dan Campbell
Charles Conner
Ms Dede Frazier
Merlin Grade
David Holmes
Fred W. Huenefeld, Jr.
Joe Lodridge
Bill Lucas
Al Mechana, Jr.
Coy Neal

Al Copeland
James Davison
William J. "Bill" Dugan
Dick Duhe
Richard Englander
Michael A. Erwin
Ralph Fagan, Sr.
Paul Fournet
Rick Oeder
Jeff Pecook
Clifford Rice
Walter W. Smith
Mickey White
George D. Williams
Rusty Williams

Then there were those wonderful friends who provided "special services"—whom I never seem to have thanked sufficiently:

Ms Michele Abadie
Lloyd Arbo +
Vincent J. Arena
Richard Arsenaux
Dottie and Murphy Arsenaux
Leo Bazile +
Ellen and Ted Brennan
Harry G. Caire
Mac Casse
B. J. (Mrs. Anthony) Corcoran
Irving B. Cohen +
Mrs. Irving B. Cohen (Rose)
Ernest Colbert, Jr.
Ms Ora Cosse
Ms Michele M. Daigle
George H. Diedrich, Jr.
Mrs. Patrick E. Duvall (Rosemary)
Col. Phares "Whitey" Fleig +
Glenn Gennaro
Jack Green +
Mrs. Jack Green (Mollye)
Floyd Guillot
The Hon. Warren J. Harang, Jr.
Mrs. Elaine Hartley
Ronnie Kole
Ms Denise Redmann Krouse
Gilbert C. "Whitey" Lagasse
Rita and Nicholas J. Lapara, Sr.
Mrs. Jennie LeBlanc
The Hon. Edwin A. Lombard
James T. Mehle +
Mrs. James T. Mehle (Jo)
Mrs. Mary Lynn "Cissy" McShane
Ricardo Pardo
Claude J. Pumilia, Sr. +
Mary (Mrs. Claude J.) Pumilia
Erik M. Skrmetta
Mrs. Everett H. Seeger (Elaine)
Brig. Gen. Karl N. Smith (Ret.)
Mrs. Hebert L. Stanton (Lillian)
Robert H. "Bob" Tucker, Jr.
Hollas U. Young, Jr.

And last—yet certainly not least—to the thousands of volunteers who worked tirelessly in each and every campaign—to the thousands of generous contributors—and to the hundreds of thousands of voters who returned me to office over and over again—my deep love, affection, and gratitude.

INDEX